THE
INEQUALITY
CRISIS

The facts and what we can do about it

ROGER BROWN

First published in Great Britain in 2017 by

Policy Press
University of Bristol
1-9 Old Park Hill
Bristol BS2 8BB
UK
t: +44 (0)117 954 5940
e: pp-info@bristol.ac.uk
www.policypress.co.uk

North American office:
Policy Press
c/o The University of Chicago Press
1427 East 60th Street
Chicago, IL 60637, USA
t: +1 773 702 7700
f: +1 773-702-9756
e: sales@press.uchicago.edu
www.press.uchicago.edu

© Policy Press 2017

British Library Cataloguing in Publication Data
A catalogue record for this book is available from the British Library.

Library of Congress Cataloging-in-Publication Data
A catalog record for this book has been requested.

ISBN 978-1-4473-3758-4 paperback
ISBN 978-1-4473-3760-7 ePub
ISBN 978-1-4473-3761-4 Mobi
ISBN 978-1-4473-3759-1 epdf

The right of Roger Brown to be identified as author of this work has been asserted by him in accordance with the 1988 Copyright, Designs and Patents Act.

Cover design by Lyn Davies
Front cover image: 123RTF
Printed and bound in Great Britain by TJ International, Padstow
Policy Press uses environmentally responsible print partners

For Josie

Roger Brown is the former Vice-Chancellor of Southampton Solent University. He has been a professor or visiting professor at 10 other universities and held other senior posts in higher education. In 2013 he received the Times Higher Education Lifetime Achievement Award.

Before that, he was a senior civil servant at the Department of Trade and Industry and an administrator with the Inner London Education Authority. He has served on many national committees and boards.

He has written four books and many articles and lectures on different aspects of higher education as an international authority on the application of market-based policies to higher education.

CONTENTS

Foreword by Kate Pickett vii

Preface ix

List of acronyms xii

1   The meaning and extent of inequality 1

2   Inequality: for and against 19

3   Structural causes of rising inequality 49

4   Institutional causes of rising inequality 79

5   Tackling rising inequality through taxes, 111
    transfers and social expenditure

6   Tackling rising inequality through policy 141
    reform

7   Looking ahead 169

Suggestions for further reading 207

Notes 209

References 227

Index 281

FOREWORD

As I write this foreword to Roger Brown's lucid and thorough examination of the impact of inequality I confess to feeling very worried about the direction our society seems to be taking. Despite the fact that economic inequality has risen sharply up the political agenda since the Global Financial Crisis of 2007/08, with accompanying rhetoric – in 2013 alone President Obama said it was 'the defining challenge of our time', Pope Francis said 'inequality is the root of social ills' and UN Secretary General Ban Ki-Moon stated that 'social and economic inequalities can tear the social fabric, undermine social cohesion and prevent nations from thriving' – so far rhetoric has not led to action. Every year, when the World Economic Forum meets in Davos, Switzerland, it issues a report on global risks. Inequality entered the list in 2012, and this year rising income and wealth disparity was ranked as the most important trend likely to determine development across the world over the next decade. At the same time, Oxfam reported that just eight men own the same wealth as the poorest half of the world. And the 2017 *Sunday Times* Rich List showed that the richest 1,000 people in Britain had a combined wealth of £658 billion. This total *increased* by £82.5 billion during the previous year alone, which The Equality Trust calculates would be enough to pay the nation's adult social care bill for 4 years, or the fuel bills of every household in the UK for the next 2.5 years. As Roger Brown shows so clearly, consecutive Coalition and Conservative governments in the UK have failed to deliver on promises of creating a fairer, more equal society. Instead we have rising child poverty, rising infant mortality rates and rising deaths among the elderly, especially among the oldest and frailest. Over a million families accessed food banks last year and admissions to hospital for malnutrition are up 50% since 2010, as is homelessness. The Institute for Fiscal Studies predicts that the poorest tenth of households will lose one tenth of their income by 2020, while the rich continue to gain.

We all need to educate ourselves about this growing crisis and arm ourselves with evidence against those who continue to believe that inequality is a precondition for economic growth, a spur to innovation and aspiration, or simply a natural manifestation of human nature. Roger Brown undertook a journey to critically examine and learn for himself what the evidence showed. In this book, he shares his learning with us all and shows that, as well as undermining population health, tearing the social fabric and undermining social cohesion, inequalities in income and wealth cause economic instability and act as a roadblock to environmental sustainability, poverty alleviation and development. His research is bang up-to-date, comprehensive and rigorous; he has done us all a great service. Please pay that service forward – when you've finished this book, please pass it on. When enough of us understand, things will begin to change.

Kate Pickett,
Professor of Epidemiology and University Champion
for Research on Justice and Equality,
University of York
May 2017

PREFACE

I thought it might be helpful to say briefly how and why I came to write this book. I should also like to take this opportunity to thank a number of friends who have helped me with it.

After stepping down as Vice Chancellor of Southampton Solent University in 2007 I edited, wrote or co-wrote a number of books and other pieces on the introduction of market forces into higher education (see References). In 2011 I reviewed for *Times Higher Education* a book by Phillip Brown, Hugh Lauder and David Ashton called *The Global Auction: The Broken Promises of Education, Jobs and Incomes* (see References). The book's central argument was that, together, globalisation and technological change were undermining the central 'opportunity bargain' whereby – in return for several years' investment in their higher and professional education – graduates in the West were rewarded with secure, stimulating and well-remunerated careers. Finally, in 2014 I published an article in the *Higher Education Review* entitled 'The real crisis in higher education'. In this I argued that the most pressing problem facing higher education was that everyone, but especially the universities, was pursuing status at the expense of education (partly because the expansion of higher education had created a greater wedge between graduates and non-graduates).

All this led me to believe that rising economic inequality was, after climate change, the greatest challenge facing the Western economies and societies, a judgement that the Brexit vote and the election of President Trump have done nothing to invalidate.

But I was unable to find a single comprehensive text. So I set out to produce my own, and this is the result.

The aim was to provide a book that would be evidence based (drawing on close reading and analysis of both popular and scholarly studies); balanced, in not starting from any specific ideology or position (beyond a view that there should be some proportionate relationship between what people put into and get out of participation in society); comprehensive, in discussing the main theories for the growth in inequality and the likeliest remedies; accessible, with a clear text and avoidance of jargon wherever possible (and explanations, where not); and up to date, taking account not only of historical trends but also of the policies of the two Conservative governments since May 2015 and the proposals in the Conservative election manifesto in May 2017. Although the description and analysis covers the industrial West as a whole, the proposed responses are aimed at Britain (although most would also be relevant to the other major Anglophone countries). Finally, since I started work on the book in mid-2014 a number of major studies of inequality have appeared, and more continue to do so. While the book covers the main issues, I have included a short section on 'Suggestions for Further Reading' so that readers with sufficient interest and curiosity can explore these for themselves.

It should be noted that most of the work on the book was done before the Prime Minister announced the Government's intention to invoke Article 50 of the Lisbon Treaty in order for the UK to leave the EU. Given that we shall not know the terms of Brexit and the UK's future trading relationship with the EU for several years, any view about the implications for inequality is necessarily speculative. However, a short passage on the possible implications for inequality is included in Chapter Seven.

Many people have given me help or encouragement. I should especially like to mention the late Tony Atkinson, Tony Bruce, Danny Dorling, Ron Glatter, John Holmwood, Diane Reay, Prem Sikka and Richard Upson. I should also like to acknowledge with great gratitude the help I have had from three current or former colleagues at Solent: Sarah Belkacem, Mark Dixon and Lilian Winkvist-Woods. Finally, I should like to thank my editor, Alison Shaw, Laura Vickers, Kathryn King and other friends at Policy Press for their support and professionalism. Above all, I should like to express my appreciation for the steadfast support and forbearance I have enjoyed from my wife, Josie, to whom the book is dedicated.

LIST OF ACRONYMS

ALMP	active labour market programme
CEO	chief executive officer
CGT	Capital Gains Tax
FTSE 100	Financial Times Stock Exchange 100 index
GDP	Gross Domestic Product
GVA	gross value added
HMRC	Her Majesty's Revenue and Customs
IFS	Institute for Fiscal Studies
IHT	Inheritance Tax
ILO	International Labour Organization
IMF	International Monetary Fund
NI	National Insurance
OBR	Office for Budget Responsibility
OECD	Organisation for Economic Co-operation and Development
ONS	Office for National Statistics
PFI	Private Finance Initiative
SBTC	skill-biased technological change
UC	Universal Credit
VAT	Value Added Tax

1

THE MEANING AND EXTENT OF INEQUALITY

Rising income inequality creates economic, social and political challenges. It can stifle upward social mobility, making it harder for talented and hard-working people to get the rewards they deserve. Intergenerational earnings mobility is low in countries such as Italy, the United Kingdom and the United States, and much higher in the Nordic countries, where income is distributed more evenly (OECD, 2008). The resulting inequality of opportunity will inevitably impact economic performance as a whole, even if the relationship is not straightforward. Inequality also raises political challenges because it breeds social resentment and generates political instability. It can also fuel populist, protectionist and anti-globalisation sentiments. People will no longer support open trade and free markets if they feel that they are losing out while a small group of winners is getting richer and richer. (OECD, 2011a, p 40)

Introduction: four key questions

Rising economic inequality has come to be seen as the greatest challenge, after climate change, facing the advanced Western economies. It was a major factor in the UK referendum vote to leave the EU, as well as in the populist election campaigns of Bernie Sanders and Donald Trump in the US. There seems in fact to be a wide measure of understanding that, to paraphrase a famous 18th-century parliamentary motion, economic inequality has increased, is increasing and ought to be decreased. This book seeks to answer four questions:

1. Has there been an increase in economic inequality in the rich countries of the West over the past 30 or so years?

2. If there has been, should we be worried about it?

3. If we should, what are the causes and what should we do about it?

4. What will be the effect of the policies introduced by the post-2015 Conservative governments and promised in the Conservative Party's 2017 election manifesto, including the May Government's decision to trigger Article 50 of the Treaty of Lisbon?

Some short preliminary responses are set out in Box 1.1. These will form the basis of the arguments to be developed throughout the rest of the book.

Box 1.1 Preliminary responses to four key questions

1. Has there been an increase in economic inequality in the rich countries of the West over the past 30 or so years?

There has been a general increase in inequalities of income and wealth in most Western countries over the past 30 or so years, although the extent varies considerably, especially between the major Anglo-Saxon economies, on the one hand, and continental Europe and Japan, on the other (the northern European countries have also seen a rise, but from a much lower starting point).

2. If there has been, should we be worried about it?

Some degree of economic inequality has often been held to be both inevitable and desirable in providing the necessary stimuli to enterprise, innovation and efficiency. But there are large and growing discrepancies between what certain groups and individuals are contributing to society, and the rewards they receive as a result. This 'contribution gap' is leading to a wide and substantial range of costs and detriments for society. While recent attention has focused on the increased wealth of the very rich – those households at the top of the income distribution – there is also a problem for the middle- and lower-income groups.

3. If we should, what are the causes and what should we do about it?

Many explanations have been offered for the rise in economic inequality. While the main drivers are structural phenomena such as globalisation, technological change and financialisation, the key to understanding why inequality has increased so much in the major Anglophone economies, in particular, lies in the neoliberal reforms of deregulation, privatisation, tax reductions and welfare cutbacks adopted in many countries (but especially in the US and the UK) since the mid-1970s/early 1980s.

Deflationary economic policies and an associated concentration of political (and media) power have reinforced these effects. If we are to reverse, halt or slow increasing inequality we should revisit these reforms, and change or modify some of the main ones. Recent work by International Monetary Fund (IMF) and Organisation for Economic Co-operation and Development (OECD) economists suggests that this can be done without damaging – and indeed restoring – economic growth.

The main areas to be covered in this book are:

- information and transparency;
- tax avoidance and rent seeking;
- taxes on people and property;
- direct and indirect taxes;
- personal savings;
- taxes on top incomes and wealth;
- corporate taxation;
- social expenditure;
- active labour market programmes;
- labour market institutions;
- industrial and competition policy;
- corporate governance;
- the funding of political parties;
- education policy; and
- macroeconomic policy.

In many of these areas, there will need to be action on an international basis.

4. What will be the effect of the policies introduced by the post-2015 Conservative governments and promised in the Conservative party's 2017 election manifesto, including the May Government's decision to trigger Article 50 of the Treaty of Lisbon?

While one or two of the measures introduced or announced since May 2015 will be helpful, the two governments' programmes overall will increase inequality, quite apart from the various complications of Brexit.

This chapter considers the meaning and extent of inequality. Chapter Two looks at the effects of increased inequality. Chapters Three and Four consider the various theories that have been put forward to explain the increases: Chapter Three looks at what have been called 'market' theories, while Chapter Four discusses 'institutional' theories. Chapters Five and Six outline various responses: Chapter Five focuses on taxes, transfers and social expenditure, Chapter Six reviews a wide range of further areas, starting with labour markets. Finally, Chapter Seven discusses the likely impact of the policies and programmes introduced or announced since May 2015.[1]

The meaning and extent of inequality

In general, the definition of within-country inequality used here is an economic one, to refer to significant variances in the distribution of income and wealth. These are often linked to other differences, such as gender, ethnicity, disability, location and so on. The issue is not the existence of inequality of economic resources – hardly anyone argues that everyone should or can be completely equal – but the extent of such inequality and whether this can be justified, for example by the relative contributions that different people make to society. What we are talking about in fact is a marked and increasing imbalance between the contributions that various groups and individuals are making to society, on the one hand, and the economic and other benefits that they derive from it, on the other.[2]

The book is chiefly concerned with *economic* inequality. At least one international survey puts the UK near the bottom of the international table on gender equality (Goodley, 2014). There are also growing intergenerational inequalities (Broughton et al, 2015; Whittaker, 2015; Gardiner, 2016), although these often have an economic dimension: far from generation replacing wealth as a social divider, it accentuates the importance of wealth as the better-off 'baby boomers' pass on their wealth and connections to their children and grandchildren. There are also large and increasing geographical inequalities (Haldane, 2016b). Within-country economic inequality is not confined to the wealthy West. The leading BRICs (Brazil, Russia, India and China) actually have higher levels of inequality as measured by Gini coefficients (see next section) than even America and Britain: South Africa, China, India and Mexico all have inequality well above the US and UK, Russia is just below the US and UK. Milanovic (2011) noted that while between-country inequalities were more important in accounting for global inequality than within-country ones, they do of course contribute to the associated instabilities.[3] Finally, although there are obvious links between inequality and poverty, it is inequality that this book focuses on rather than poverty.[4]

The Gini coefficient

The commonest measure of economic inequality is the Gini coefficient (named after an Italian statistician, Corrado Gini). This measures inequality across the whole of a society rather than simply comparing different income groups. If all of the income in a society went to a single person, and everyone else got nothing, the Gini coefficient would be 1. If it was shared equally, and everyone got exactly the same, the Gini value would be 0. In short, the lower the Gini value, the more equal a society (for details of Gini and other measures, see Equality Trust, 2014a). But while the Gini coefficient is a useful measure for making between-country comparisons, it is less helpful for analysing within-country inequality. Several writers (for example, Voitchovsky, 2005; Cingano, 2014) argue that at least to capture the impact of inequality on economic growth a more differentiated approach is needed based on examining inequality at different points in the income distribution.[5]

Figure 1 shows changes in the values of the OECD member countries' Gini coefficients between the mid-1980s and 2013. As can be seen, the values range from 0.48 (Mexico) to 0.25 (Denmark). The great majority of countries have seen rises over the period, although these have been most marked among the Anglophone countries: the US and GBR (Great Britain) are among the highest 'scorers'.

The actual level of measured inequality in a country is a function of both market incomes (incomes before taxes and transfers such as welfare benefits) and post-tax transfers. A 2012 OECD survey divided the member countries into five groups (see Box 1.2).

Figure 1: Income inequality increased in most OECD countries since 1985

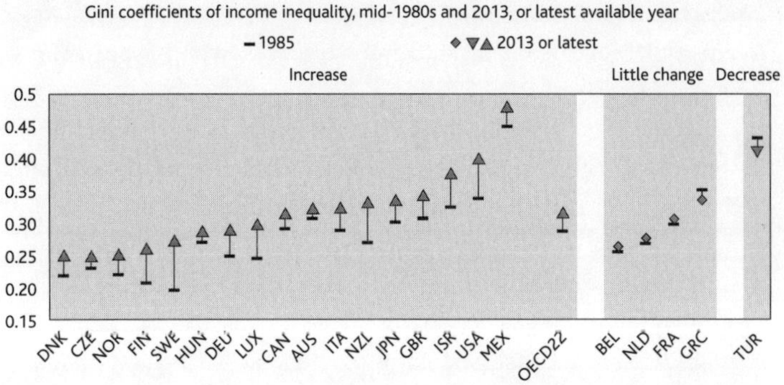

Gini coefficients of income inequality, mid-1980s and 2013, or latest available year

— 1985 ◆ ▼▲ 2013 or latest

Note: 'Little change' in inequality refers to changes of less than 1.5 percentage points.

Source: OECD Income Distribution Database (IDD), www.oecd.org/social/income-distribution-database.htm (OECD, 2015b).

Box 1.2 Inequality in OECD member countries

1. Countries with below-average inequality
Examples: Four Nordic countries, plus Switzerland

In such countries there is little wage dispersion (variations in wages), in particular at the upper end, combined with a high employment rate. Cash transfers (for example, welfare payments) are often universal and household taxes tend to be proportional to household income, implying only moderate redistribution through taxes and transfers. Overall, both the dispersal of disposable income and the poverty rate are well below the OECD average.

2. Countries where inequality arising from the labour market is slightly below the OECD average
Examples: Belgium, the Czech Republic, Estonia, Finland, France, Italy, the Slovak Republic and Slovenia

In most of these, a high concentration of self-employment or capital income (for example, income from shares) brings inequality in household market income close to the average. But the share of tax and cash transfer systems in Gross Domestic Product (GDP) is also large, reducing household income inequality to or below the average.

3. Countries with average inequality

Examples: Seven other continental European countries (Austria, Germany, Greece, Hungary, Luxembourg, Poland and Spain), plus Japan and Korea

In these countries the dispersion in household disposable income and the poverty rate are close to the OECD average.

4. Countries with above-average inequality in labour earnings

Examples: Five English-speaking countries (Australia, Canada, Ireland, New Zealand and the UK) and the Netherlands

In these countries a large share of part-time employment drives inequality in labour earnings, partly offset by a higher employment rate (except in Ireland). Taxes and transfers have some redistributive impact, but not enough to reduce household disposable income to the OECD average, except in the Netherlands.

5. Countries with high inequality

Examples: Chile, Israel, Mexico, Portugal, Turkey and the US

In the above six countries both above-average labour market inequality and low rates of taxes and transfers mean that both inequality in household disposable income and poverty are well above the OECD average (OECD, 2012, pp 188–90; see also, Bogliacino and Maestri, 2014)

Before we get too much further, we should perhaps note that both tax records and household surveys have deficiencies as sources of authoritative data on inequality (Brandolini, 2010, p 212; Atkinson, 2015, pp 46–54; Milanovic, 2016, pp 12–18).

In the US, the Federal Reserve Bank's most recent (2013) triennial Survey of Consumer Finances showed that the share of total income to the top 5% of households (a threshold of $230,000 in gross income in 2013) rose from 31% of income reported by all correspondents in 1989 (the earliest survey), to 37% in 2007. There was then a fall with the financial crisis, but the top 5%'s share of all income was now again 37%. The share of the next 45% fell from 53% in 1989 to 49% in 2013. The bottom half of the distribution (the remaining 50%) saw its share fall from 16% in 1989 to 14% in 2013. This concentration of income reflected incomes and living standards rising much more quickly for those at the top. After adjusting for inflation, the average income of the top 5% rose by 38% between 1989 and 2013, whereas the average income of the remaining 95% grew by less than 10%. The distribution of wealth was even more unequal. The share of all wealth held by the wealthiest 5% of households (over $1.9m) rose from 54% in 1989 to 63% in 2013. The share of the next 45% fell from 43% to 36%, that of the remaining 50% from 3% to 1%. In the UK, the Gini coefficient rose from just under 0.24 in 1977 to 0.34 in 1990 and just under 0.35 in 2007 before moving to its present level (0.34). Jenkins (2015), Belfield et al (2016) and ONS (2017) provide surveys of recent inequality trends in Britain.[6]

Top incomes

In both the US and the UK there have been particularly large increases in the shares of total income taken by the very top earners: the top 1% and, even more, the top 0.1%. In the UK, the share of income taken by the top 1% rose from 5.93% in 1977 to 10.36% in 1993 and 12.7% in 2012; the US percentages at the same dates were 7.9, 12.82 and 22.83. For the top 0.1%, the share in the UK rose from 1.27% in 1977 to 3.09% in 1993 and 4.8% in 2011; the US percentages were 2.04, 4.72 and 7.38.[7] These changes matter because they are likely to affect the entire income distribution. In particular, an increased income share to top earners will increase overall inequality, at least in terms of income before taxes.

Saez (2008) illustrated the significance of the rise in the top income share in the US by comparing trends in real income growth per family between the top 1% and the remaining 99% between 1993 and 2006. Average real incomes per family grew at an average annual rate of 1.9%. This implied a cumulative rise of 28% over the 13-year period. But if the top 1% were excluded, the average growth figure was nearly halved, to about 1.1%, implying a much lower cumulative increase of 15%. Top 1% incomes grew at a much faster rate of 5.7% per year, implying a cumulative growth of 105%. This meant that the top 1% captured about half of all economic growth during the period. Saez blamed the discrepancy on the post-war retreat from the institutions developed during the New Deal and the Second World War, such as progressive taxes, powerful trades unions, corporate provision of health and retirement benefits, and changing social norms regarding pay inequality. These are all matters to which we shall return.

In a further study (2013), Saez calculated that the top 1% had captured 95% of America's economic growth since 2009, although they had also lost three times as much income (relatively) as the remaining 99% during the recession in 2007–09. Over the entire 20-year period 1993 to 2012 the cumulative real growth in top 1% incomes was 86%, compared to 6.6% for the 99%. This implied that the top 1% captured 68% of the total growth during the period. These are amazing, if not actually shocking, figures.[8]

In the UK, Atkinson and Voitchovsky (2011) provided an account of the evolution of top earnings since 1945. Using a number of new data sources, they found a fall in the top (top decile and above) income share up to 1978 and a rise thereafter. They attributed this to a combination of increases in the skill premium, due to globalisation and technological change, and greater individualisation of pay, the latter reversing the systematisation of pay according to position that had dominated the earlier post-war period. Atkinson et al (2011, p 10) also drew attention to the importance of the top 1% for overall inequality:

> if the Gini coefficient for the rest of the population is 40 percent, then a rise of 14 percentage points in the top share, as happened with the share of the top 1 per cent in the United States from 1976 to 2006, causes a rise of 8.4 percentage points in the overall Gini. This is larger than the official Gini increase from 39.8 percent to 47.0 percent over the 1976–2006 period based on U.S. household income in the Current Population Survey (U.S. Census Bureau 2008, table A3).[9]

As Piketty and others have emphasised, these figures for top income shares need to be put into some sort of longer-term perspective (Piketty and Saez, 2006). Atkinson et al (2011) showed how in the US the top-decile income share peaked at nearly 50% in the late 1920s and then fell in the post-Second World War period before rebounding from the mid-1970s: what Paul Krugman (2007) has termed 'the Great Divergence'. A similar pattern could be seen with the top 1% income shares in both the US and the other major English-speaking countries: the UK, Canada, Australia, New Zealand and Ireland. Top 1% shares were also highest in the early part of the century in France, Germany, the Netherlands, Sweden and Japan but there was not the same recovery after 1945 as in the US and UK.

Alvaredo et al (2013) provided a similar analysis of trends in top incomes. They explained the growth in top income shares in terms of four factors (see Box 1.3).

Box 1.3 Four reasons for the increase in top incomes

1. Changes in top tax rates

Tax rates had moved in the opposite direction from top pre-tax income shares, and without any significant benefits to either economic growth or corporate performance.[10]

2. A richer model of pay determination

Highly skilled workers and executives had both gained greater bargaining power as a result of globalisation and technological change and also, because of changes in tax rates, had more incentive to divert effort into personal remuneration issues, at the expense of corporate investment, employment and growth.

3. U-shaped path of private wealth over time

In Europe, though less so in the US, (relative to national income) there has been a spectacular U-shaped path of private wealth over time, with the possibility that inherited wealth could be making a comeback (see next section). This in turn implied that inheritance and capital income taxation could again become central policy tools for curbing inequality.

4. The increasing correlation between earned and capital income

Earned and capital income had become more closely associated in the US.

Source: Alvaredo et al (2013).

These again are all matters we shall return to.

Top incomes and wealth

The recent surge in top incomes, especially labour incomes, is also a major cause of the increased concentration of wealth in the US that has been the counterpart to increased income inequality.

Owing to the development of the offshore wealth management industry, changes in tax avoidance behaviours and indirect wealth ownership through trusts and foundations, as well as the intangible nature of many assets, the difficulties of getting reliable data about wealth are even greater than those in getting good information on incomes. Using tax data, Saez and Zucman (2014) found that, as with incomes, the distribution of wealth in the US had followed a U-shaped pattern since the early years of the last century, with a decline from the late 1920s and a marked rebound after 1980. By 2012, the top 10% owned 77.2% of all wealth, the top 1% owned 41.8%, the top 0.1% owned 22% and the top 0.01% (1 in 10,000 households) owned 11.2%. This rise was almost entirely due to the increase in the top 0.1% share, from 7% in 1979. They commented that:

> Income inequality has a snowballing effect on the wealth distribution: top incomes are being saved at high rates, pushing wealth concentration up; in turn, rising wealth inequality leads to rising capital income concentration, which contributes to further increasing top income and wealth shares. Our core finding is that this snowballing effect has been sufficiently powerful to dramatically affect the shape

of the US wealth distribution over the last 30 years.
(Saez and Zucman, 2014, p 3)

What about the rest of the population? Over the 20th century, the wealth share of the bottom 90% rose from a low point of 15% in the late 1920s and the start of the Great Depression to 35% in the mid-1980s, thanks to rising pension and housing wealth. It then dropped back to 23% in 2012 because of an increase in mortgage and other debts:

> The key driver of the declining bottom 90% share is the fall of middle-class saving, a fall which itself may partly owe to the low growth of middle-class income, to financial deregulation leading to some forms of predatory lending, or to growing behavioural biases in the savings decisions of middle-class households. (Saez and Zucman, 2014, p 3)

As regards the last of these possible causes, the authors commented that many individuals do not know how to invest properly, and often end up spending too much on servicing short-term debt at high interest rates.

In Britain too, wealth is even more unevenly distributed than income. Taking all forms of wealth other than accrued pension rights, Hills (2014, pp 149–52) showed that in 2008–10 on average each household had wealth of £220,000. But nearly two-thirds of households had wealth below this. Half of them had less than £145,000 – two-thirds of the average or less. A tenth of households had wealth of less than £7,500, and 2% had 'negative' wealth – debts bigger than assets, even including personal possessions. At the other end of the scale, 1 in 10 households had non-pension wealth of over £489,000, and 1% had more than £1.4m. If pension rights were included, the slope sharpened and the ratio of wealth at the 90th percentile to the 10th percentile increased from 65.2 to 71. A more recent study (Crawford et al, 2015) estimated median household wealth in Britain in 2010–12 at £172,000. While 9% of households had no positive net wealth, 5% had more than £1.2m. The Gini coefficient for total household wealth was 0.65, compared with

0.40 for household net income. Financial wealth was the most unequally distributed component of wealth, with a coefficient of 0.91, followed by private pensions (0.73) and property net of mortgage debt (0.64) (see also Alvaredo et al, 2016).

A squeezed middle?

As well as looking at top incomes we need to look at what is happening at the middle and lower ends of the income distribution. In analysing the impact of inequality on economic growth, Cingano (2014, p 6) argued that what matters most is the gap between low-income households and the rest of the population. By 'low-income' households Cingano went up to the 40th percentile:

> The analysis in this paper suggests ... that it is not just poverty (i.e., the incomes of the lowest 10% of the population) that inhibits growth. Instead it suggests that policymakers need to be concerned about the bottom 40% more generally, including the vulnerable lower middle classes at risk of failing to benefit from the recovery and future growth. Anti-poverty programmes will not be enough. (Cingano, 2014, p 29)

A very recent (December 2016) analysis (Piketty et al, 2016) combines tax, survey and national accounts data to estimate the distribution of income in the US since 1913. It finds that while average pre-tax national income per adult has increased by 60% since 1980, it has stagnated for the bottom half of the distribution at about $16,000 a year. Interestingly, the pre-tax income of the middle class – adults between the median and the 90th percentile – has grown 40% since 1980. This was due very largely to the rise of tax-exempt fringe benefits. A recent Institute for Fiscal Studies (IFS) report (Belfield et al, 2016) finds that in many key respects middle-income families with children now more closely resemble poor families. Half are now renters (rather than owner-occupiers) and, while poorer families have become less reliant on benefits as employment has risen, middle-income households with children now get 30% of their income from benefits and tax credits, compared to 22% 20 years ago.

The impact of the recession

A recent OECD survey (2016e) finds that, at least up to 2013/14, the recession had little overall impact on income inequality for the member countries as a group. However, as we shall see in Chapter Four, a number of commentators believe that the concentration of wealth has increased as a result of the monetary policies – ultra-low interest rates and 'quantitative easing' (the purchase of government debt by the monetary authorities, so releasing money into the economy) – that were adopted to cope with the crisis and that have increased the value of assets, especially financial assets. This has increased the wedge between those with substantial assets – a small minority – and those who rely on wages and salaries (as well as fixed incomes, like annuity holders) – the great majority.[11]

Inequality of consumption

There is an argument that, in welfare terms, analysing trends in inequality of consumption could be more informative than looking at trends in inequality of income. To quote the authors of a wide-ranging review:

> Since individuals' utility is typically defined over consumption goods rather than income per se, one may argue that measures of consumption inequality get closer to an ideal measure of inequality in household welfare than income inequality. Moreover, large changes in income inequality may reflect transitory variations, and these may have small welfare effects if households can smooth their consumption against transitory shocks. In other words, consumption might be a better proxy of 'permanent income'. Consumption inequality might therefore provide a more reliable measure of inequality in long term living standards than income. (Attanasio et al, 2013)

However, the authors found that consumption inequality within the US between 1980 and 2010 had increased by nearly the same amount as income inequality. This finding was very robust to alternative measures of consumption, and across all data sets (see also Atkinson, 2015, pp 33–7).

Functional income inequality

Hitherto we have been talking about inequalities in personal or household incomes or wealth. It is also necessary to consider the *functional* distribution of income, and especially the share of national income taken by the wages on which the great bulk of the population depends for its income.

A number of studies (Daudey and Garcia-Penalosa, 2007; Arpaia et al, 2009; Kristal, 2010; Peters, 2010; Bailey et al, 2011; Reed and Himmelweit, 2012; Karabarbounis and Neiman, 2012, 2013; Lansley and Reed, 2013; Stockhammer, 2013; Piketty, 2014a; Atkinson, 2015; ILO, 2015) chart reductions in the share of national income taken by wages over the past 30 or so years. In Britain, according to Office for National Statistics (ONS) data, the wage share of GDP (strictly, employee compensation including both wages and salaries and employers' social contributions) fell from 60.1% in 1975 to 49.7% in 2015. For the US, the comparable percentages are 56.7 and 53.1 (shares of gross domestic income: Compensation of employees, paid, percent, annual, not seasonally adjusted – Federal Reserve Data).[12]

There is a clear link between changes in the wage share and changes in levels of inequality. Daudey and Garcia-Penalosa (2007) demonstrated that a larger labour share in national income was associated with a lower Gini coefficient of personal incomes (that is, a greater compression of incomes). Stockhammer (2013) looked at changing wage shares in GDP in 71 countries (28 advanced, 43 developing or emerging) between 1970 and 2007. He found that wage shares had fallen in most countries over the period, whereas previously they had been stable or even increasing. Overall, real wage growth had lagged behind increases in productivity since around 1980. The International Labour Organization (ILO) noted (2015, p 10) that because capital is more concentrated than labour endowments, declining labour shares are frequently associated with greater income inequality. It found quite a high correlation (0.57) between a falling labour share and widening market income disparities. It also noted that declining labour shares had important macroeconomic consequences, with a negative impact on consumption not being offset by increases in investment or job creation. Yet again, these are matters that we shall come back to.

Trends in real wages

The recent OECD survey (2016e) also mentions falls in real disposable income since the 2007–09 financial crisis: an average decline across all member countries of 2.1% between 2007 and 2010, with the strongest decline (5.3%) for the bottom decile. In a recent speech the Governor of the Bank of England, Mark Carney, referred to data showing that over the past decade real earnings in Britain had grown at their slowest rate since the mid-19th century. He remarked that 'Inequalities which might have been tolerated during generalised prosperity are felt more acutely when economies stagnate' (Carney, 2016, p 5). Moreover, several respected independent agencies – including the Office for Budget Responsibility (OBR), the IFS and the Resolution Foundation – have forecast that average wages will not recover to pre-crisis levels until the end of the decade at the earliest (Tetlow and O'Connor, 2016). The US position is broadly similar (Pew Research Center, 2015). The continuing stagnation of wages will have a very bad impact on future social mobility, as several studies (for example, Dobbs et al, 2016) have pointed out (social mobility is discussed in Chapter Two).

Conclusion

There has clearly been an increase in economic inequality in the wealthy West over the past 30 years or so. But there have also been different inequalities at different points in the income distribution. It is understandable that attention has been focused on the increasing shares of income (and economic growth) taken by the rich and very rich, not least because of the political consequences (which we shall examine in Chapter Two). But it is also vital to attend to inequalities at the middle and lower ends of the spectrum, not only for social cohesion but also for economic growth and efficiency. There is a particular concern about the 'lower middle class', those households between the 30th and 70th points on the income distribution, who have suffered from worsening employment conditions without as much social protection as those lower down the income spectrum.

There appear in fact to have been two main things going on: a longer-term weakening in the position of the lower middle and upper working classes through the increasing compression of wages, and a strengthening of the position of the wealthy and very wealthy through increased returns on capital as well as much higher levels of top remuneration and lower rates of tax. Both phenomena reflect the fact – accepted by almost everyone – that the proceeds of economic growth have been shared more and more unequally, and that both involve a redistribution of income and wealth to households towards the top of the income distribution. In the circumstances it is hardly surprising that economic inequality has become a major political issue in Britain and America, where populist candidates from a wide range of affiliations have attacked the elite establishment for its protection of high incomes and wealth. However, these are only some of the detriments of inequality, as we shall see in Chapter Two.

2

INEQUALITY: FOR AND AGAINST

Inequality is not necessarily bad in itself, the key question is to decide whether it is justified, whether there are reasons for it. (Piketty, 2014a, p 19)

Introduction

Chapter Two looks at what we know about the impact of the rising economic inequality described in Chapter One. It looks first at the claimed benefits of inequality before turning to the alleged costs and detriments. It concludes that the latter far outweigh the former, especially in view of the extent to which inequality has increased in most Western countries over the past 30 or so years.

The case for inequality

One of the difficulties in studies looking at market-based policies on higher education (Brown, 2011; Brown with Carasso, 2013) was the fact that books and articles advocating marketisation were much harder to come by, and much less specific, than evidence-based critiques. There is a similar problem here. The negative effects of inequality, or at least the degree of inequality that we now have in most Western societies, are much more fully written up than the positive ones. In broad terms, however, some measure of inequality has been held to be justified on the basis that (a) full equality is unattainable because economic actors usually start with very different amounts of the various forms of capital, and (b) even if it could be achieved, equality would be undesirable because it would reduce incentives to work, study, save, take risks and/or invest (richer people save more and this provides the basis for capital accumulation and investment). On this view, some inequality is the price that has to be paid for economic growth and prosperity. To quote a former Mayor of London:

> Some measure of inequality is essential for the spirit of envy and keeping up with the Joneses that is, like greed, a valuable spur to economic activity. (Johnson, 2013)

Or, for a more scholarly view:

> Inequality of wealth and incomes is the cause of the masses' well being, not the cause of anyone's distress ...Where there is a lower degree of inequality, there is necessarily a lower standard of living for the masses. (Ludwig von Mises' Ideas on Liberty {Irvington, New York, 1955} quoted in Lansley, 2011, p 36; see also Okun, 1975)

As Bartels (2008, p 14) noted, even the great liberal philosopher John Rawls (1971) argued that inequality was just in so far as it contributed to the well-being of the least well-off members of society. Of course, Rawls was writing before US levels of income inequality returned to those of the so-called Gilded Age before the First World War. But it is also arguable that inequality is less important in an economy that is many times as productive as it was 200 years ago: even the poorest members of society enjoy goods and services that were unavailable to even the richest a few decades ago.

Welch (1999) argued that without inequality of priorities and capabilities there would be no trade, no specialisation and no surpluses produced by cooperation. But he went on to say:

> So if we agree that inequality is good in principle, why then must we assume as an article of faith that increasing inequality is necessarily bad? I would argue that inequality is destructive whenever the low-wage citizenry views society as unfair, when it views effort as not worthwhile, when upward mobility is viewed as impossible or as so unlikely that its pursuit is not worthwhile. Even more extreme, inequality can be literally destructive if it leads to 'illegal' attempts to redistribute. (Welch, 1999, p 2)

Yet these are conditions that already exist, as the popular support for Brexit and President Trump surely indicates.

Milanovic (2011, pp 53–60) showed how greater equality, reinforced by political coercion, damaged the economies of the major socialist countries during the 20th century, although this also suggests that distribution can be changed by different political arrangements. Milanovic estimated that socialism reduced inequality as measured by Gini coefficients by about a quarter in the countries concerned, compared with what it would have been under capitalism. This was achieved through the nationalisation of production and land (which obliterated the large industrial and landowning fortunes); full employment (which cut the bottom of the income distribution as nationalisation cut the top); generalised compulsory and free education (which increased overall educational levels); and a network of different social transfers, from subsidised transport and vacations to child allowances and pensions (which were received by almost everybody). But socialism also lowered incentives, so that productivity stagnated, and reduced innovation. Of course, the fact that the economic price of greater equality was so high does not necessarily justify the current levels of inequality in some wealthy capitalist economies. Indeed, Milanovic contrasted 'good' inequality (creating the right incentives for economic growth and innovation) with 'bad' inequality (where inequality provides the means to preserve acquired positions). The issue of course is: what is the 'right' level of inequality, and how to achieve it.

In any event, the economic case for inequality has been holed, if not demolished, by the work of economists at two of the most important international organisations, the IMF and the OECD.

Using a cross-country dataset that distinguished market income inequality from net income inequality, and that enabled them to calculate redistributive transfers for a large number of country-year observations, IMF economists found that lower net inequality was robustly correlated with faster and more durable growth, for a given level of redistribution. At the same time, redistribution appeared generally benign in its impact on growth. Only in extreme cases was there some evidence that it might have had some direct negative effects on growth (Ostry et al, 2014; see also, Ostry, 2014). A further IMF analysis (Dabla-Norris et al, 2015) examined how individuals' income shares at various points in the distribution matter for growth. A higher net Gini coefficient – a measure of inequality that nets out taxes and transfers, that is, disposable income – was associated with lower output growth over the medium term:

> More importantly, we find an inverse relationship between the income share accruing to the rich (top 20 per cent) and economic growth. If the income share of the top 20 percent increases by 1 percentage point, GDP growth is actually 0.8 percentage point *lower* in the following five years, suggesting that the benefits do not trickle down. Instead, a similar increase in the income share of the bottom 20 percent (the poor) is associated with 0.38 percentage point *higher* growth. This positive relationship between disposable income shares and higher growth continues to hold for the second and third quintiles (the middle class). (Dabla-Norris et al, 2015, pp 6–7; original emphases)

What is of particular interest in the present context is the means through which rising inequality damages growth.

- **It reduces the ability of lower-income households to stay healthy** and accumulate physical and human capital, for example by investing in education or training.
- **It dampens investment** by fuelling economic, financial and political instability.
- **It can lead to a backlash** against market-based policies to promote growth.
- **It hampers poverty reduction**. (Dabla-Norris et al, 2015, pp 8–9)

In December 2014 the OECD published a study by one of its economists (Cingano, 2014) that also suggested that income inequality has a negative, statistically significant impact upon subsequent growth. The study drew on harmonised data covering the OECD countries over the past 30 years. It estimated that between 1985 and 2005 rising inequality had knocked 10 percentage points off growth in Mexico and New Zealand. In the US, the UK, Sweden, Finland and Norway the growth rate would have been more than a *fifth* higher, had income disparities not widened (the Nordic countries did of course start from a lower level of inequality in the first place). On the other hand, greater equality helped to increase GDP per head in Spain, France and Ireland prior to the economic crisis.

According to the OECD (2015a, p 67), had inequality not increased between 1985 and 2005, the average OECD country would have grown by nearly a third. One of the main ways in which this occurs is through raising the relative cost of education of an increasing fraction of families in the bottom half of the income distribution: note again, not just the bottom 10%, this is not simply about poverty.

The analysis looked at three sets of indicators:

1. **the quantity of human capital accumulated by the individual**, including the probability of attaining tertiary education, and the number of completed years of formal education;

2. **skill proficiency**, capturing cognitive ability and therefore also accounting for the quality of the education completed;

3. **probability of employment**.

To quote:

> The results of all three approaches indicate that widening income disparities lowers [sic] the outcomes of individuals from low socio-economic backgrounds, but does not affect those of individuals from medium and high backgrounds ... the results strongly support the idea that higher inequality lowers opportunities for education (and social mobility) for disadvantaged individuals in the society, an effect that dominates the potentially positive impacts [on economic growth] through incentives. (OECD, 2015a, p 74)

In other words, policies that limit or reverse the long rise in inequality would not only make societies fairer, but also make them richer. Both the OECD and the IMF have long been cheerleaders for free markets and deregulation, so this is quite a policy turnaround. It is also of interest that both sets of economists have highlighted investment in education as the principal channel through which increased inequality damages the economy. This takes us quite neatly to a discussion of the detriments of inequality.

The case against inequality

> Where the riches are in few hands these must enjoy all the power, and will readily conspire to lay the whole burthen on the poor, and oppress them still further, to the discouragement of all industry. (David Hume, *Of Commerce*, p 15, quoted in Thompson, 2007, p 45)

The literature surveyed points to five main sets of costs and detriments of inequality: social, educational, economic, environmental and political. There is also, of course, a moral dimension. The greater the amount of inequality, the harder it is to achieve real equality of opportunity, the ability to achieve something entirely through your own ambition and efforts (Barry, 2005).

Social impacts

One influential review of the social effects of increased inequality is that of Wilkinson and Pickett (2009). They identified associations between significant levels of within-country inequality and a wide range of social problems: levels of trust (essential not only for social cohesion but also for efficient market transactions), mental illness (including drug and alcohol addiction), life expectancy and infant mortality, obesity, children's educational performance, teenage births, homicides, imprisonment rates and social mobility. They combined all the health- and social-problem data for each major developed country and each US state to make an Index of Health and Social Problems. For each dataset (that is, country and state) a higher score on the Index was strongly associated with income inequality (but weakly related to average incomes). The UNICEF index of child well-being in rich countries was also related to income inequality (Wilkinson and Pickett, 2009, pp 19–26). Underlying these specific symptoms, there had been a general deterioration in community life, social relations and social cohesion, something also highlighted by the UK Social Integration Commission (2015). Finally, rising inequality contributes to rising insecurity, not only for workers competing in increasingly difficult labour markets but also for the wealthy living in separate, sometimes protected, enclaves (Judt, 2010).

In his most recent book, Milanovic (2016, p 197) suggests that 'rather than financing public education, the rich might prefer to use public funds on increased policing and what Marx called "guard labor"'. Bowles and Jayadev (2005) used the guard labour model to identify the resources devoted to the exercise of power in the US. They showed a considerable increase in its extent since 1890. Furthermore, cross-national comparisons showed a significant statistical association between income inequality and the fraction of the labour force that was constituted by such labour, as well as with measures of political legitimacy (inversely) and political conflict: the more unequal the society, the greater the use of such labour. The late Tony Judt (2010, p 107) commented on the irony that it is the states that have been foremost in market-based reforms – rather than the cradle-to-grave 'nanny states' – that have also gone furthest in keeping tabs on their citizens.

Studying health, Marmot (2015) wrote of a 'social gradient' whereby increasing differences in power, money and resources translate into increasing inequities in health. Early child development, education and lifelong learning, employment and working conditions, and the provision of welfare are all areas where widening inequalities play out in differential health outcomes. Social and community cohesion are also put at risk (see also Bambra, 2016; Bennett et al, 2016; ONS, 2016b).

Dorling (2014, p 24) highlighted the social and cultural attitudes that go with and exacerbate inequality:

> Inequality is more than just economics – it is the culture that divides and makes social mobility so painful, both for those dropping down the income and wealth scales and for those going up.

In an earlier book (2011) Dorling noted evidence that unequal societies tend to breed superiority and inferiority complexes, while people in more equal societies will see themselves as more similar to their peers. Some of the other social detriments of inequality include poorer relationships and social segregation, greater insecurity and mistrust, and valuing money for what it represents rather than for what it can buy: a 'multiplication' approach to money rather than an 'additive' one. Inequality of all kinds was sustained by five specific sets of beliefs: elitism (some children can be better educated than others); exclusion of some people from society is necessary (the poor are always with us); prejudice (people are born with inherent differences); greed is good; and despair is inevitable (for Dorling's theory about the origins of these beliefs, see Chapter Four).

A number of writers (for example, Chang, 2013) draw attention to the way in which the poorer members of society are scapegoated for society's ills – the 'strivers or skivers' approach – where increased welfare spending is blamed for the recent collapse in the public finances, rather than the true cause, the fall in economic activity and tax receipts due to the world-wide recession:

> The beauty of this worldview – for those who disproportionately benefit from the present system – is that, by reducing everything down to individuals, it draws people's attention away from the structural causes of poverty and inequality. (Chang, 2013)

Television programmes like *Benefits Street* provide a regular diet of what David Sayer (2016, p 299) calls 'poverty porn', while both television and newspapers indulge viewers' and readers' fantasies about the lives led by the rich and famous. There have even been instances of successful entrepreneurs attacking the poor, homeless or unemployed, with the implication that their predicament was essentially of their own making (Levin, 2016). Of course, this is a familiar trope in British media coverage of these issues (for some examples, see Jones, 2014, pp 87–8).

The cost of inequality

In 2014 the Equality Trust estimated that if UK inequality was reduced to the average OECD level the UK could expect to:

- increase healthy life expectancy by 8½ months (at a value of £12.5bn)
- reduce mental health illness rates by 5% (£25bn)
- imprison 37% fewer people (£1bn)
- experience 33% fewer murders (£678m).

When broken down to an individual level, the impact on each man, woman and child was the equivalent of £622 (Equality Trust, 2014b). It has not been possible to find other or more recent estimates.

Social mobility

> More people believe it is difficult to move between classes today than did 10 years ago. Nearly 3 in 4 (73%) believe it is fairly or very difficult to move between classes, compared with 65% who held this view in 2005. People who identify as working class are more likely than middle class identifiers to think moving between classes is very difficult. (Nat Cen Social Research, 2016)

Falling social mobility, and especially declining intergenerational social mobility – the possibility of moving up (or down) the income or wage scale relative to one's parents – has become a major concern in a number of Western countries. It is a particular worry in the US, given the strong historical attachment to the notion that any child, however modest their origins, can grow up to be president. Yet, with high inequality, economic advantage is more likely to be inherited than earned.

In his magisterial review of the historical relationship between economic growth and well-being, Angus Deaton equated social mobility with equal opportunity:

> Even if we believe that equality of opportunity is what we want, and we don't care about inequality of outcomes, the two tend to go together, which suggests that inequality itself is a barrier to equal opportunity. (Deaton, 2013, p 107)

Wilkinson and Pickett (2009, pp 157–69) reviewed the evidence linking rising income inequality to falling social mobility based on the eight countries (Canada, Denmark, Finland, Germany, Norway, Sweden, UK and US) for which there was reasonable mobility data. They found a clear association between higher inequality and lower mobility. They noted that, after slowly increasing from 1950 to 1980, US social mobility declined rapidly as income differences widened. They also identified an international relationship between public expenditure on education (elementary/primary and high/secondary school) and inequality, with the countries with the lowest levels of social mobility having the lowest shares of public expenditure. Wilkinson and Pickett further drew attention to the way in which, in both America and Britain, as inequality has grown, greater social distances have been translated into greater geographical segregation between rich and poor.

In a speech in 2012, the then Chairman of the US Council of Economic Advisers, Alan B. Krueger, drew attention to the evidence that as inequality had increased, year-to-year or generation-to-generation economic mobility had diminished. He highlighted a measure known as Intergenerational Income Elasticity (IGE). This means that if someone's parents earned 50% more than the average, their child could be expected to earn 20% above the average in their generation. The US IGE was predicted to increase from 0.47 to 0.56. In other words, the persistence in the advantages and disadvantages of income passed from parents to children could rise by a quarter for the next generation as a result of the rise in inequality that the US had seen over the preceding 25 years. Krueger introduced the

Figure 2: The Great Gatsby curve: inequality and intergenerational mobility

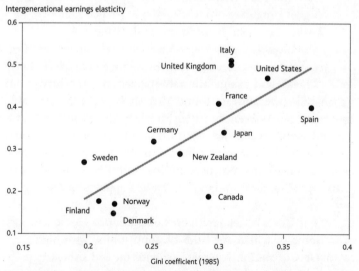

Source: Economic Report to the President (2012, p 177) quoted by Jerrim and Macmillan (2014, p 32)

'Great Gatsby Curve': a graph that plots the relationship between inequality as measured by the Gini coefficient (the horizontal axis) and intergenerational social mobility as measured by the IGE (the vertical axis) for the major Western countries (Figure 2).

There was a close relationship between the two variables: the greater the degree of inequality, the higher the IGE. The US came out at the top of the curve (highest on both measures), with the UK and Italy not far behind. The countries at the other end of the curve were Finland, Denmark, Norway and Sweden, followed by Germany and New Zealand. A more recent study (Chetty et al, 2014b) found that children entering the US labour market today have the same chances of moving up in the income distribution (relative to their parents) as those born in the 1970s and 1980s. But because inequality has risen in the meantime, the consequences of the 'birth lottery' – the parents to whom a child is born – are larger today than in the past:

> A useful visual analogy is to envision the income distribution as a ladder, with each percentile representing a different rung. The rungs of the ladder have grown further apart (inequality has increased), but children's chances of climbing from lower to higher rungs have not changed (rank-based mobility has remained stable). (Chetty et al, 2014b, p 1)

In a parallel paper using data from the 1980–86 cohorts (Chetty et al, 2014a), and using commuting zones as the primary unit of analysis, the authors found that there were considerable geographical differences *within* the US: the probability that a child would reach the top quintile of the national income distribution starting from a family in the bottom quintile was 4.4% in Charlotte, North Carolina, but 12.9% in San Jose, California. So, far from being a 'land of opportunity':

> The U.S. is better described as a collection of societies, some of which are 'lands of opportunity' with high rates of mobility across generations, and others in which few children escape poverty. (Chetty et al, 2014a, p.1; see also, *Economist*, 2015)

Education was important: by electing their own local school boards, and by funding their schools through property taxes, the Americans had all but ensured that the quality of their children's education would be determined by zip code (Klein, 2014).

Miles Corak (2013) noted that it was the very strong attachment to the 'American Dream' that made Americans less intolerant of inequality than most European countries and that, together with a suspicion of or antipathy towards government, rendered them resistant to redistributive policies. Yet greater inequality of incomes meant that family background played a stronger role in determining young people's adult outcomes than did their own talents and effort. Increasingly, indeed, it is the differential investments in the human capital of children that determine their adult earnings and socioeconomic status (as argued in the IMF and OECD work). In turn, the parents' incentive to invest rises as the returns on tertiary education increase as a function of increased inequality, and especially the significant increase in the share of total earnings and incomes accruing to the very top of the distribution.

Corak reviewed a range of studies that unpack the ways in which increasing economic inequality feeds through into differential educational attainment (McLanahan, 2004; Belley and Lochner, 2007; Bailey and Dynarski, 2011; Corak et al, 2011; Reardon, 2011). Duncan and Murnane (2011, p 11) have a figure (1.6) showing how spending on 'child-enrichment' goods and services (books, computers, high-quality childcare, summer camps, private schools and so on) has increased for American families in the top quintile to a far greater extent than for those in the bottom one (the figure is based on consumer expenditure surveys by the US Bureau of Labor Statistics). In 1972/73 high-income families spent about $2,700 more per year on such activities; by 2005/06 this gap had almost tripled, to $7,500. Francis and Hutchings (2013) provided a general survey of how better-off parents in the UK were using their money and information to boost their children's chances of success.

In the UK, there have been a number of studies that show declining intergenerational social mobility since the 1970s (for example, Blanden et al, 2005). In an issue of the *British Journal of Sociology* (Bukodi et al, 2014), Erzsebet and colleagues reported on a study of more than 20,000 Britons born in 1946, 1958, 1970 and 1980–84. They compared the class of each individual when in their late 20s or 30s with that of their father. They found that social mobility was now more likely to be downward in nature. Across all birth cohorts, about three-quarters of men and women ended up in a different class to the one they were born in, a proportion that has stayed roughly stable over time. However, the study found that inequalities in the *relative* chances of mobility were greater than thought, with the child of a higher-professional or managerial father 20 times more likely to end up in a similarly high-status job than a child with a working-class father was to end up in a professional job. The conclusion was that society needs to actively renew its stock of 'top jobs' if we do not want to consign graduates to lower-level jobs than their parents (see also Clark and Cummins, 2014, and Jerrim and Macmillan, 2014).

In a wider review, McKnight and Cowell concluded that the evidence was split between cross-country studies showing a clear relationship between higher cross-sectional inequality and lower intergenerational mobility, and the limited evidence from across-time studies within countries, where the findings were less conclusive. However:

> Recent increases at the top of the income distribution in a number of countries may influence future trends, as 'stickiness' at the top of the income distribution, even in countries such as Sweden with relatively high levels of intergenerational mobility, appears to be leading to rich dynasties. Evidence from the USA examining a number of precursive factors predicts that intergenerational mobility will fall in the future. (McKnight and Cowell, 2014, p 194).[1]

Educational impacts

> One major systemic failing in the UK education system is the 'long tail' of poorly performing schools and pupils compared with other countries, particularly at the secondary level. A significant

part of the explanation for this is the stubborn link between pupils' socio-economic background and their educational attainment. For example, a fifth of children in England on free school meals (a common measure of disadvantage) do not reach the expected maths level at age 7 (Key Stage 1) and this proportion rises to a third by age 11 (Key Stage 2). The correlation between disadvantage and poor academic attainment is particularly strong in the UK. (Aghion et al, 2013, pp 16–17)

It seems clear that as income inequality rises, there is a greater and greater disparity in the resources that rich and poor families are able to invest in their children's education. There is indeed ample evidence of the association between family poverty and educational attainment, what has been termed the 'attainment gap' or the 'achievement gap'(for example, Clifton and Cook, 2013). Moreover, this association becomes clear even before children start school (Machin, 2009; Government Equalities Office, 2010; Crawford et al, 2014; Fair Education Alliance, 2014).

Wilkinson and Pickett (2009, pp 103–17) reviewed the evidence showing that more unequal countries and, within the US, more unequal states, have worse educational attainment (as well as more drop-outs). It also appears that the steepness of the social gradient affects the absolute levels of educational performance achieved. The quality of family life in less-equal societies clearly has an impact on subsequent educational achievement. But inequality also has a direct effect on children's cognitive abilities and learning. Finally, greater inequality creates a bigger gap between children's aspirations and their chances of realising them.

A 2013 review of 34 studies with strong evidence about whether money affects children's outcomes (Cooper and Stewart, 2013) found that children in lower-income families have worse cognitive, social-behavioural and health outcomes, in part because they are poorer, and not just because low income is correlated with other household and parental characteristics. The evidence was strongest for cognitive development and school achievement, followed by social-behavioural development. Income also affects outcomes that indirectly affect children, including maternal mental health, parenting and the home environment. The impact of increases in income on cognitive development appears to be broadly comparable to that of spending similar amounts on school or early education programmes. Increasing household income could substantially reduce differences in schooling outcomes, while also improving wider aspects of children's well-being (see also, Connelly et al, 2014, and Sammons et al, 2015).

The Commission on Inequality in Education (Social Market Foundation, 2016a) found that only 40% of pupils receiving free school meals achieved five A★ to C GCSEs, compared with 70% of other pupils. The performance gap between the richest and the poorest pupils had remained persistently large between the mid-1980s and the mid-2000s. One reason for this might be that teachers serving lower-income communities have more characteristics that are associated with lower rates of educational progress – unqualified, lacking experience, not having an academic degree in the subject being taught – together with higher teacher turnover (Social Market Foundation, 2016b).

As well as damaging a country's educational performance, educational inequality also has an economic impact. In his analysis of the causes of the financial crash and the subsequent Great Recession, Wolf (2014b) agreed with Stiglitz (2013a) that, in addition to weakening demand, rising inequality causes lagging progress in raising educational levels. This in turn will impair an economy's longer-term success, on both the demand and supply sides. There is ample evidence from both the US and Britain that, as inequality increases, students from poorer households are falling behind those from wealthier backgrounds in participation and achievement in tertiary education.[2]

Economic impact

As extensive an analysis as any of the economic costs of increased inequality is that of the Nobel Prize winner Joseph Stiglitz (2013a). Greater inequality both reduces output and increases instability, which in turn further reduces growth by disincentivising investment (Alesina and Perotti, 1993; for a review of the relevant literature, see Bartels, 2008, p 14). Output is lower because demand is lower: the rich save a larger proportion of their wealth than the less well-off, who also have less to spend (see also Herzer and Vollmer, 2013). Greater inequality is a major contributor to what Laurence Summers (2013) has termed 'secular stagnation', an economic period of persistently insufficient demand relative to the aggregate savings of households and corporations, which the main Western economies are now experiencing. Inequality increases the level of debt as the less well-off borrow to maintain their standard of living, with the excess savings of the rich providing the necessary credit. With deregulation, increased debt also increases risks and was a major contributor to, if not the underlying cause of, the 2008 financial crash (Kumhof and Ranciere, 2010; Rajan, 2010; Milanovic, 2011; Onaran, et al, 2011; Galbraith, 2012; Kumhof et al, 2012; Sturn and van Treeck, 2013; Mian and Sufi, 2014; Wolf, 2014a; Piketty, 2014a).[3]

On top of this, the economy is less productive and efficient. To quote the June 2016 OECD Ministerial Council:

> there is a risk of a vicious cycle setting in, with individuals with fewer skills and poorer access to opportunities often confined to operate in low productivity, precarious jobs, and … in the informal economy. This reduces aggregate productivity, widens inequality, and ultimately undermines policy efforts to increase productivity and growth. (OECD, 2016c, p 5)

As the OECD says, while incentives are important, so are opportunities. There is reduced public investment in infrastructure and education (leading to declines in opportunities and social mobility); massive distortions in the economy through rent seeking and 'financialisation';[4] and a reduction in the motivation of the workforce, especially through the undermining of conventional notions of fairness (Stiglitz, 2013a, pp 115–32). Finally, reduced rates of personal and corporate tax – owing to depressed levels of economic activity and widespread tax avoidance, as well as lower rates of tax generally – further jeopardise the supply of public goods. As the supply of public goods diminishes, people in turn feel less and less like paying for them.[5]

Economic growth

Reference has already been made to the work of economists from the IMF and the OECD on the relationship between income inequality and economic growth. This comes on top of a much earlier study by Persson and Tabellini (1991). To recap, Ostry et al (2014) established that even large redistributions through taxes and transfers do not seem to carry a clear cost to growth. Cingano (2014) referred to what has been called 'human capital accumulation theory' (Galor and Zeira, 1993). In essence, this holds that higher inequality leads to under-investment in human capital by the poorer segments of society. Cingano tested this by reference to three generally accepted measures of educational and labour market outcomes: the probability of graduating from tertiary education, test scores for numeracy and the probability of not being unemployed (on average) over the working life. In each case, the results showed that widening income disparities lower the outcomes of individuals from lower socioeconomic backgrounds without affecting the outcomes of individuals from middle- and upper-income backgrounds.

Fitoussi and Saraceno (2010) argued that the rise in inequality depressed aggregate demand and prompted monetary policy to react by maintaining low interest rates, which itself allowed private debt to increase beyond sustainable levels. On the other hand, the search for high-return investment by those who had benefited from the increases led to bubbles. Net wealth became overvalued, yet high asset prices gave the false impression that high levels of debt were sustainable. The crisis revealed itself when the bubbles exploded and net wealth returned to a normal level. So, while the crisis may have emerged in the financial sector, its roots go much deeper and lie in the structural change in income distribution that has been going on for the past three decades (see also King, 2013; Stockhammer, 2013; Sturn and van Treeck, 2013).

In a July 2014 World Bank Research Paper, Van der Weide and Milanovic assessed the impact of overall inequality – as well as inequality among the poor and the rich – on income growth rates along various percentiles of the income distribution. The analysis used micro-census data from US states from 1960 to 2011. The authors found that high levels of income inequality reduced the income growth of the poor and, if anything, helped the income growth of the rich. When inequality was deconstructed into bottom and top inequality, they found that it was mostly top inequality that was holding back growth at the bottom.

What is of special interest here is what the authors hypothesised as the main channels through which these effects occurred. The poor suffered more than the rich from what the authors termed 'social separation', whereby the wealthy prefer to opt out of publicly funded and provided education, health, urban infrastructure and other services because their private equivalents may be of better quality (and also signal the wealth and power of those that can afford them). At the same time, the poor find it harder to escape poverty because the lack of interest of the rich in using, let alone paying for, the public services on which many of the poor rely means that the quality (and quantity) of those services declines. On the other hand:

> Segmentation among the poor can ensure that the rich are provided [with] some services and amenities at cheaper rates than they would pay if the poor were more homogeneous. In other words, the poor who have a choice between facing destitution or being willing to work for a very low remuneration, may prefer the latter. Segmentation among the poor … creates perhaps what Marx called 'the reserve army of the unemployed' which may be conveniently used to improve real incomes of the rich. (Van der Weide and Milanovich, 2014, p 23)

Finally, one justification for reducing marginal tax rates and allowing top incomes to take off has been that the resultant additional wealth will 'trickle down' to the rest of society. This view was refuted in a much-quoted article in the *New*

York Times (Frank, 2007); one of the main pieces of evidence was the clear historical association between lower levels of inequality and higher levels of growth. In fact, Bertrand and Morse (2013) coined the term 'trickle-down consumption' to describe how, as inequality increases, middle- and lower-income households spend more on visible goods and services (possibly more than they can afford) in order to keep up with higher-income households. Bowles and Park (2005) explored whether the desire to emulate the better-off influenced the choices of the less well-off as between work and leisure. Data on working hours in 10 countries between 1963 and 1998 showed clearly that greater inequality was associated with longer work hours, as Veblen (1934) would have predicted (given his theory that consumer spending is driven as much by status concerns as by the enjoyment of the goods purchased). These effects were both substantial and robust. Such inequality of consumption is a social bad because it generates social costs not accounted in the private calculations of the consumer. So, what is needed is a progressive tax on personal consumption. We shall return to this in Chapter Five.

Housing and the environment

The growth of geographical segregation as a consequence of greater inequality has already been noted. Dorling (2014, p 96) observed that one of the most important consequences of increased inequality in the US was increased residential segregation by income: 'rich areas have become richer, poor areas have become poorer'. At the same time, neighbourhoods in many places have become more alike (see also, Dorling, 2011, p 171). In Britain, one of the major instances of market failure in housing has been the capture of so much property for rent by the wealthiest 1%. Dorling quoted a 2014 *Financial Times* analysis (Allen, 2014) to the effect that over the previous five years the total equity of mortgage holders had fallen by £169bn while that of landlords had risen by £245bn. He commented:

> Growing wealth inequality leads to an increasingly less efficient use of our existing housing stock, and

> rapidly increases prices as a result, because less efficient
> use reduces supply. This forces up rents, forcing even
> those on a living wage into effective poverty. First
> time buyers are also harmed. (Dorling, 2014, p 107)

Atkinson (2015, pp 161–2) noted that while the historic increase in owner-occupation had been positive for inequality, shortages of supply had meant average prices rising in relation to incomes and less-wealthy households increasingly being priced out of more attractive locations. This made relative wealth even more important than before for life chances and opportunities for education, health and employment. Social tenants and private tenants had missed out altogether. At the same time, government policies to stimulate demand, such as the 'Help-to-Buy' scheme, had mostly benefited rentiers and the better-off (see also Meek, 2014). A recent report for the Labour Party (Redfern, 2016) finds that the key drivers for the fall in homeownership in England, from a peak of 70.9% in 2003 to 63.6% in 2014–15, have been a collection of macroeconomic issues, including in particular changes in the earning and borrowing power of young people. Even with a significant increase in supply, rates of homeownership will not necessarily increase unless this is reversed.

In a report for the Fabian Society, Wilkinson and Pickett (2014) argued that reducing inequality was also necessary for environmental sustainability. The main barrier to such sustainability, and especially to reducing carbon emissions, was consumerism (found not only in the West, of course). This in turn was created or exacerbated by the increased status anxieties and status competition that are some of the main concomitants of increased inequality. The authors also made the point that, in general, more equal societies have a much better record on development aid and recycling; indeed, lowering within-country inequality in rich countries will help to improve understanding of poorer countries, which might in turn lead to less between-country inequality as well. Sayer (2016, pp 337–8) argues that through the over-production of debt and rent seeking, the businesses that sustain the rich are mortgaging our future and that of the planet. Brazil, for example, is clearing forests to generate hard currency to pay off its foreign debts. It is also very hard to persuade the majority in the rich countries to make sacrifices to stop or slow global warming if the rich minority is clearly not doing so. This takes us neatly to the final, and perhaps the most serious, of all the detriments associated with rising inequality.

Political impacts

> It is the next big scandal waiting to happen. It's an issue that crosses party lines and has tainted our politics for too long, an issue that exposes the far-too-cosy relationship between politics, government, business and money. (David Cameron, Leader of the Opposition, quoted in the *Telegraph*, 8 February 2010)

Stiglitz (2013a) argued that besides damaging the economy, increased inequality was weakening the political process in America. He outlined

> a process of disempowerment, disillusionment and disenfranchisement that produces low voter turnout, a system in which electoral success requires heavy investments, and in which those with money have made political investments that have reaped large rewards – often greater than the returns they have reaped on their other investments. (Stiglitz, 2013a, p 183)

Stiglitz stressed the importance of the Supreme Court's 2010 decision in the case of *Citizens United v. Federal Election Commission* that essentially allows unlimited corporate campaign spending. He gave the repeal of the estate tax, the recapitalisation of the banks, and mortgage restructuring as examples of ways in which the financial power of the wealthiest had been exercised politically to damage the great majority. In a further article, Stiglitz (2014) referred to the follow-on *McCutcheon* decision that eliminated aggregate limits on individual contributions to national candidates and parties. America now has a political system where 'one dollar, one vote' has replaced 'one person, one vote'.

Another Nobel Prize winner, Paul Krugman (2007), noted some parallels between today's political system and what pertained during the previous era of high US inequality (1870–1930): the effective disenfranchisement of many American workers, extensive election fraud and high levels of campaign spending. On this last, the independent Center for Responsive Politics, which monitors American political spending, estimates (2016b) that in 2015/16 presidential candidates had by 11 February 2016 raised $1.31bn, House candidates $1.028bn and Senate candidates $727m. These are extraordinary sums, by any standard.

Hacker and Pierson (2010) observed that direct spending on electoral contests in the US was only a small fraction of the amount of spending on politics. They estimated that over $3bn was spent every year by lobbyists. They also noted that if you looked at the 100 biggest-contributing firms since 1989, the contributions of the financial sector totalled more than those of the energy, healthcare, defence and telecoms sectors combined. A report in the *Financial Times* (Mishkin and Chon, 2014) suggested that Google had now overtaken Goldman Sachs as a political donor in the US: its political action committee (NetPAC) had spent $1.43m on political campaigns in 2014 as against Goldman's $1.4m. In 2010, Google spent only a third as much as Goldman. Yet only 36.3% of the electorate voted in the mid-term elections, the lowest turnout in over 70 years (Younge, 2014). Elizabeth Drew (2015) provided an overview of how the restraints on US political party funding had gradually been removed:

> We are now at the point where, practically speaking, there are no limits on how much money an individual, a corporation or a labor union can give to a candidate for federal office (though the unions can hardly compete). (Drew, 2015, 22)

Moreover, many of these donations do not have to be disclosed, contributions known as 'dark money'. Finally, we should note the growth of other links between wealthy corporations and government, for example, through 'revolving doors' where large companies hire former politicians and officials and governments employ former corporation staff.[6]

How much does the increasing importance of capital in political funding matter?

Page et al (2013) found that the top 1% of US wealth holders were both extremely active politically and far more conservative than the American public as a whole on taxation, economic and (especially) social welfare. These distinctive policy preferences might help to explain why many public policies in the US appear to deviate from what the majority of US citizens want the government to do. There is indeed plenty of evidence that, to quote a major study:

> When the preferences of economic elites and the stands of organised interest groups are controlled for, the preferences of the average American appear to have only a miniscule, near-zero, statistically non-significant impact upon public policy. (Gilens and Page, 2014, p 575)

In their vigorous rebuttal of criticisms of their study, the same authors wrote:

> To summarize, U.S. government policy depends strongly, although imperfectly, on what the well-to-do want but weakly, if at all, on what middle-income Americans prefer. We believe this massive inequality of influence is a serious indictment of the quality of American democracy. (Gilens and Page, 2016)

We are not quite at this point in the UK. But in December 2014 the *Observer* noted (Boffey, 2014) that the Government had increased the totals that the candidates of each party in a general election can spend from £26.5m to £32.7m. This was done through the use of a Statutory Instrument, which avoided a House of Commons debate and vote. It went against a recommendation of the independent Electoral Commission that there should be no increases in spending limits during the so-called 'long campaign' from December 2014 to the election in May 2015. In October 2014 the *Guardian* reported on a Conservative fundraising event earlier in the year where the combined publicly disclosed wealth of the 500 or so guests was an estimated £22bn. The guests included a doorstep lender, a host of property tycoons and a Ukrainian-born energy magnate (Goodley et al, 2014). At another event, a bronze statuette of the then Prime Minister on a bicycle was reportedly sold for £22,000 (Syal, 2014).

Mason (2015) reported that £100m in donations had been reported to the Electoral Commission in the year prior to the May 2015 election; this compared with £72m over the period before the 2010 election and £44m in 2005. In the same month, the Prime Minister's former chief strategist, Steve Hilton, attacked the growing influence of money on British politics (Martin, 2015). Nevertheless, several major Conservative donors received knighthoods or other awards in the Queen's Birthday Honours List (Pickard, 2015). In June 2015 the Press Association reported that only 76 people accounted for nearly half (41%) of all individual and corporate donations to the political parties and other political causes in the previous five years. Finally, a study by the University of Oxford Department of Economics (Mell et al, 2015) found that of the 92 people nominated for peerages since 2005 who did not meet the usual criteria (having been a politician or being active in politics), 27 were major political party donors. This could not be a coincidence: the chances of such people randomly ending up in Parliament were 1 in 73,500 decillion (the same as winning the National Lottery for five successive weeks).

The fact that both the main British political parties are increasingly reliant on donations from large organisations and wealthy individuals is largely due to the steep post-war decline in individual party membership, as well as the increasing cost of elections. This in turn reflects a wider disengagement with politics, to which growing inequality may have contributed (as well as an electoral system where the parties' representation in Parliament bears little relationship to the numbers or proportion of votes cast for them). There are also concerns that government-led changes in the system of electoral registration, so that now every voter has to register individually whereas previously voters could apply by household, will mean a much smaller proportion of those entitled to vote actually voting, with possibly 8 million people not correctly registered at their proper address in December 2015 (Merrick, 2016).

Another important area where increased wealth confers quite disproportionate influence concerns the ownership of the media.

Media Reform Coalition (2015) estimated that just three companies – News UK (*Sun*, *The Times*), DMGT (*Daily Mail*) and Trinity Mirror (*Mirror*) – controlled 71% of the national newspaper market. Just six major regional newspaper groups owned 81% of local papers. There is less concentration in the broadcast media, mainly because of the BBC, but even here Sky is the largest generator of revenue, and Mr Murdoch's 21st Century Fox has (December 2016) launched a bid to acquire the share of Sky (60.9%) not already owned by Mr Murdoch. Jones (2014, Chapter 3) described how the views of a small number of wealthy individuals or families dominate the mainstream press in Britain as well as some of the broadcast media. Accordingly:

> While polls consistently demonstrated that a large majority of the British public wanted, say, renationalization of the railways, energy and the utilities; rent controls; the introduction of a living wage; and increased taxes on the rich – no mainstream newspaper endorsed such calls. Quite the reverse. (Jones, 2014, p 97)[7]

More broadly, there seems to be a link, at least in the US, between increased inequality and increased political partisanship (Krugman, 2007, p 5; see also, McCarty et al, 2006). However, Krugman saw the link as being from politics to economics, rather than from economics to politics. At the same time, increased inequality may have reinforced a rightward trend, as the number and wealth of potential Republican Party donors grew.

Bartels (2008) noted that income inequality rose much more under Republican administrations than under Democrat ones. Bartels shared Stiglitz's and Krugman's views about the effects of increased inequality on politics. He pointed to a 'debilitating feedback cycle' linking the economic and political realms:

> increasing economic inequality may produce increasing inequality in political responsiveness, which in turn produces public policies that are increasingly detrimental to the interests of poor citizens, which in turn produces even greater economic inequality, and so on. If that is the case, shifts in the income distribution triggered by technological change, demographic shifts, or global economic development may in time become augmented, entrenched and immutable. (Bartels, 2008, p 286)

Tony Judt (2010) claimed that not only will a more equal society evince greater trust and cooperation between its members, it is also more likely to be able to accept change:

> it is not just a question of income: where people have similar lives and similar prospects, it is likely that what we might call their 'moral outlook' is also shared. This makes it much easier to institute radical departures in public policy. In complex or divided societies, the chances are that a minority – or even a majority – will be forced to concede, often against its will. This makes collective policymaking contentious and favours a minimalist approach to social reform: better to do nothing than to divide a people for and against a controversial project. (Judt, 2010, pp 66–7)

In a wide-ranging historical survey, Acemoglu and Robinson (2012) contrasted 'inclusive' and 'extractive' economic and political institutions:

> Inclusive economic institutions that enforce property rights, create a level playing field, and encourage investments in new technologies and skills are more conducive to economic growth than extractive economic institutions that are structured to extract

resources from the many by the few and that fail to protect property rights or provide incentives for economic activity. Inclusive economic institutions are in turn supported by, and support, inclusive political institutions, that is, those that distribute political power widely in a pluralistic manner and are able to achieve some amount of political centralization so as to establish law and order, the foundations of secure property rights, and an inclusive market economy. Similarly, extractive economic institutions are synergistically linked to extractive political institutions, which concentrate power in the hands of a few, who will then have incentives to maintain and develop economic institutions for their benefit and use the resources they obtain to cement their hold on political power. (Acemoglu and Robinson, 2012, pp 429–30)

The authors saw the Glorious Revolution of 1688 in Britain as the first clear development of an inclusive polity. It would appear that in Britain and the US we are moving back towards a more extractive political and economic system, where organised interests with strong financial backing are able to outweigh the general public interest (see also, Pincus and Robinson, 2010).[8]

Finally, there is an even deeper issue, that of control. As R.R. Reno (2014) has argued:

Only utopians imagine that everyone can be the same and treated in the same way. Instead, we use equality to describe an inclusive social order, one in which ordinary people count, have a say, and are involved in their society's consequential activities and decisions. In a hierarchical society, those at the top do most of the shaping of affairs, not just in their own lives but in those of others as well. Social equality reflects a different ideal, one that empowers everyone to use their own agency.

As Thomas Palley (2012, p 19) wrote:

> Ultimately, people will only value a system that values them. If the system does not value them, then they may cease to value it and turn against it.

Conclusion

The recent work by economists at the IMF and OECD indicates that the economic costs and detriments of increased inequality outweigh any benefits through incentives. It is also clear that increasing inequality gives rise to a wide range of social costs and detriments, notably in health, education, crime and social relations. But perhaps the most serious damage is to democratic politics, and the way in which – at least in the US, and to an increasing extent in Britain – such inequality is enabling the better-off, and especially the top 1%, to have a quite disproportionate influence on political choices and decisions. This in itself will make it very hard to unwind the inequality we see in most major Western countries. We shall return to this issue in Chapters Six and Seven.

In the meantime, we can conclude that a society with less inequality will be socially more cohesive, have greater social mobility, be better educated, more tolerant, healthier, have less crime, be more environmentally sustainable, be wealthier and more productive, and will have a better political system, where ordinary citizens are involved in governance in some way, and where the policies adopted reflect in a significant degree the views and interests of all its members rather than of a small, wealthy subset. Chapters Five and Six suggest how some of this might be achieved. But first we need to consider, in Chapters Three and Four, how we arrived at this position.[9]

3

STRUCTURAL CAUSES OF RISING INEQUALITY

Most explanations can be classified into market driven
changes vs. institution driven changes. (Piketty et al,
2011, p 2)

Introduction

In Chapter Two we concluded that reducing inequality by
adjusting the discrepancies between the contributions that
various groups and individuals make to society and the
concomitant rewards is not only desirable on moral and social
grounds – crucial as these are – but is also necessary for economic
growth, efficiency and innovation as well as for achieving a more
responsive and representative democratic process. Unfortunately,
though, there is much less agreement about the causes of these
'contribution gaps', and how the increase in inequality should
be tackled. This chapter and the next consider the main current
explanations for the rise in inequality. Following this suggestion
of Thomas Piketty and his colleagues, we distinguish (a) theories
that identify structural changes that go wider and deeper than
any individual country or set of social and political arrangements
('market theories'), and (b) theories that emphasise the political
and societal choices made by individual countries or societies
('institutional theories'). This chapter looks at the former,

Chapter Four at the latter. In each case, we identify one or more current representations of each theory. The discussion begins with an overview of all the main explanations considered. It concludes at the end of Chapter Four.

Box 3.1 Overview of the explanations for rising inequality considered in Chapters Three and Four

Structural causes (Chapter Three)

• **Globalisation**
Rising inequality is due to globalisation, not only the increased mobility of jobs and labour but also of goods, knowledge and (especially) capital.

• **Skill-biased technological change**
Rising inequality is due to technological advances that put a premium on the skills needed for non-routine tasks and reduce the value placed on low-skill, routine tasks: 'skill-biased technological change' (SBTC). This has led to important changes in the organisation of work. Educational under-achievement, under-investment or under-supply may also be a factor.

• **Changes in the organisation of work**
Rising inequality is due to changes in the organisation of work: the 'gig economy'.

• **Changes in household structure**
Rising inequality is due to changes in household structures, especially the increase in single-headed households and the greater likeliehood of people choosing partners in the same earning bracket.

• **'Winner-take-all markets'**
Rising inequality is due to the rise of 'winner-take-all markets', where small differences in performance translate into large differences in reward.

• The inherent nature of capitalism

Rising inequality is an inherent property of capitalism, and in particular its relentless drive to extend production and cut costs through technological innovation, something only kept in check when capital is destroyed by, typically, war and its attendant policies.

Institutional causes (Chapter Four)

• Neoliberal government policies

Rising inequality is the result of the neoliberal policies of deregulation, privatisation, tax reductions and welfare cutbacks pursued especially in the major Anglophone countries since the early 1980s, and for long espoused by such influential international organisations as the IMF, the OECD and the World Bank (the so-called 'Washington Consensus').

• Changing role of labour market institutions

A key element in these reforms was the weakening of the trades unions and other labour market institutions and norms that have historically kept inequality in check.

• Financialisation and rent seeking

Rising inequality is the result of the increasingly important role played by the financial sector in most Western countries – 'financialisation' – together with increased rent seeking by wealthy individuals and corporations.

• Macroeconomic government policies

Rising inequality is the result of the deflationary macroeconomic policies pursued by most Western governments over the past 30 or so years.

It should be noted that the main theories have been separated for expository purposes. As we shall see, it is actually very hard to distinguish between them, not to mention teasing out the causes and effects of each (Salverda et al, 2014, pp 4–5).

Globalisation

> There is substantial evidence, from countries of different sizes and different regions, that as countries 'globalize' their citizens benefit, in the form of access to a wider variety of goods and services, lower prices, more and better-paying jobs, improved health and higher overall living standards. (IMF, 2008, p 1)

> Globalization is a system characterized by high real rates of interest, low investment, high unemployment, low wages and high rates of debt. (Pettifor, 2006, p 51)

Freeman (2006) estimated that the global labour pool doubled in the early 1990s following the fall of communism, China's move towards market capitalism and India's decision to undertake market reforms and enter the global trading system. However, the world's capital stock did not increase to the same extent. This meant that the ratio of capital to labour fell, so shifting the global balance of power towards capital and away from labour. This had had three main impacts on the well-being of workers in the US and other advanced countries. First, it created downward pressures on the employment and earnings of less-skilled workers. Second, where developing countries were becoming competitive in technologically advanced industries – as China is in nanotechnology, for instance – it reduced the advanced countries' comparative advantage and might mean displaced workers having to shift to less-desirable sectors at home. Third, the development of computers and the web enhanced the ability of firms to move work to low-cost operations abroad.

Freeman's preferred response – his 'good transition scenario' – was for the US to invest in science and technology and keep attracting the best and brightest scientists, engineers and others from the rest of the world. This meant the country maintaining itself as an attractive, open society. The US also had to make more effort to encourage its own citizens to enter these fields. This required more spending on basic research and development, allocating a larger share of research grants to young (as opposed to senior) researchers, and giving more and higher-valued scholarships and fellowships. For less-skilled and lower-paid Americans there was a need to restructure the labour market for their services so that they did not fall further behind. This meant strengthening their rights at work so that they could gain a share of the profits in non-traded sectors; higher minimum wages; the expansion of earned-income credit; and the provision of social services such as health insurance that make workers less costly to hire. Part of this programme was implemented through President Obama's healthcare reforms, but even now more than 13% of Americans have no health insurance (Woolf, 2014).[1]

In a later paper, Freeman (2009) emphasised that trade is only part of the story and that international capital flows, immigration and technology transfer – all of which increased substantially after 1970 – also affect incomes around the world, in most cases in the same direction as trade. Freeman repeated his earlier advice that the neoliberal emphasis on protecting capital and deregulating labour markets should be rethought in favour of finding ways of protecting labour. For the longer term, the globalisation of knowledge could turn out to be more important in determining global economic outcomes than trade in goods and services:

> If this is the case, we need to focus on the diffusion of knowledge across locales, of the ways firms transform knowledge into products and activities of economic value, and of how intellectual property rights, pure research and development, education and training impact these processes. If in the knowledge economy, knowledge is the key determinant of outcomes, then globalization of knowledge should lie at the heart of analyses of how globalization affects inequality. (Freeman, 2009, p 595)

In a comprehensive review, Stiglitz (2007) noted that the issue was not just the number of jobs that were being outsourced to China and India, but the fact that even a relatively small gap between labour supply and demand could create real problems, leading to wage stagnation and decline, and creating high levels of anxiety among the many workers whose jobs were at risk. But even without globalisation, there would be increasing inequality because changes in technology had increased the premium on certain skills so that the winners in today's economy were those who had or could acquire those skills. This led him to a similar policy prescription to Freeman's:

> The advanced industrial countries have to continue upskilling their labor forces, but they also have to strengthen their safety nets and increase the progressivity of their income tax systems; it is the people at the bottom who have been hurt by globalization (and, probably, by other forces, like changing technology); it seems the right thing to do, to lower taxes on them and to increase taxes on those who have been so well served by globalization. Regrettably, in America and elsewhere, policies have been moving in precisely the opposite direction. (Stiglitz, 2007, p 275)

Jaumotte et al (2008) estimated that world trade, measured as the ratio of imports to exports over GDP, had grown five times in real terms since 1980, and its share of world GDP had risen from 36% of GDP to 55%. This reflected greater openness, especially to financial transactions: total cross-border financial assets had more than doubled, from 58% of global GDP to 131% in 2004. Trade globalisation had reduced income inequality overall by increasing agricultural exports (especially benefiting the poorer countries) and reducing the cost of consumer goods (helping the poor in all countries). But financial globalisation, especially Foreign Direct Investment (FDI), had increased it. This was because FDI mainly occurs in relatively higher-skilled and technologically intensive sectors, and thus increases the demand for and wages of more skilled workers. In other words, a disproportionately large share of increased financial rewards goes to those who already have higher incomes and assets (to serve as collateral). They are thus able to take greater advantage of increased financialisation to further raise their income and earnings potential. A more recent study (Furceri and Loungani, 2015) notes that FDI is only one of the channels through which greater openness in financial markets can increase inequality.

Chusseau et al (2008) looked at the competing explanations of globalisation and SBTC (see below). They found that both had contributed to increasing wage inequality but that impacts varied as between countries and sectors. They identified outsourcing ('off-shoring') as the main way in which globalisation had affected demand for worker skills. A further study (Chusseau and Dumont, 2012) came to similar conclusions. Elsby, Hobijn and Sahin (2013) identified off-shoring of the labour-intensive component of the US supply chain as 'a leading potential explanation' of the decline of the American labour share over the preceding 25 years. Moreover, the decline would have been even greater had it not been for the greatly increased earnings of the super-rich; in fact, the increase in inequality *within* labour income 'dwarfed' the movements in the labour share (Elsby et al, 2013, p 47).[2]

Immigration

While the main impact of low-cost labour on employment and wages in the West has come from overseas workers via off-shoring and other devices, it is also possible that direct immigration from low-income sources affects employment and earnings. A 2013 paper by Blau and Kahn surveyed both the theories and the evidence on the effects of immigration on inequality. They looked first at composition impacts and then at factor prices, primarily on wage differentials across skill groups of 'natives'. They found that in the US the composition effects – the impact on the make-up of the population – were relatively small as of 2009, although that could change. On the second, most research had not found quantitatively important effects of immigration on either native wage levels or the wage distribution (for broadly similar findings, see Card, 2009, and Ottaviano and Peri, 2011).

Globalisation and inequality: critique

One of the main difficulties with globalisation as the proposed main cause of increased inequality since the 1980s is the fact that, as already noted in Chapter One, the extent of the increase has varied considerably. Thus continental Europe (France, Germany,

Switzerland, the Netherlands), the Nordics and Japan still have considerably lower levels of inequality than the major English-speaking countries. All of these countries have been exposed to the various aspects of globalisation but their experiences and responses have differed considerably. There is also a timing issue even with the more unequal countries. Was the fall in inequality between the early decades of the 20th century and the late 1970s the result of 'de-globalisation'?

Next, it is accepted even by advocates of globalisation that its potential impact varies considerably within an economy: for example, as between different sectors, what is actually being traded (goods vs services, services that can be delivered remotely vs those that cannot, and so on) and, indeed, the relative openness of the economy. It is interesting that the US, which has the highest inequality of any rich developed country, is much less reliant on international trade than most other developed countries. Finally, there has very recently been a move to repatriate some manufacturing and service operations back to the West. Automation means that labour costs are no longer such a deal-breaker. A Boston Consulting Group report in 2013 estimated that over half of all large US manufacturing companies were either actively re-shoring activity or considering it as America was becoming a more competitive destination (see also Tett, 2015). The Trump Administration is of course encouraging this.[3]

Skill-biased technological change and other employment and societal factors

The view that technological change (SBTC) is a major factor, if not the main cause, of increased economic inequality goes back some years (Bound and Johnson, 1989; see also Autor et al, 1998; Autor et al, 2003; Autor et al, 2006; Acemoglu and Autor, 2010; Goos et al, 2011). A clear statement of the case is *The Second Machine Age: Work, Progress and Prosperity in a Time of Brilliant Technologies* (Brynjolfsson and McAfee, 2014).

A second machine age – through digital hardware, software and networks – is doing for brains what the steam engine did for production in the Industrial Revolution (the first machine age). As a result, we now have real, useful artificial intelligence and connections through common digital networks. This has come in parallel with increased investment in 'organisational capital' – investments in training, hiring and business process redesign – to eliminate more routine tasks, including routine cognitive tasks. Together, these changes are 'exponential, digital and combinatorial' in character.

There are clear benefits in productivity, in an increased consumer surplus, and in the quality and range of goods and services available. But there is also a downside: less demand for less-skilled workers, leading to a 'polarisation' of the labour market between 'lovely' and 'lousy' jobs (Goos and Manning, 2003; Goos et al, 2011); the substitution of technological capital for workers (increasing the profits of the owners of capital and reducing the share of income going to labour); and an increasing gap between the 'superstars' in each field and the rest (see below, 'Winner-take-all markets'). This is reflected in the way in which, since the late 1990s, productivity and employment have become uncoupled, with productivity pulling away from employment. However, capital's profits may also be under threat as the marginal value of capital declines because of the ability to replicate capital at ever lower levels of cost (there are echoes here of Marx). Finally, there will be an increase in political inequality as the better-off use their resources to protect themselves.

There is a key role for the state in helping society to come to terms with and adapt to these changes. Schools need to be improved by upgrading the status of teaching; business start-ups need greater encouragement; immigration needs to be facilitated, which helps in the creation of new firms; and there should be more support for science and investment in infrastructure. Better tax policies would help, with taxes on negative externalities like pollution and traffic, higher marginal rates for the highest earners, and taxes on economic rents such as a land tax (already common in states like Florida and California). For the longer term, the authors mention guaranteed incomes; recognising the value of mastery, autonomy and purpose in employment; and subsidising low-paid work through a negative income tax (when a worker's income is below the level at which tax starts to be paid, they receive a proportion of the difference back from the government). Other recent proponents of the 'march of the robots' include Frey and Osborne (2013); Manyika et al (2013); Bank of America Merrill Lynch (2015); Ford (2015); Haldane (2015); Kaplan (2015); and Susskind and Susskind (2015).

In Chapter One we noted several studies showing a significant fall in labour shares in national incomes in most countries since the 1970s. Conventional economic theory sees the labour share of corporate gross value added (GVA) within an economy as stable over time (corporate value added represents about 60% of total GVA, with households and government as the other chief contributors). But in a series of papers (2012, 2013) Karabarbounis and Neiman identified a 5% fall (from 64% to 59%) in the labour share of GVA in most countries (and within the US) between 1975 and 2012. This could not be explained by shifts between industrial sectors: more than 90% of the labour share decline reflected *within-industry* declines. This, incidentally, ruled out globalisation: the declining labour share was found even in labour-abundant China (see also Timmer et al, 2014). The main cause was the lower price of investment goods from 1980, often attributed to advances in information technology and the computer age. As labour shares have reduced, both business earnings and corporate savings have risen. However, increased dividends to shareholders have not absorbed all of the consequent increase in company profits, so that the supply of corporate savings increased by 20 percentage points as a share of total global savings, mainly at the expense of household savings (for a similar finding, see Arpaia et al, 2009).[4]

Labour force participation

A number of recent reports have highlighted the long-term decline in US labour force participation by prime-age males (between 25 and 54). A June 2016 report by the Council of Economic Advisers found that after peaking in 1954 the participation rate had fallen by an average of 0.16% a year from 1965, totalling an 8.3% decline by May 2016. This was a greater rate of decline than that of almost any other advanced country. The fall was concentrated among those with a high school degree or less. More than a third of prime-age males outside the workforce were living in poverty (suggesting that dropping out was not a choice because of other sources of income). The main reason was reduced demand for lower-skilled workers, which in turn reflected the broader evolution of technology, automation and globalisation in the US economy. However, institutional factors were also important, especially the absence of labour market support, as well as the rapid rise in incarceration (on one estimate, between 6% and 7% of the prime-age male population in 2008 were incarcerated at some point in their lives). Another recent study (Eberstadt, 2016) estimates that if these trends continue, a quarter of US men aged between 25 and 54 will be out of the workforce by the middle of the century. The UK does not have quite the same issue with labour force participation; the problem is more the persistence of low wages and poor productivity (Saunders, 2017).[5]

US female labour force participation also lags behind that in most OECD countries, even Greece and Japan that have always had low female participation. In a widely reported paper Case and Deaton (2015) drew attention to the marked increase in the all-cause mortality of middle-aged white non-Hispanic men (and women) in the US between 1999 and 2013. This reversed decades of progress and was unique to the US. There was a parallel increase in morbidity. While not advancing an overall explanation, the authors did mention a number of economic factors including the slow growth in real median earnings and the switch to defined contribution pensions. It would appear that this group gave strong support to President Trump in the November 2016 election.

The growth of non-standard work

The OECD (2015b) and others have drawn attention to the rise of various forms of non-standard work, typically part-time and temporary work and self-employment, as a barrier to the reduction of inequality if not an actual cause. This is an issue highlighted by the October 2016 Employment Tribunal ruling in the UK that Uber taxi drivers should not be treated as self-employed but be paid the national living wage and receive holiday pay (Osborne, 2016b), and also by the parliamentary inquiry into employment practices at Sports Direct (House of

Commons Business, Energy and Industrial Strategy Committee, 2016), which was triggered by the findings of an undercover investigation by the *Guardian* at the company's main warehouse at Shirebrook, Derbyshire. More people, often low skilled, have obtained access to the labour market, but at a cost. The OECD (2015b) estimated that between the 1990s and the start of the Great Recession almost half of all job creation was in the form of non-standard work: including the crisis years brings the figure to 60%. By 2013, non-standard work accounted for about a third of all employment in OECD countries. The OECD noted that people are more likely to be poor or in the struggling bottom 40% of society if they have non-standard work, especially if they live in a household with other non-standard or non-employed workers. It attributed the phenomenon to increased job polarisation, which in turn was due to technological changes and the associated evolution of labour demand.

A recent ILO report endorses this view. As well as being harmful to many workers, the growth of non-standard work poses dangers for firms and the wider economy and society:

> An over-reliance on non-standard employment can lead to a gradual erosion of firm-specific skills in the organization, limiting its ability to respond to changing market demand. While there may be some short-term cost and flexibility gains ... in the long run these may be outweighed by productivity losses. There is evidence that firms that use [such] employment more, tend to underinvest in training, both for temporary and permanent employees, as well as in productivity-enhancing technologies and innovation. (ILO, 2016, Executive Summary, p xxiv)

Moreover:

> Widespread use of non-standard employment may reinforce labour market segmentation and lead to greater volatility in employment with consequences for economic stability. Research shows that for temporary and on-call workers, it is more difficult

to get access to credit and housing, leading to delays in starting a family. (ILO, 2016, Executive Summary, p xxiv)

However, Lisa M. Lynch (2014) observed that the critical development in the US labour market since the early 1970s was not so much job polarisation (which was associated with both rising *and* falling wage inequality) as the changing relationship between wages and productivity reflected in the decline in labour's share of national income over the period. Besides technology, other causal factors included declining unionisation, the falling real value of the minimum wage and immigration, as well as increased off-shoring. But she also drew attention to the restructuring of the workplace and the increasing use of temporary hires, sub-contracting and third-party management, which together challenged the regulation of working conditions and the setting of wages within a firm (what has become known as the 'gig economy').

In *The Fissured Workplace* David Weil (2014) showed how a combination of increased capital market pressures and the reducing costs of coordination (through developments in computing and digital technology) had since the 1970s led major US firms to restructure their working arrangements to focus on 'core competences', shedding employment to partners but controlling the outputs through more effective monitoring and standards (off-shoring and the deregulation of workplace standards had also contributed):

> By shifting work from the lead company outward – imagine the outsourcing of janitorial or security workers – the company transforms wage setting into a pricing problem … this pushes wages down for workers in the businesses now providing services to the lead firm, while lowering the lead business's costs. Fissuring results in redistribution away from workers and towards investors. It therefore contributes to the widening income distribution gap. (Weil, 2014, p 20)

Moreover:

> The implications of fissuring go even beyond workplace conditions to more macro-level outcomes. The productivity of U.S. workers has grown steadily since 1973, increasing particularly rapidly from the mid-1990s until 2010. Over the same time period, median hourly compensation stagnated. Yet some people were indeed doing quite well. While wages stagnated over the past quarter of a century, the pay received by top business executives soared. In 1979 the ratio of the pay received by the average CEO in direct compensation to that of the average production worker was 37.2:1. By 2007 ... it had grown to 277:1. (Weil, 2014, p 22)

In 2014 the ratio was 303.4:1, having risen as high as 376.1:1 in 2000 (Economic Policy Institute, 2016; see also Mishel et al, 2012, p 175). Ironically, American firms' rates of return on assets have fallen steadily since the mid-1960s, from around 5–6% in 1965 to around 1% today (Deloitte Shift Index, 2013). Only 35% of Standard and Poor's 1500 companies generated both five-year positive Total Shareholder Returns and five-year (2008–12) positive cumulative economic profit (return on capital exceeding the cost of capital) (Van Clief et al, 2014). So the huge increases in CEO pay have occurred over exactly the same period as US firms' performance has deteriorated!

In the UK, the gap between top pay and that received by the average worker has roughly tripled, from about 50 times in the late 1990s to about 150 times today (High Pay Centre, 2016). In September 2016 the Trades Union Congress published an analysis showing that the median total pay (excluding pensions) of top FTSE 100 directors increased by 47% between 2010 and 2015, to £3.4m. Over the same period the average worker's wages rose by 7%. The average FTSE 100 top director was earning a year's worth of the minimum wage in one day.[6]

As well as lowering wage rates (and corporate benefits such as healthcare contributions), fissuring has a macroeconomic impact:

Historically, large businesses led recoveries: as demand returned, large firms directly increased employment. Now, employment decisions on many industries are mediated by fissured structures. Not only does this mean that the timing of recoveries may be slowed, since they must 'flow through' the fissured relationships; but the composition of jobs added also will reflect those relationships. Seen in this light, it is not surprising that the first jobs to be added following the Great Recession of 2007–2009 were predominantly at the low-wage end of the spectrum, nor that 93% of total income growth during the recovery from 2009 to 2010 went to the top 1% of the income distribution. (Weil, 2014, p 23; see also Robert Kuttner's review of the book in the *New York Review of Books*: Kuttner, 2014)

There are also implications for tax revenue, as the Chancellor of the Exchequer acknowledged in his November 2016 Autumn Statement (see Chapter Seven). However, we need to bear in mind the fact that although they often overlap – especially in low-wage, low-benefit and low-security sectors like food and drink, hospitality and tourism and security – non-standard employment and fissured work organisation are not synonymous, and many forms of fissuring still result in what is characterised as standard full-time work (Weil, 2014, p 273).

Sustainable employment portfolios

Declining levels of labour force participation in the US and the growth of non-standard employment more widely are both illustrations of what Buchanan et al (2014) described as the failure of employers, especially in the private sector, to create sustainable employment 'portfolios' as hedges against an uncertain future when the labour market remains the primary mechanism through which income and employment are generated and distributed for most citizens. Using case studies from the US, the UK and Australia, the authors argued that over the past 30 years or so labour market deregulation had failed to provide workers with employment portfolios of sufficient size and quality. They recommended (a) a more active state role in promoting and coordinating labour market infrastructure (training and skills development, minimum standards and access) and (b) a more positive approach to public sector employment (as complementary to, rather than as displacing, private sector employment).

Increasing variability in firms' returns on capital

One of the foremost American critics of growing inequality is the former Labor Secretary Robert Reich. In his latest book Reich (2016) emphasises the role of large corporations in using their market and political power at the expense of consumers and workers. Reich identifies five main ways in which this has been done: through greater exploitation of the rights of property, especially intellectual property rights; through the extension of market power, not only through mergers and acquisitions but also by expanding ownership of monopolies through economies of scale; through the exploitation of contracts; through the use of bankruptcy rules; and by weakening regulation and enforcement. Reflecting this, in 2014 US corporate profits before taxes reached their highest share of the total economy in at least 85 years. From 2000 to 2014 quarterly after-tax corporate profits rose from $529bn to $1.6tn. Meanwhile labour's share of non-farm incomes fell from 63% in 2000 to 57% in 2013, an annual transfer of some $750bn (Reich, 2016, pp 83–4). The consequences have included a decline in social mobility, excessive levels of management remuneration, taxpayer support for excessive rewards on Wall Street, the declining bargaining power of the middle as earnings and job security have become detached from productivity growth, the growth of the working poor and the rise of the non-working rich.

Reviewing Reich's book in the *New York Review of Books*, Paul Krugman (2015) drew attention to a paper by Jason Furman and Peter Orszag (2015) arguing that, at least since 2000, most of the rise in income inequality in the US had been due to an increasing disparity of earnings *between* firms rather than *within* them (see also Barth et al, 2014, and Song et al, 2015). Furman and Orszag hypothesised that a rising share of firms were earning super-normal returns on capital, that their workers were both producing and sharing in those super-normal returns (driving up wage inequality) and that these high returns (to both labour and capital) reduced labour mobility by discouraging workers from leaving them (see also Atkinson, 2015, pp 98–9). There does not appear to be any comparable analysis for the UK. We shall consider the role of rent seeking as a contributor to rising inequality in Chapter Four.

Changes in household structure

A number of writers (for example, Deaton, 2013) have identified changes in household structure as a contributing factor to inequality, especially the rise in single-headed households and the greater likelihood of people choosing partners in the same earnings bracket, the latter being known as 'assortative mating' (Chadwick and Solon, 2002; Ermisch et al, 2005; Schwartz, 2010; Charles et al, 2013; Greenwood et al, 2014). Both developments increase inequality, the former by reducing the benefits from sharing savings and household costs, the latter by diversifying income less across husband and wife (but more over others). However, surveying the evolution of household earnings inequalities for 23 OECD countries between the mid-1980s and the mid-2000s, Chen et al (2013) found that changes in labour market factors – and especially increases in men's earnings disparities – were far more important than such demographic or 'societal' factors.

The supply of education

One important reason for increased assortative mating has been the rise in the education of women. We reviewed in Chapter Two the extensive evidence about the impact of increasing economic inequality on educational participation and achievement and social mobility. But it has also been suggested (for instance, Rajan, 2010) that deficiencies in the supply of education may also be a *cause* of increased inequality. We also noted the view that under-investment in education by the poorer members of society, as a result of increased inequality, was harmful to economic growth. The same analysis (Cingano, 2014) proposed that education policy should focus on improving access for low-income groups: their educational outcomes are not only worse on average than those of middle- and high-income groups but are also more sensitive to increases in inequality. This may be difficult in view of the economic, cultural and social advantages of students from better off – or, at least, better-educated – backgrounds (see also Thrupp, 1999; Jenkins et al, 2006; Burgess et al, 2014; Connelly et al, 2014). For these reasons, education policy needs to take into account the fact that low socioeconomic groups in unequal societies are likely to have under-invested in formal education. Strategies to foster skills development should therefore include improved job-related training and education for the low-skilled (including on-the-job training) as well as better access to formal education throughout their working lives (Cingano, 2014, p 29).

A similar emphasis on the need for increased investment in the education of students from poorer backgrounds is found in Claudia Goldin and Lawrence Katz's influential 2008 book, *The Race Between Education and Technology*. Goldin and Katz explained the rise in US income inequality since around 1980 in terms of an increasing shortage of workers with the skills needed to exploit technological advances. Growing wage differentials between more and less-skilled workers reflected the plateauing of American educational performance, seen especially in high school and college retention and graduation rates. Goldin and Katz put forward three main sets of reform proposals: creating greater access to high-quality pre-school education for children from disadvantaged families; improving the operation of K-12 (upper secondary) schooling so that more young people graduate from high school and are ready for college; and making financial aid sufficiently generous and transparent so that those who are college-ready can complete a four-year college degree course or gain marketable skills at a community college. Juhn et al (1993) and Rajan (2010) are among those who offer a similar analysis and prescription.[7]

A number of other studies make a link between greater participation in education and higher levels of attainment, on the one hand, and reduced income inequality or greater wage compression, on the other (De Gregorio and Lee, 2002; Machin, 2009; Fournier and Koske, 2012; Hanushek and Woessmann, 2012; Ballarino et al, 2014). This of course takes us back to the role of education in this context: does it just reflect economic inequality, or could changes in the organisation of education actually be a means of *reducing* inequality? This is discussed further in Chapter Six.

SBTC and inequality: critique

It has been seen that one of the problems with the globalisation theory was the fact that while the major Western economies have faced similar challenges from the increased mobility of goods, services, labour, knowledge and capital, not all have experienced the same amount of inequality. The same reservation applies to SBTC as a general explanation. Once again, too, there is a timing issue. Reviewing some of the literature critical of the theory, Dew-Becker and Gordon (2005, p 119) asked: 'are we to believe that technical change over 1920–1970 was "unskilled biased"?' In common with others who have stressed the importance of increases in top salaries, they argued that such a shift was much too narrow a group to be consistent with a widespread effect from SBTC, although they did accept that what they call 'new media inventions' might have contributed to the skewing at the top associated with 'superstars' and top CEOs.

Card and DiNardo (2002) reviewed the evidence for SBTC, focusing on the implications for economy-wide trends in wage inequality and for the evolution of wage differentials between various groups. A fundamental problem was that wage inequality had stabilised in the 1990s, despite continuing advances in computer technology. SBTC also failed to explain the closing of the gender gap, the stability of the racial wage gap, or the dramatic rise in education-related wage gaps for younger versus older workers.

Analysing data from the US Current Population Survey over several decades, Lawrence Mishel and colleagues (2013) cast doubt on both versions of SBTC: the race between technology and education, and the impact of computerisation on occupational employment trends and the resulting 'job polarisation':

> there is little or no connection between decadal changes in *occupational employment* shares and *occupational wage* growth, and little or no connection between decadal changes in *occupational wages* and *overall wages*. Changes within occupations greatly dominate changes across occupations so that the much-focused-on occupational trends, by themselves, provide few insights (Mishel et al, 2013, p 5; original emphases)

Another argument is that while SBTC can make some kinds of work redundant, it can also create complementarities (Shestakovsky, 2015).

Several writers (for instance, Atkinson et al, 2011) have pointed out that just as there has been a growing discrepancy in the remuneration of college- and non-college-educated workers, there has been a growing dispersion in the labour market returns of college-educated ones. This is certainly not an argument against investment in education and skills. But it does suggest that, at least in the short run, other measures, including reforms to labour market policies and institutions, may be more effective in combating inequality (see below, Chapter Six). In a thoughtful survey of the then-existing literature on SBTC, Chennells and Van Reenen (2002) wondered if the explanation for the apparent association between computerisation and increased wage differentials might be the fact that the newest technologies tended to be used by the most-skilled workers, who were already earning the highest wages. In any case, while there are certainly plenty of proponents of the march of technology, there are also a number of respected authorities who do not foresee dramatic technological breakthroughs in the near future, particularly bearing in mind the world-wide shift to services, which are less easily automated than manufacturing (Gordon, 2012; Nordhaus, 2015; Gregory et al, 2016; Nordhaus, 2016).

Globalisation and SBTC: conclusion

Most recently, the tendency has been to combine globalisation and SBTC as major drivers of inequality. In his most recent survey of the causes of rising inequality, Branko Milanovic writes:

> Technology and globalisation are thus wrapped around each other, and trying to disentangle their individual effects is futile. Removing either of them would do away with almost half of the increases in wage inequality. And, conversely, adding either of them to the existing level of the other (for example, 'adding' globalisation to existing computerisation) would on its own explain almost the entire increase in wage inequality. Policy changes are endogenous to these. (Milanovic, 2016, p 110)

In other words, globalisation facilitates the spread of new technologies, and technological innovations facilitate globalisation (see also Baldwin, 2016).

It is hard not to sympathise with Milanovic's frustration with attempts to explain rising inequality in terms of one main or dominant cause. It seems clear that it is the *combination* of greater openness across borders and rapid technological change that is of the greatest relevance. To quote a comprehensive literature review:

> Increasing trade openness has contributed to the spread of technology whereas technological progress has helped to widen trade integration. (Foerster and Toth, 2015, p 1770)

We should also not overlook the point (OECD, 2011a) that whatever the *direct* impact on inequality, globalisation and SBTC did create pressures (or at least a rationale) for the deregulation of labour and product markets (to safeguard growth, productivity and employment) that has characterised most Western countries since 1980, and which we shall be reviewing in Chapter Four. There can also be little doubt that the combined impact of globalisation and technological change, on top of labour market deregulation, was a major factor in the support for President Trump.[8]

Winner-take-all markets

One theory that brings globalisation and SBTC together, and which is certainly relevant to understanding recent developments in higher education, is that of 'winner-take-all markets'.

In the preface to the revised and updated edition of their 1995 book *The Winner-Take-All-Society: Why the Few at the Top Get So Much More than the Rest of Us*, Robert Frank and Philip Cook (2010) rejected rent seeking and market manipulation, skills premia and the impact of globalisation on lower-level wages as explanations of growing inequality, although they did acknowledge the weakening of the norms and institutions that had previously constrained top earnings. But they continued to argue that the main cause of rising income inequality, at least towards the top of the earnings distribution, was the emergence and intensification of 'winner-take-all markets'. These are markets where small differences in performance, often assisted by luck, can lead to large differences in economic reward, together with a concentration of such rewards in the hands of a few top performers. Previously confined to sectors like entertainment, sports and the arts, these are now ubiquitous across the professions (see also Rosen, 1981).

The main causes were (a) the expansion and intensification of competition, including through globalisation, the lowering of trade barriers, deregulation and reductions in transport costs and (b) the information revolution that has transformed our ability to collect, process and transmit information, including information about performance. Executive compensation has been the most obvious instance of runaway incomes at the top, assisted by increases in company size and executive mobility, although the authors recognised that the huge multiples of executive salaries found in the US (and the UK) are much less common in Japan or Germany. Other high-profile examples include book publishing, professional tennis, business consulting, motion pictures and television, fashion models, and college and professional team sports (with football coaches often paid more than college presidents). But the 'really important' new source of inequality was the escalating earnings of the near-rich: the sales people, administrators, accountants, physicians and millions of other 'minor league superstars' who dominate the smaller niche markets of everyday life. They too had benefited from the changes in the economic environment that had increased the value and compensation associated with positions with relatively great scope and leverage.

Another important contributor to winner-take-all markets was the tendency to value many goods according not just to their absolute properties but also to how they compare with those acquired and consumed by others: 'status' or 'positional' goods (Veblen, 1934; Hirsch, 1976). As prosperity grows, such goods assume greater importance. But:

> By its very nature, the demand for top rank can be satisfied by only a limited number of products in any category. And this, together with the fact that people are often willing to pay substantial premiums for top-ranked products, often gives rise to intense winner-take-all competitions between the aspiring suppliers of those products. (Frank and Cook, 2010, p 41; see also Frank, 1985, Chapter 2)

As the authors say, higher education is a classic case of such a market, at least in the major Anglophone countries. Students, donors, employers and even public authorities all compete to be associated with the 'top' colleges, and are prepared to pay handsomely for the privilege. At the same time, the providing institutions put ever-increasing amounts of time and effort into activities designed to raise their status, at the expense of their core activities of educating students, conducting research and serving their local and regional communities (Brown, 2014). There are clear and obvious parallels here with the marketing and status-building activities of the leading English private schools (Brown, unpublished paper).

Besides excluding a significant proportion of the population from access to elite educational credentials, what many commentators (for example, Winston, 2000) have termed 'the academic arms race' exhibits the second main consequence of winner-take-all markets, namely, a substantial waste of resources. This arises from (a) attracting too many 'contestants' ('overcrowding'), and (b) giving rise to unproductive patterns of consumption and investment as competitors vie with one another for top positions. On the first, most of the contestants contribute very little to national output; in other words, the cost of identifying top performers is much higher than it should be. On the second, competitors jockey for position in a host of expensive but mutually offsetting ways. National efficiency and income would be higher if there were fewer contestants in these markets and if more of the most talented individuals went into socially more productive sectors. Incidentally, higher education again exemplifies this, with many low-prestige institutions diverting resources into research when they can never become research-based elite universities, although the pressures from staff here should not be under-estimated (Brown, 2011).

One way of limiting these detriments and inefficiencies would be through 'positional arms control agreements': arrangements, norms and rules that aim to curtail patterns of mutually offsetting investment in enhanced performance, such as limits on competitors' expenditure, revenue sharing and so on. To be fully effective, such agreements would require state sanction, or at least acquiescence. Other remedies could include higher and more progressive taxes on income or consumption, with the latter clearly preferable, given the low level of US savings rates; reforming the law on torts so that there are fewer such cases, which can be extremely lucrative for lawyers (the evidence of overcrowding is greatest in law, although finance runs it a close second); reducing the cost of healthcare by tailoring reimbursements to the nature of the procedures being performed, rather than to the physician's qualifications; using student tuition and support subsidies to encourage students to choose socially valuable disciplines; and using anti-trust laws appropriately. On the last, Frank and Cook noted the early 1990s suit that the Justice Department filed against the Ivy League colleges and Massachusetts Institute for Technology for price fixing through collusion on their student aid policies, when such collusion would actually have been beneficial in limiting tuition fee increases (there was a similar case in the UK in the early 2000s involving a number of leading private schools).[9]

Dew-Becker and Gordon (2005) used Inland Revenue Service data to try to explain why American workers generally had failed to share in the benefits of increases in productivity since the mid-1960s (a fact that virtually everyone accepts). They found that the total labour income share had remained constant over the period. Only the top 1% of the income distribution had enjoyed a growth rate of total real income (excluding capital gains) equal to or above the average rate of economy-wide economic growth. The dominant share of real income gains accruing to the top 1% (and the top 0.1%) was almost as large for labour income as for total income. As an explanation, the authors suggested a version of winner-take-all, namely, the increased concentration of income to superstars in fields like sport and entertainment – major league athletes and 'power celebrities' – together with corporate CEOs.[10]

The nature of capitalism

Thomas Piketty must wait in the wings no longer. His 2014 book *Capital in the Twenty-First Century* was a best seller. It is indeed a 'must read' for anyone with a serious interest in the relationship between capitalist economies and the distribution of income and wealth.

Using tax records, Piketty argued that, historically, capital – traditionally, land and buildings; more recently, financial and business capital plus physical property – had always dominated income. This was because the return on capital – by definition, wealth accumulated in the past – usually exceeds the growth rate of the economy. Because the ownership of capital is always less widely distributed than labour income, this leads to greater and greater concentrations of wealth. The only period when this was not the case was between the first decade of the 20th century and about 1950. Since then, the longer-term relationship, where the ratio of the total capital stock to a year's national income was six or seven to one in Europe (somewhat lower in the US), had reasserted itself, albeit to somewhat lower levels because of the ability, after 1945, of what Piketty calls the 'patrimonial middle class' to begin to share some of the rewards of capital. To quote:

> The entrepreneur inevitably tends to become a rentier, more and more dominant over those who own nothing but their labour. Once constituted, capital reproduces itself faster than output increases. The past devours the future. (Piketty, 2014a, p 571)

As Paul Krugman said in his review of *Capital in the Twenty-First Century* (Krugman, 2014), Piketty sees economic history as basically the story of a race between capital accumulation and other factors driving growth, chiefly population growth and technological progress.

The main reasons for the 20th-century weakening in the dominance of capital were the two world wars, which both destroyed capital and necessitated policies to control capital: rent controls, more stringent financial regulation and the taxation of dividends and profits, as well as higher rates of progressive taxation. The loss of capital overseas (Britain and France) was another factor, together with the many bankruptcies that accompanied the Great Depression. Only through a combination of (much) higher economic growth and a depression of the returns on capital, ideally through some sort of global wealth tax applied steadily over time, as well as much higher rates of income tax, can we begin to unwind the position.

In a parallel study to Piketty's, Frederiksen (2012) found the distribution of wealth within OECD countries to be much more concentrated than the distribution of income. Wealth inequality had declined during the 20th century until the mid-1970s to early 1980s, since when it had been rising again. This reflected (a) soaring financial markets in the aftermath of financial market deregulation from the 1970s, (b) lower marginal tax rates on top incomes and lower capital gains and wealth taxation, which had made the accumulation of wealth easier for the rich and (c) (at least in France) rising inheritances and inter vivos gifts, which now stood at nearly 15% of national income (almost as high as a century ago).

Using country balance sheets, Piketty and Zucman (2014) found increases in the private wealth–national income ratio nearly everywhere, from about 200–300% in 1970 to about 800–900% today. This was due to the long-run recovery in asset prices, in turn driven by changes in capital policies since the Second World War and by the slowdown in productivity and population growth. Since the ownership of wealth is always more concentrated this has major implications for inequality. Moreover, with imperfect capital markets and home portfolios bias – domestic capital typically accounts for 90–110% of the total wealth of rich countries today, while the net foreign asset position accounts for only -10% to +10% – structurally large wealth–income ratios can contribute to domestic asset-price bubbles. Finally, the fact that capital now takes so many forms means that the possibilities for substituting capital for labour increase, so raising capital shares in national income at the expense of wages.

Turning from capital to income, labour increased its share of income from capital plus labour between 1910 and 1970, but this has since fallen back because of the substitution of labour by technology, together with policies aimed at reducing labour's bargaining power, which globalisation has reinforced. There are also some important income inequalities that have increased, with the top 1% in the US receiving a fifth of all income (as already noted, capital ownership was always less dispersed). This reflects the rise of 'supermanagers', and also the renewed importance of inherited wealth, as well as the considerable reductions in top marginal tax rates that have occurred as a result of neoliberal reforms (see Chapter Four).

In a widely read blog, Bill Gates (2014) agreed with Piketty that high levels of inequality are a major problem, that capitalism does not self-correct towards equality and that the state can play a constructive role in offsetting the 'snowballing tendencies' of inequality if it chooses to do so. However, Gates argued that we should distinguish between the different kinds and uses of wealth. On the first, he noted that about half of those in the Forbes 400 list were entrepreneurs of successful companies whose fortunes could wane as well as wax: they were not simply inheritors or rentiers. On the second, we should distinguish those who put their wealth to socially valuable activities, such as building a business or philanthropy, from those who simply spent their money on yachts or planes. As well as continuing with estates tax, therefore, we should levy progressive taxes on consumption, where there was anyway much less inequality than with income or wealth. However, a recent report by the US Institute for Policy Studies (Collins et al, 2016) suggests that charitable giving may be skewing non-public funding towards particular donors and pet causes. This will hardly come as a surprise to anyone who has been involved with university fundraising.

Marx again

As John Holmwood, in a perceptive review of *Capital in the Twenty-first Century*, put it, 'the logic of capitalism is to produce a patrimonial order where inheritance increasingly triumphs over merit' (Holmwood, 2014, p 608). Although Piketty dissociates himself from Marx, there is more than an echo in his work of Marx's theory of the fundamental structural weakness of capitalism, namely its unceasing tendency to raise productivity through technical innovation, leading inexorably to reduced prices and profits for producers. This in turn leads to economic crises that can be avoided only through the destruction of capital value to restore profitability. If factors exist that prevent this, such as state intervention in the economy for social reasons, then profits will not recover and the level of economic activity – the creation of economic value – will not revive.

In a contemporary reworking of Marx, Andrew Kliman (2012) argued that the failure of the world economy to recover after the 1973–80 period was due to the failure to destroy capital. This had a negative impact on corporate profits and profitability, since without profits there is insufficient investment. The failure to destroy capital led to reduced tax revenues and increased government deficits and debt. The resultant economic sluggishness will continue unless and until profitability is restored, or there are radical changes in the socioeconomic system.

Kliman therefore agreed with those like Stiglitz who blame the Great Recession, in whole or in part, on the build-up of debt. But in his view the cause was not under-consumption because of falling wages. If you added in non-wage compensation (benefits paid for by employers, such as health and pensions) and state benefits, and if national income rather than GDP was used as the denominator, there had been little change in the workers' share of US national wealth, and in fact their share would have increased if total corporate income had increased (on average, before-tax profits declined from 11.6% of US GDP in the period 1947–69 to 8.8% in 1970–2007; Kliman, 2012, p 64). The solution to the problem of continued stagnation was not state intervention, which would only lead to moral hazard, excessive risk taking and government bail-outs (with austerity to pay for the deficits incurred). Nor was regulation the answer because it doesn't touch the fundamentals. The only sure way was through the full-scale destruction of capital value (for a similar view, see Scheidel, 2017).

Conclusion

In this chapter we have discussed the main market theories for the rise of inequality, theories that emphasise the role of structural drivers such as globalisation, SBTC, changes in the organisation of work, changes in household structures, winner-take-all markets, the historic importance of capital and the inherent properties of capitalism. We also noted the difficulty, even perhaps the futility, of trying to disentangle them. In Chapter Four we review theories that, in contrast, draw attention to the institutional and policy choices made by individual countries or societies, partly at least in response to these factors.

4

INSTITUTIONAL CAUSES
OF RISING INEQUALITY

It is not true that inequality is an inevitable byproduct
of globalization, the free movement of labor, capital,
goods and services, technological change that
favours better-skilled and better-educated employees.
(Stiglitz, 2013b)

Introduction

Chapter Three reviewed the main 'market' explanations for
increased inequality, underlying structural drivers such as
globalisation and technological change. Chapter Four looks at
'institutional' explanations, beginning with the neoliberal policies
pursued especially by governments in the major Anglophone
countries since the early 1980s and also espoused, at least until very
recently, by major international organisations such as the OECD,
the IMF and the World Bank. We then turn to the changing
role of labour market institutions, financialisation, corporate rent
seeking and macroeconomic policies (financialisation can also
be seen as a structural development, but it is more convenient
to deal with it here).

Neoliberal policies

Under these policies, as described in Lansley (2011), freer markets, smaller government and lower taxes have replaced full employment, progressive taxation and inclusive welfare as state priorities. Together, the resultant squeeze on wages, the boost to corporate profits and booming fortunes at the top have upset the equilibrium needed for economic stability. Increased debt has been the inevitable response, alongside huge and mobile financial surpluses that are in part a consequence of greater inequality as companies and wealthy individuals pile up savings.

Labour market deregulation weakened the trades unions and the share of wages in the economy. There was a fundamental shift in macroeconomic policy from reducing unemployment to preventing inflation, together with an attempt to restructure the economy around services, and especially financial services. The outcomes were higher unemployment (in spite of the assumed trade-off between wage levels and employment); a shift from manufacturing to finance ('de-industrialisation'); and a polarisation of the labour market, with a growth in high- and low-skilled jobs at the expense of the middle. While the richest have pulled away, the rest of society has become increasingly bunched in the bottom half of the income distribution, with increased downward occupational and social mobility – what one American commentator described as 'chasing a speedboat with a rowboat' (Bob Herbert in the *New York Times*, 6 June 2005, p A23, quoted in Dew-Becker and Gordon, 2005, p 67).

The assumption underpinning these policies was that, in return for lighter regulation, the City and Wall Street would pay for those displaced or immiserated. The City and Wall Street have indeed benefited from the Big Bang (the relaxation of restrictions on share dealing in London from 1986), and also from the increased capital flows that accompanied globalisation. But much of the additional revenue and profits have gone not into productive investment and innovation but into increasing 'shareholder value' – maximising the share price (especially in the short term) and linking executive remuneration to shareholders' interests – as well as into more mergers and acquisitions activity, with dubious returns on productivity as well as a depressive effect on demand:

> On only one count – curbing inflation – can the post-1980 era be judged a clear success. Inflation rates tailed off during the 1980s and have remained lower ever since. On all other counts, the economic record of market capitalism has been inferior to that of managed capitalism [the period from 1950 to 1973]. Growth and productivity rates have been slower, unemployment levels higher. As the proceeds of growth have been very unequally divided, the wealth gap has soared, without the promised pay-off of wider economic progress. [At the same time] financial crises have become more frequent and more damaging in their consequences. (Lansley, 2011, pp 141–2)

Similarly:

> GDP and productivity have grown *more slowly* since 1979 than over previous decades, contrary to widespread belief. Although inflation and industrial disruption were reduced after 1980, unemployment and inequality have been higher. The volatility of the economic growth has also been much greater. (Coutts and Gudgin, 2015, p 5, original emphasis)[1]

What is needed is radical reform. We need a better balance in corporate objectives, away from shareholder value. Labour markets should be re-regulated: countries with a higher coverage of collective bargaining tend to have lower earnings dispersion. Tougher policies are needed on personal taxation and tax avoidance. There should be reforms to make finance serve its proper function of providing the levels of credit and liquidity to finance trade and investment (for a similar critique, see Krugman, 2007; Brandolini, 2010; Galbraith, 2012; Palley, 2012; Stiglitz, 2013b; Gamble, 2014; Palley, 2015). Rajan (2013, p 3) suggested that income inequality 'emerged, not primarily because of policies favouring the rich, but because the liberalized economy favoured those equipped to take advantage of it'.

In a more recent book, Lansley argues:

> Creating a more equal society requires a wholly different economic and social model, one aimed at building a new 'sharing economy', one which builds a basic floor below which nobody would ever fall, a lower ceiling at the top and which ensures that the fruits of economic activity are more evenly shared than in recent decades. (2016, p 2)

He proposes that the revenue from the better management of public assets and the reduction of 'corporate welfare' (rent seeking) should form the core of a single, ring-fenced social wealth fund that could be used to tackle the various weaknesses in the current UK economic model, including investment in infrastructure and social capital (see also Atkinson, 2015, pp 174–8).

Peet (2011) argued that both the Great Recession and the austerity measures that followed in many countries were manifestations of 'global finance capitalism', the international investment community that controls access to global investment funds. The fiscal deficit was due to the failure of tax rates to keep up with the increases in the incomes of the rich. In effect there was a massive redistribution of the tax burden onto working-class people at a time when their incomes were stagnant:

> the highest income 1% of taxpayers (the super-rich) received a total of $21tn in income between 1987 and 2008, on which they paid $5.3tn in income taxes, an effective tax rate (after deductions, and so on) that averaged 25%, while the highest income 5% of taxpayers received $36tn in that period, on which they paid $8.3tn in taxes, an effective tax rate that averaged 23%. If the richest 5% had been taxed at an effective rate of 50%, by comparison, the deficit would have been $4.6tn. Raising the corporate tax rate to 50% would have resulted in a budget surplus.

But progressively taxing rich people does not feature in the public discourse on crisis, while corporate taxation if mentioned is only in reverse (lowering the corporate tax rate). (Peet, 2011, p 397)

Meek (2012) argued that the privatisation of public utilities is a clear form of (upward) redistribution:

By packaging British citizens up and selling them, sector by sector, to investors, the government makes it possible to keep traditional taxes low or even cut them. By moving from a system where public services are supported by general taxation to a system where they are supported exclusively by the fees people pay to use them, they move from a system where the rich are obliged to help the poor to a system where the less well-off enable services, like a road network, that the rich get for what is, to them, a trifling sum.

In Chapter Two we noted Dorling's identification of the beliefs that stem from and sustain inequality. Dorling located the origins of these beliefs in the choices made in the US and Britain in the mid-1970s. The period up to that point and since the Second World War was one of both growth and relative equality: a time of shared prosperity. But such growth could not continue. Rather than have to share the more limited growth that seemed likely, the rich decided to keep the proceeds to themselves:

When the choice had to be made ... as to how to manage the fall in resources, those with more did not choose to limit their own consumption but to curtail the consumption of those with less. (Dorling, 2011, p 136)

The outcome was increasing divisions in wealth, votes, housing, education, income and much more of the fabric of life than just these basics.[2]

Sant'Anna (2015) drew on Besley and Persson's (2011) notion of 'common-interest states' to argue that the post-war existence of a powerful socialist bloc acted as a disciplining device to Western inequality. In the common-interest states a social cohesion emerged because of the presence of a powerful external enemy, leading to reduced top income shares. The researchers ran a panel of 18 OECD countries between 1960 and 2010, controlling for variables that the literature sees as important factors. They found a negative and robust significant relation between the Soviet Union's relative military power and top income shares.

Hacker and Pierson (2010) attributed the rise in inequality in America to the failure to maintain the policies of redistribution that would have been required to offset the concentrationist tendencies of globalisation and technological change. A key factor here was the strengthening of business representation and lobbying in the early to mid-1970s through organisations such as the National Association of Manufacturers, the Chamber of Commerce, the National Federation of Independent Business and the Business Round Table. These interests became better organised and more willing to use their financial muscle not only at federal level but also in state and even local politics. They in turn were reacting to the liberal and redistributive programmes associated not only with Democrat presidents and Congress but also with Republican presidents like Eisenhower and Nixon. At the same time, the position of the labour unions was weakening while the liberal opposition tended to get into non-economic single issues such as abortion. As a result:

> From 1979 until 2006, the top 1 percent received 36 percent of all the income growth generated in the American economy, while the highest-income 1/10th of 1 percent – one out of every 1,000 households – received nearly 20 percent, even after taking into account all federal taxes and all government and employer-provided benefits ... To explain *this* split – how the United States morphed from the Broadland of shared prosperity that defined the immediate decades after World War II into our present Richistan of hyperconcentrated rewards at the top – technological change and globalization

prove to be of surprisingly limited relevance. They matter, to be sure. But what matters more is how these forces have been chaneled by major changes in what government has done and not done over the course of the thirty-year war [between labour and capital]. Where the conventional wisdom confidently declares, 'It's the economy', we find, again and again, 'It's the politics'. (Hacker and Pierson, 2010, p 290, original emphasis; see also Drutman, 2015, and Katz, 2015)

The changing role of labour market institutions

One of the central points in John Kenneth Galbraith's work was that a successful capitalist economy relies upon 'countervailing powers', with strong companies being counterbalanced by robust trades unions. Yet one of the key planks in the neoliberal reforms was the deregulation of labour markets. In an influential paper, Freeman (1980) concluded that:

1. Trade unions have adopted wage policies designed to reduce dispersion of earnings within and across establishments, for what can be rationalized as plausible economic reasons.

2. Other things equal, the dispersion of earnings is significantly lower among organised blue-collar workers, in part because of a reduced effort of standard wage-determining factors on earnings, and in part because of smaller dispersion within categories of workers having the same wage-determining characteristics.

3. Dispersion of average compensation is also lower among establishments that are unionized than among those that are not.

4. Unionism reduces white-collar/blue-collar earnings differentials in the organized sector, further contributing to within-sector reductions in dispersion.

5. Overall, the within-sector effect of unionism on dispersion appears to more than offset the increase in dispersion of earnings across industries, so that on net unionism reduces inequality. (Freeman, 1980, p 23)

Card et al (2003) studied the link between unionisation and wage inequality in the US, the UK and Canada. They found that unions had remarkably similar qualitative impacts in each country. Unions tended to systematically reduce wage inequality among men, but had little impact on wage inequality for women. They concluded that (a) unionisation helped to explain a sizable share of cross-country differences in male wage inequality among the three countries, and (b) de-unionisation explained a substantial part of the growth in male wage inequality in the US and the UK since the early 1980s. Up to 29% of all wage inequality between British men in the 1980s and 1990s was due to the decline of the unions (see also Levy and Temin, 2007).

In a 2007 IMF Working Paper, Harjes noted that while income inequalities had increased in most industrialised countries, this development was quite uneven, and was much less pronounced in continental Western Europe. This led him to question globalisation and technological change as explanations. Instead, changes in labour market institutions – the role and strength of the trades unions and the existence and level of a minimum wage – had played an important part in determining the level of inequality.

Krugman (2007) emphasised the collapse of the American labour movement as a key contributor to increased inequality. The percentage of unionised wage and salary workers fell from 30.4% in 1960 to 13.5% in 1999; this percentage is now 11.1 (Bureau of Labor Statistics, 2016). He contrasted General Motors (GM) in the late 1960s with today's Walmart. In 1969, auto-industry workers earned on average almost $9,000 a year, the equivalent of $40,000 today; they also received excellent health and retirement benefits. This partly reflected a long-standing agreement between the company and United Auto Workers that guaranteed that wages would rise with productivity. By contrast, Walmart's non-supervisory employees in 2005 earned an average of $18,000 a year, less than half of what the GM workers had been paid 35 years earlier (after adjusting for inflation). In addition, Walmart's Chairman earned five times the salary of GM's CEO, again after allowing for inflation.

Krugman attributed the decline of the American unions to the way in which American firms took advantage of the change in the political climate after the mid-1970s/early 1980s to engage in union-busting activities and punish workers who supported union organisation. The change in climate was symbolised by President Reagan's suppression of the air traffic controllers' union. The Thatcher Government's determination to weaken the unions provides a clear parallel. Krugman noted that the sharpest increases in inequality had occurred in the two Western countries with the greatest falls in union membership, the US and the UK.

Achur (2010) estimated that, with a union density of 26.6%, the UK was well below many other European countries, and especially the North: Finland with 69.2%, Sweden with 68.4% and Norway with 54.4%. The term 'density' here means the proportion of people in employment (including self-employment) who are members of trades unions. The current percentage of all UK employees who are union members is 24.7; in the private sector alone it is 13.9 (BIS, 2016).

Kristal (2010) sought to account for the increase in labour's share of national income in the aftermath of the Second World War, followed by a decrease since the early 1980s in terms of changes in the levels of working-class bargaining power. This was reflected by changing indicators for working-class organisational power in the economic sphere (unionisation and strikes), in the political sphere (government civilian spending) and in the global sphere (Southern imports and foreign direct investments). A further indirect indicator was the degree of centralisation of collective bargaining. The analysis did not support the SBTC explanation: although productivity growth had certainly had a negative effect on labour's share, this effect had not increased over the past two decades. Likewise, there was no evidence that research and development intensity (as a directly observed, comparable measure of technological change) was related to changes in labour's share (for a similar conclusion, see Peters, 2010).

Krugman (2007, pp 141–9) also emphasised the importance of changing norms about fairness. Previously, it was seen as bad for worker morale and labour relations if there was too great a differential between workers' and bosses' salaries (see also, CIPD, 2015). But now it was only what Bebchuk and Fried (2004) christened the 'outrage constraint' – the risk that excessive compensation would create a backlash from usually quiescent shareholders, workers, politicians, the media and/or the general public – that acted as a check on top executives' salaries. Greatly reduced tax rates might also have played a part: there is more incentive for a top manager to exploit their position because they get to keep more of their (excessive) pay.

Reviewing the then-available literature, Lemieux (2008) concluded:

> Wage-setting institutions are a fairly successful explanation for recent changes in inequality in the United States. De-unionization implies increasing inequality at the top end but decreasing inequality at the low end, which is consistent with changes in the wage distribution observed over the last 15 years. Adding another institutional factor, the minimum wage, can also account for the fact that inequality also expanded in the low end of the distribution in the 1980s, when the real value of the minimum wage fell sharply. Finally, changes in the way wages are set due to the growth in performance-pay jobs can also help to explain a large share of the growth in inequality above the 80th percentile of the wage distribution. (Lemieux, 2008, pp 36–7).[3]

Other studies that see changes in labour market institutions as major contributors to rising inequality include Piketty and Saez (2003); Dew-Becker and Gordon (2005); Kolev and Saget (2010); ILO (2014); and Jaumotte and Buitron (2015). Even the OECD now accepts the need for reform of labour institutions as a way of reducing inequality (OECD, 2015b, pp 42–4).

Finally, there is the broader relationship between changes in labour market institutions and economic demand. Lavoie and

Stockhammer (2013) looked at the interaction between different policies for distribution – pro-labour or pro-capital – and the different kinds of demand regime. An economy is in a *wage-led* demand regime when an increase in the wage share of national income (or a fall in the profit share) increases the sum of the components of aggregate demand: private consumption, private investment, government expenditure and net exports. A *profit-led* demand regime is one where the rise in the profit share (or a fall in the wage share) has this effect. For long-term growth and stability there has to be a match between the distributional policies chosen and the nature of the demand regime.

Demand in most major economies is wage led, even taking account of external components (net exports). Global demand is also wage led (Onaran and Galanis, 2013). It follows that only distributional policies that are pro-labour will produce long-term growth. These policies include the welfare state, labour market institutions, labour unions, unemployment benefit levels, minimum wages and reductions in wage/salary dispersion. Only when wages grow with productivity growth will consumption expenditures grow without rising debt levels. This will require international coordination and labour standards to prevent a 'race to the bottom' on wages. It is important to emphasise that we are talking here about *long-run* growth and stability. In the short run, there are many other factors that influence demand, such as monetary policy, fiscal policy, changes in the price of oil and so on. But if there are long-lasting and major changes in income distribution, such as have occurred over the past 30 or so years in most Western economies, they will end up having a substantial effect on demand.

The crucial assumption underpinning the ability of wages or profits to stimulate growth is the well-established differing propensity to consume: if the propensity to consume out of wages is greater than the propensity to consume out of profits, then a shift to wages in the national income will boost demand, other things being equal. The authors acknowledged that it is also necessary to look at the supply side, and the effects of such a shift on productivity. But they were able to point to several studies that show that higher real wages induce firms to increase labour productivity (Storm and Naastepad, 2013). The link between low wages and low productivity has recently been confirmed by Michael Saunders (2017).[4]

Financialisation

It seems to be generally accepted that, together, globalisation and rising productivity through technological innovation have contributed to major structural shifts in the main Western economies, away from manufacturing to services, and especially financial services: financialisation. One authoritative estimate (Haldane et al, 2010) was that in the UK financial intermediation (services bringing together suppliers and consumers of finance accounted for more than 8% of GVA in 2007, compared with only 5% in 1970. In the US it quadrupled from 2% of total GDP in the 1950s to about 8% today. The US financial sector's share of profits – gross operating surpluses – is much higher: 28% in November 2016 (Bureau of Economic Analysis, 2016). Peet (2011, p 392) estimated that US financial corporate profits exceeded manufacturing companies' profits in every year since 1999 apart from 2008. According to Kotkin (2015), whereas in 1995 the assets of the six largest bank holding companies accounted for 15% of US GDP, by 2011 this share had risen to 64% (aided of course by the massive bail-outs of the biggest banks after 2008).

Philippon and Reshef (2013) looked at the evolution of the finance sector in 10 advanced countries since 1850. They noted that the income share of finance had grown in all of them, but especially in the US. There was no particular correlation between the size of the sector and economic growth. Wages in finance – average and skilled – had grown relative to wages in the economy as a whole in many countries, although in some cases finance wages were relatively high to begin with. Financial services had become more skill-intensive since 1970, with both computerisation and deregulation playing their part; increased competition between financial sectors was another factor. Overall, the authors concluded that 'at the very high end of financial development, rapidly diminishing social returns may have set in' (Philippon and Reshef, 2013, p 94; see also Greenwood and Scharfstein, 2013).

There is in fact a substantial literature on the (often, negative) impact that a larger and generally buoyant financial sector may have on the rest of the economy (for example, Young and Scott, 2004). But how far has the expansion of the financial sector caused or contributed to rising inequality?

Kaplan and Rauh (2010) looked at the contribution to top (0.1%) incomes in 2004 of four identifiable groups: top executives of non-financial firms ('Main Street'); financial service sector employees from investment banks, hedge funds, private equity funds and mutual funds ('Wall Street'); corporate lawyers; and professional athletes and sports stars. While these groups represented a substantial proportion of the top income group, there were also large numbers outside them. These included trial lawyers, executives of privately held companies, highly paid doctors and individuals who were independently wealthy. The authors had little doubt that the contributions of lawyers, hedge fund managers, private equity and venture capital professionals (Wall Street) had increased since 1994, almost certainly to a much greater extent than those of top Main Street executives.

Of the various theories as to why this should be so, the authors favoured SBTC, increased firm scale and superstars. Computers and advances in information technology increased the marginal product of professional athletes by allowing them to reach more consumers. They also enabled professional investors to acquire more information and trade large amounts more easily and efficiently. Financial services and law firms had all grown larger, in many cases by orders of magnitude. Similarly, the amount of capital per employee at the top 50 firms in the securities industry increased by almost nine times in real terms between 1987 and 2004 (there was a similar expansion in the UK after Big Bang). Technological change, especially in information and communications, also increased the relative productivity of superstars or highly talented individuals.

Philippon and Reshef (2009) examined wage trends in the American financial sector from 1909 to 2006. They found that until 1933 the sector was a high-skill, high-wage industry. It then rapidly lost its high human capital and its wage premium relative to the rest of the private sector. The decline continued at a more moderate pace from 1950 to 1980, when wages in finance were similar, on average, to wages in the rest of the economy. From 1980 another dramatic shift occurred. The financial sector became once again a high-skill, high-wage industry, and relative wage and education levels went back almost exactly to their pre-1930s levels. The authors attributed these shifts to changes in the intensity of regulation.

Another factor making for increases in human capital intensity in finance was increases in aggregate IPO activities and credit risk, that is, corporate finance activity (IPOs are initial public stock offerings). Information technology and computers also played a role, but a much more limited one. However, financiers were now overpaid. The authors reckoned that rents accounted for 30–50% of the wage differentials with the rest of the economy since the late 1990s. Because the financial sector was not in a sustainable labour market equilibrium, however, these short-term differentials would diminish over time.

In another important study, Philippon (2014) looked at the costs of financial intermediation in the US since 1890. He found that, unlike in almost every other industry, unit costs had hardly changed: financial intermediation had not become more efficient. There had certainly been fluctuations, with a first main peak in the early 1920s, then a fall in the middle decades of the century and then again an increase from the 1970s. Since these fluctuations match quite closely to shifts in US income inequality over the same period, we asked Professor Philippon if this might be cause and effect. His response was that there might indeed be a causal effect but one would need more data to show it, perhaps for several countries. He referred to another study, by Guillaume Bazot (also 2014), which identifies broadly similar patterns of stagnation or increase in the unit cost of financial intermediation in Europe since 1950.

Dorling (2014, p 85) has a figure (3.5) showing a very close association between levels of US financial regulation and top 1% income shares, with the latter falling with increased regulation after the scandals of the late 1920s/early 1930s, and rising with deregulation from the early 1980s.

Bell and Van Reenen (2013) looked at the growth in pay at the very top of the wage distribution in the UK. Using tax records, they found that between 1998/99 and 2007/08 the top percentile increased its share of all income by 2.9%. Almost all of this was earned income, mostly from employment rather than self-employment. No less than 60% of this increase in income share (accruing to the top percentile) went to financial services employees, even though they account for only a fifth of such workers (that is, workers in finance). However, none of the gains in wage share accruing to finance workers occurred through changes in salary: the entire increase took the form of bonuses. In the US, Kaplan and Rauh (2010) suggested that Wall Street might conservatively account for around 5% of the top 0.5% of the income distribution (and more at the very top). Of course, the City is much larger in relation to the UK economy than Wall Street is to the (far larger) American economy.

Philippon and Reshef (2009) also pointed to the considerable gains made by corporate CEOs over the same period, although much of this increase was in the form of contingent, equity-based pay that, at least in principle, depends on relative performance. Smithers (2013) argued that recent changes in the way in which top executives were remunerated, with bonuses and share options linked to short-term performance (sales, profits, share prices), were actually a major obstacle to economic recovery. Such incentives reduced investment in favour of share buy-backs and maintained the cash surpluses that – along with high levels of household debt and the unwillingness of countries like Germany and China to stimulate domestic consumption – prevent countries like the US, the UK and Japan from tackling their fiscal deficits. The extensive use by the financial sector of 'convex contracts' – ones where mildly good profits will produce a useful rise in total remuneration, but the impact becomes massive if profits per share or the return on corporate equity are a bit better still – has increased the extent to which companies generally have attended to cash flow.

Moreover, financial margins are now greater than both those in the non-financial sector and those in finance previously. This reflects both increased riskiness (which therefore needs higher returns on capital to compensate) and decreasing competition. Matters have been made even worse by (a) the explicit and implicit subsidies that financial firms receive and (b) the way they have used their excessive profits to protect themselves politically.

Overall, therefore, financialisation contributes to increased inequality both directly – by increasing wage differentials and the share of profits in the economy – and indirectly – by dampening economic growth.[5]

Jamie Galbraith (2012) also argued that what drove increases in income inequality in the US from the 1980s was not changes in pay structures or levels but the behaviour of the capital markets and the incomes of those most closely associated with them: rising stock prices, asset valuations and the incomes drawn from stock options realisations and capital gains, as well as wages and salaries paid in sectors that were financed by the new equity:

> Since ownership of stocks is skewed to the top of the distribution, the parameters of the power law vary with valuations in the stock market. This, along with the comparative stability of pay-based incomes, accounts for the high degree of correlation between stock market prices and the income distribution. It also demonstrates that the distribution of taxable income is a poor proxy for inequality in wages, making data from this source largely ill suited for investigation of issues related to pay for work. Finally, it shows that the issue of rising income inequality in the United States is not, by and large, a phenomenon that has run from the top to the bottom of the structure. It is, rather, a phenomenon that reflects, in the main, an extreme increase in incomes of a tiny group at the very top. (Galbraith, 2012, p 41)

This was borne out by a geographical analysis:

> Basically, fifteen counties contributed all of the rise in inequality measured between counties from 1994 to 2000, meaning that if they had been removed from the dataset the rise in overall inequality would not have occurred. Of these, just five (New York; three counties in Northern California associated with Silicon Valley; and King County, Washington) contributed about half the rise in total inequality,

> again measured between counties, in the late 1990s.
> An American resident in Ohio or Georgia saw very
> little of this directly. (Galbraith, 2012, p 13)

In his most recent book, Galbraith also draws attention to changes in corporate structures in explaining this incidence of increased inequality:

> as the digital revolution came into view, the top technologists in the big corporations realized that they would be far better off if they set off on their own, incorporated themselves as independent technology firms, and then sold their output back to the companies for whom they had formerly worked in salaried jobs. In that way, technologists could become owners, taking advantage of venture finance, and could, in effect, upset the previous structure of American corporate valuation. Fairchild Semiconductor is the firm commonly credited with pioneering this model, and the 'Fairchildren' soon followed, of which the most prominent is the now-dominant micro-processor manufacturing firm Intel. Microsoft, Apple, Oracle, and now Google, along with many others, have followed a similar path ... (Galbraith, 2016, p 86)

There does not appear to be any comparable UK analysis, but Danny Dorling (personal communication) suggests that as the top 1% become richer, they are more likely to cluster geographically. For example, family doctors used to be in the top 1% and were spread very evenly across the country; now only 2% of doctors are in the top 1%. It is also interesting that the great majority of the English private schools, which are a major contributor to inequality (see below, Chapter Six), are located in London and the South East.

Stockhammer (2013) argued that financialisation has two important impacts on the bargaining position of labour. First, firms have more options for investing, being able to invest in financial as well as in real assets, and at home as well as abroad.

Second, financialisation has empowered shareholders in relation to workers by putting additional constraints on firms, and the development of a market for corporate control has aligned management's interest with that of shareholders, as just noted. Strengthening the welfare state, in particular changing union legislation to foster collective bargaining, could help to increase the wage share with little if any cost in economic efficiency (see also Stockhammer, 2012).

Lansley and Reed (2013) noted that since the early 1980s the share of output going to the bottom half of the workforce – the lower-half wage share – has been falling sharply in the UK. This reflected changes in the structure of the economy – with a shift away from sectors with a high wage share – and changes in the rate at which pay had risen – with the biggest increases at the top end. This trend was mainly driven by a combination of financialisation and a weakening of the bargaining power of labour. They recommended 'a new social contract with labour' with four main elements: a more generous minimum wage, an increase in the number being paid the Living Wage, an extension of collective bargaining and a reduction in unemployment. There should also be a more active industrial strategy to rebalance the economy towards sectors that can support higher-waged employment.[6]

In Chapter Two we noted the growing dependence of political parties on private funding as party membership has fallen, and the increased importance of Wall Street and the City for party finance. It has been estimated that no less than a quarter of the £78m that the Conservative Party raised between 2009 and 2013 came from hedge fund donors (Wintour and Syal, 2014). A more recent analysis (Watt and Wintour, 2015) suggests that 27 of the wealthiest City fund managers have together donated £19m to the Conservative Party. In America, in 2016, up to 11 October, 27% of all political contributions came from securities and investment: two-thirds went to 'Conservatives', one-third to Liberals (Center for Responsive Politics, 2016a). King (2013, p 107) quoted President Roosevelt in 1936: 'We know now that Government by organized money is just as dangerous as Government by organized mob.' Yet Kotkin (2015) showed how the Democratic Party under Bill Clinton and Barack Obama had also worked closely with Wall Street, which has provided recent Democrat administrations with most of their main economic advisers, a tradition President Trump has continued.[7]

Rent seeking

Smithers (2013) also argued that financialisation is a major example of rent seeking, which he also termed 'rent extraction' or 'rent gouging':

> Looked at from a national standpoint, the ability of one sector to extract rent from the others is bad for the economy. It encourages resources of skilled labour to be misdirected. It does social damage by aggravating disparities of income and encourages political contributions to prevent necessary reforms. (Smithers, 2013, p 105)

It seems clear that the financial sector has three characteristics that make it especially prone to rent-seeking behaviour: concentration, size and scale ('too big to fail'); complexity and opacity; and the ability to capture or control regulators, as Daniel Aronoff pointed out in a letter in the *Financial Times* on 29 May 2015 (see also Zingales, 2015).

As already noted, one major set of neoliberal reforms was to reduce the ability of the trades unions to secure wage levels above those that would otherwise have been obtained, by providing members with a monopoly over certain jobs and thus preventing employers driving down wages by setting union against non-union workers. However, Weeden and Grusky (2014) argued that just as rents were being abolished at the lower end of the income distribution, they were being created at the upper end. They identified four main kinds of 'top-end' rents.

Occupational rents arise where entry to a profession or occupation is controlled through licensing or accreditation. Educational rents result from institutionalised bottlenecks that limit access to high-value education. Capitalist rents are those that are extracted by capitalists that workers were previously able to secure but that have become more elusive through the weakening of unions, globalisation and technological change. Finally, managerial rents stem from three sources: pay-setting institutions that provide managers with performance-based bonuses, pay-setting institutions that allow board members to intrude and acquiesce to the CEO and new forms of managerial closure through credentialism (MBAs) and other means. Rather than accepting redistributive tax and welfare policies as ways of remediating or mitigating the income inequality that is an inevitable concomitant of market competition, the aim should be to eliminate the corruption, closure and bottlenecks that are clear and avoidable market failures (see also Krueger, 1974, and Bhagwati, 1982).

We referred in Chapter Three to a 2015 paper by Jason Furman and Peter Orszag drawing attention to the increasing variability in US firms' returns on capital. In a more recent survey Furman (2016) identifies increased economic rents as a major contributor to increased inequality. Furman argues that (a) the division of rents between capital and labour has become skewed as a result of changes in labour market institutions (the decline of the unions and the fall in the real value of the Minimum Wage) and (b) increasing concentration in product markets is generating additional rents that are not being shared fairly across the economy: 'super-successful' firms are able to share rents with their workers by paying them more than they would have received if they were employed at less-successful or less-dominant enterprises (such concentration can also damage productivity and efficiency).

Sikka (2014a) highlighted the range and scale of the subsidies to companies that he and others have christened 'corporate welfare'. As well as the City (not only the banks), the beneficiaries included a major energy provider (EDF) to build a nuclear power plant; private rail operators; food producers (not necessarily farmers) under the Common Agricultural Policy; BT, to install highspeed broadband in rural areas; and the sports car maker Lotus. There was also the Private Finance Initiative (PFI).

Farnsworth (2013, p 51) defined corporate welfare as 'public policies that directly or indirectly meet the specific needs and/ or preferences of private businesses'. His most recent (2015) estimate, using 2012/13 data, is that direct corporate welfare ('official' subsidies, capital grants, tax benefits, hidden transport subsidies, insurance and advocacy, additional energy subsidies and procurement subsidies) is worth about £93bn a year. More indirect benefits are worth a further £52bn. Together with the legacy costs of the 2008 bank bail-outs and other crisis measures, the overall total is around £180bn a year. These figures can be contrasted with corporate tax contributions of around £42bn (2012/13). Even adding employers' National Insurance (NI) contributions brings the offsetting amount to only £100bn, and there is also legal corporate tax avoidance of £12bn.

Before we leave rent seeking, we should note that the tax and benefits system, which props up the income of the poor, also supports the resources of companies and landlords. Tax credits top up the incomes of low-paid workers, enabling employers to pay lower wages. Housing benefit protects rents. Nearly all of these benefits go to working households: Toynbee and Walker (2015) estimated that the number of people in work who also draw housing benefit will have doubled between 2010 and 2018. Overall, more than £1 in £7 from the total social security bill now goes to private landlords. The campaign group Generation Rent estimates that private landlords may be receiving £26.7bn in subsidies annually: £9.3bn of housing benefit, £1.69bn in 'wear and tear' tax relief, £6.69bn of tax that landlords do not have to pay on mortgage interest payments, and £9.06bn of tax not paid on average annual capital gains (Osbourne, 2015).[8]

Macroeconomic policies

Finally, reference has been made to macroeconomic policies as contributing to growing inequality.

As we saw in Chapter Three, Piketty (2014a) argued that with very low economic growth (which has been the case for most of recorded history), inequality will be greater because the rate of return on capital will be higher. There is, in other words, a link between low growth and capital-dominated societies. There is also a link between economic growth, with the constant creation of new functions and new skills, and social mobility:

Insofar as tastes and capabilities are only partially transmitted from generation to generation (or are transmitted much less automatically and mechanically than capital in land, real estate, or financial assets are transmitted by inheritance), growth can thus increase social mobility for individuals whose parents did not belong to the elite of the previous generation. This increased social mobility need not imply decreased income inequality, but in theory it does limit the reproduction and amplification of inequalities of wealth and therefore over the long run also limits income inequality to a certain extent. (Piketty, 2014a, p 85)

Bartels (2008) observed that the US economy had grown more rapidly under Democrat than under Republican presidents, and that this was why income inequality trended slightly downwards under Democrats and substantially upwards under Republicans. Jamie Galbraith (2012) noted a close correlation in the US between manufacturing pay inequality and unemployment:

Federal Reserve officials have regularly been at pains to deny the proposition that monetary policy can affect inequality. But the evidence for pay inequality strongly indicates that it has. Indeed, to the considerable extent that monetary policy influences the stock market, one can also argue that the pattern of overall income inequality is substantially affected as well by the stance of monetary policy – something Federal Reserve officials have also been at pains, over the years, to deny. Similar results hold for Europe, where inequality as a whole declined with declining unemployment from 1995 to 2000 (Galbraith and Garcilazo, 2005). (Galbraith, 2012, pp 41–2)

In an argument very close to Stockhammer's theory of the sources of demand, Palley (2012) observed that prior to the neoliberal reforms the main engine of demand growth was wage growth: demand growth was income led. The growth in demand led to full employment, which in turn led to investment, productivity growth and further wage growth. But deregulation and deflation had broken the link between wage growth and productivity growth, with demand being sustained (for a while) by borrowing and asset price inflation (credit-driven growth). As a result, we now have an economy that is both debt saturated and almost permanently short of demand: what has been termed 'secular stagnation' (Summers, 2013). Increasing economic inequality and exclusion were an inevitable corollary of this, as in the 1930s prior to the New Deal:

> Since 1980, each U.S. business cycle has seen successively higher debt-to-income ratios at the end of expansions, and the economy has become increasingly dependent on asset price inflation to spur the growth of aggregate demand. (Palley, 2012, p 40)

In fact, the weakness of aggregate demand actually necessitated low interest rates and asset price increases to keep the economy going.

These policies for managing the domestic economy were reinforced by two further sets of neoliberal reforms:

1. **The lifting of barriers to the movement of goods, jobs and capital** at the behest, very largely, of multinational corporations ('corporate globalisation'), leading to increased spending on imports, the loss of manufacturing jobs and the off-shoring of investment.

2. **Financial deregulation and innovation** that helped to plug the demand shortfall and stave off disaster by facilitating higher levels of borrowing through ever-greater supplies of credit, albeit at the cost of a lower level of stability.

Together these policies led to greater trade imbalances, yet external deficits were seen as a small price to pay for the perceived economic benefits. As Palley (2012, p 36) said:

under the new model, trade deficits came to be viewed as semi-virtuous because they helped control inflation and because they reflected the choices of consumers and businesses in the market place.

Britain now has the largest external deficit in its peacetime history at nearly 6% of GDP. But 'no need to panic'.[9]

Austerity

Finally, a number of studies have found that the austerity policies adopted by a number of governments in the wake of the 2008 financial crisis have increased inequality (Chick and Pettifor, 2010; Pollin, 2010; Bogliacino and Maestri, 2014; Sen, 2015; Wren-Lewis, 2015a and b). In a recent (2016) overview, Jonathan Ostry and fellow IMF economists note that while neoliberal policies have certainly delivered benefits – the expansion of global trade (leading to reduced worldwide poverty), the transfer of technology and know-how to developing countries and improved efficiency through privatisation – removing barriers to capital movements and fiscal austerity have had costs, in particular by increasing inequality and thereby limiting the level and sustainability of growth:

> since openness and austerity are associated with increasing income inequality, this distributional effect sets up an adverse feedback loop. The increase in inequality engendered by financial openness and austerity might itself undercut growth, the very thing that the neo-liberal agenda is intent on boosting. (Ostry et al, 2016, pp 40–1)

It seems clear that austerity policies to reduce fiscal deficits and debt levels increase inequality in two main ways. First, by making growth rates lower than they would otherwise have been. Second, at least in the UK case, through policy design, by making austerity bear more on the poorer members of society by cutting public expenditure on the services on which they disproportionately rely, rather than by increasing taxes on those who can more easily bear them. Given that the collapse in the public finances was largely due to the misbehaviour of the financial sector, it is hardly surprising that public anger at the banks in particular remains so strong.

There has been particular criticism of the distributional impact of the associated changes in monetary policy.

King (2013) argued that the policy of 'quantitative easing' – where a central bank buys government bonds from investors in order to strengthen demand and which, together with ultra-low interest rates, is a key element in 'expansionary monetary policy' – reinforces inequality:

> By lowering long-term interest rates, quantitative easing should, in theory, boost the value of government bond portfolios (the price of bonds goes up) as well as the value of other, riskier, assets (with government yields now lower, other assets are relatively more attractive).Yet, in the UK, the vast bulk of these assets are owned by the mature and the rich: those over 45 own around 80 per cent of financial assets (excluding pensions), while the richest 5 per cent of households own 40 per cent of those assets. Put another way, the rich become even richer even as the economy as a whole remains weak. And, on the whole, the rich have a lower marginal propensity to consume. (King, 2013, p 76; see also White, 2012)[10]

This view has now been endorsed by the Prime Minister:

> while monetary policy – with super-low interest rates and quantitative easing – provided the necessary emergency medicine after the financial crash, we have to acknowledge that there have been some bad side effects.
>
> People with assets have got richer. People without them have suffered. People with mortgages have found their debts cheaper. People with savings have found themselves poorer. A change has got to come. And we are going to deliver it. (May, 2016c)

But it has been vigorously contested by the Bank of England (Carney, 2016).

International financial relations

We noted in Chapter Three the suggestion that greater financial openness may have led to increased economic inequality.

Pettifor (2006) noted that the liberalisation of finance during the 1970s and 1980s led to the rich becoming richer and the poor becoming poorer both between and within countries. The increased availability of credit leads to an increased incidence of debt (as we noted in Chapter Two). In rich nations the burden falls disproportionately on the poor, particularly those who are 'asset poor': without existing houses, stocks and shares, and so on.

In an earlier article Galbraith (2007) traced the growth of both within- and between-country inequality since the early 1980s to changes in global financial governance:

> Up until 1973, the world lived under the globally stabilizing financial order of the Bretton Woods system, created in 1944 to provide a framework within which countries could pursue reconstruction and development, with short-term financial assistance from the IMF and long-term development aid from the World Bank. Capital movements between countries were generally controlled, and international commercial banking played a minor role in global finance. This system began to break down when Richard Nixon ceased to exchange dollars for gold in central bank settlements in 1971, and it fell apart altogether in 1973 ...
>
> From 1979 forward, with the arrival of Margaret Thatcher (and economic monetarism) in power in Britain, and then the appointment of Paul A. Volcker to chair the Federal Reserve Board in the US, and then again the election of Ronald Reagan in 1980, the global economic climate changed. Interest rates soared, the pound and the dollar rose, commodities slumped, and the currencies of Latin

America and Africa collapsed. Imports were slashed, and what was experienced as recession in the global North was full-throated depression in the global South. Now, with declining per capita incomes, the Kuznets process went into reverse, and inequality rose sharply. But it was not only a Kuznets process. Everywhere, with high interest rates, creditors gained on debtors. Everywhere, with a rising dollar, those who held dollar assets gained on those who did not. Everywhere, with collapsing local currencies, those who could sell to the outside world gained on those whose market was largely internal. Everywhere – and continually for 20 years, with just limited exceptions, global inequalities rose. (Galbraith, 2007, p 606)[11]

Kumhof et al (2012) argued that increases in inequality can account for a substantial part of the observed current account deteriorations in countries like the US or the UK. The poor and middle-class, who are assumed not to have direct access to international capital markets, start to borrow from the rich when they receive a smaller share of aggregate output. The drop in their consumption is therefore less than the drop in their income, while the consumption (and investment) of the rich increases steeply. The net effect is an increase in domestic demand and therefore a current account deficit.

Bogliacino and Maestri (2014, pp 41–2) argued that one of the underlying causes, or exacerbators, of inequality was the liberalisation of capital movements and the consequential structural imbalances between debtor and creditor nations that result, at least in the absence of arrangements to control those imbalances. Because of the presence of behavioural biases, prices do not reflect fundamentals. So capital liberalisation ends up generating financial bubbles. These in turn increase inequality by inflating the capital share and changing top shares (that is, the existence of rents for companies that allows CEOs and top executives to appropriate part of them):

Although the bubbles are created in financial markets, through increases in prices that do not reflect fundamentals, their origin is economic, in the sense that they are rooted in protracted current account deficits, reflecting diverging competitiveness conditions. (Bogliacino and Maestri, 2014, p 41)

The authors illustrated this thesis by reference to the US, the peripheral countries of the eurozone and Latin America.

So there appears to be a wide measure of agreement that while they are not a sufficient condition for reducing inequality, higher rates of economic growth are at least a necessary one, in addition to combined international action to regulate cross-border financial flows. It is therefore discouraging that most reputable forecasters expect only low growth for the foreseeable future:

With weak growth, particularly of productivity, and structural upheaval in labour markets, politics has taken on zero-sum characteristics: instead of being able to promise more for everybody, it becomes more about taking from some to give to others. The winners in this struggle have been those who are already highly successful. That makes those in the middle and bottom of the income distribution more anxious and more susceptible to racist and xenophobic demagoguery. (Wolf, 2017)

Conclusion

[I]nequality is not simply driven in a more or less uniform fashion by exogeneous forces: political processes, societal institutions, and policies matter. (Salverda et al, 2014, p 12)

It seems clear that the general increase in economic inequality in the West has been partly driven by structural changes – globalisation, SBTC and financialisation, whether singly or, much more likely, in combination – that have affected nearly every country (and that show little sign of being halted, in spite of popular support for politicians who promise to do so). But the fact that the increase has not occurred to the same extent in all the advanced countries, and also that it has not been historically continuous even in the more unequal ones, does suggest that the incidence of inequality is also a reflection of the policy choices made in each individual country at particular points. The evidence assembled here suggests that the key to understanding why economic inequality is now so much greater in the major Anglophone economies lies in the neoliberal policies of deregulation, privatisation, tax reductions and welfare cutbacks adopted especially in the US and the UK since the late 1970s. The deflationary macroeconomic policies associated with these reforms have reinforced these effects, as has an associated concentration of political (and media) power, at least in the US and, to a lesser extent so far, in Britain.

This conclusion is supported by what has been happening in some of the northern European countries. As is clear from Table 1 in Chapter One, although the overall levels of inequality there are still relatively moderate, Finland and Sweden have seen some of the biggest recent increases. As a valuable set of country case studies (Nolan et al, 2014) makes clear, these increases were largely due to the neoliberal reforms introduced in both countries in the mid- to late 1990s in response to economic difficulties.[12] It is also relevant to note that a number of Latin American countries have successfully tackled inequality in recent years, in many cases by reversing some of the neoliberal policies previously adopted (in some instances at the urging or requirement of the international organisations that previously advocated liberalisation).[13] In short, the policies that have been adopted in response to developments like globalisation may be as important in explaining how and why we are now where we are as those actual developments.

The final question to be considered under the institutional heading is whether certain advanced countries have a greater historical disposition towards inequality.

Path dependencies

It is well established that the US Gini coefficient for inequalities in market income is not greatly different from that of other countries: it is the post-taxes and transfers measure that is seriously out of line. In a discussion of the challenges to British sociology from Piketty's *Capital*, Holmwood (2014) drew attention to the work of Monica Prasad (2006, 2012) in identifying certain 'path dependencies' that might be relevant to the question of why certain advanced industrial countries were more open to having significant levels of poverty and economic inequality.

Prasad (2006) sought to explain why and how, in the aftermath of the first oil price shock, the US and the UK were more open than France or Germany to neoliberal policies of preferring capital accumulation to income redistribution and industrial policies that minimised the role of the state (and to organised labour). She argued that the key lay in their very different political economies. The US and Britain had (and very clearly still have) 'adversarial' political structures that define labour and capital as adversaries and the middle-class and the poor in opposition to one another (the middle-class paying for policies that benefit the poor) and that provide the potential to ally the majority of voters with market-friendly policies (together – in the US – with certain changes in political structures that provide politicians with incentives to mobilise this potential). In France, meanwhile, invisible and targeted taxation, a middle-class welfare state and a post-war industrial policy that put the state at the service of capital all combined to create a highly resilient political-economic structure. In Germany, corporatist institutionalisation of business and labour power dampened conflict (Prasad, 2006, pp 38–40):

> Different decision-making structures and policies mobilized the electorate in different ways in the two sets of countries, so that in West Germany and France, pro-growth policies and state structures meant that politicians were neither forced to make neoliberal appeals to the electorate to stay in power, nor able to find issues that would appeal to a broad segment of the electorate. In the United States and Britain, in the wake of the 1973 oil crisis, the adversarial structure of previous policies led to the potential popularity of neoliberalism, and adversarial state structures led

to a greater need for politicians to mobilize populist appeals to acquire or maintain power. (Prasad, 2006, pp 40–1)

5

TACKLING RISING INEQUALITY THROUGH TAXES, TRANSFERS AND SOCIAL EXPENDITURE

> Inequality is embedded in our social structure, and the search for a significant reduction requires us to examine all aspects of our society. (Atkinson, 2014, p 619)

Introduction

In Chapter Four we concluded that current levels of economic inequality in the West, and especially in the major Anglophone countries, are a function of underlying structural developments – globalisation, technological change, financialisation – combined with the neoliberal programmes of deregulation, privatisation, tax reductions and welfare cutbacks adopted in many countries, but especially the US and UK, since the late 1970s/early 1980s. The deflationary macroeconomic policies associated with these reforms may have reinforced these effects, as did an associated concentration of political (and media) power in the US and, to a lesser extent so far, in Britain.

Reversing, halting or slowing the rise in inequality will therefore require a rolling-back of some of the main planks of these neoliberal reforms, but in such a way as not to deprive us of the benefits of market competition as the main driver of growth and innovation where the necessary conditions are present. Because of the scale and complexity of the problem the approach needs to be comprehensive, and the measures recommended need to be complementary as well as technically feasible. The main areas to be considered are: information and transparency; tax avoidance and rent seeking; taxes on income and wealth; direct and indirect taxation; personal savings; corporate taxation; social expenditure; active labour market programmes (ALMPs); labour market institutions; industrial and competition policy; corporate governance; the funding of political parties; education policy; and macroeconomic policy.

However, there first needs to be sufficient agreement that (a) increasing economic inequality is, after climate change, the greatest challenge that the advanced Western societies now face, (b) it is possible to reverse it without incurring significant economic costs, and (c) as with the 2007–09 economic crisis, this is a necessary as well as an appropriate area for state action in the interests of society as a whole. The rest of this chapter focuses on reforms to taxes and transfers and social expenditure (other than ALMPs). Chapter Six looks at the other main areas identified. It should be noted that in both chapters the discussion generally reflects the position at the time of the May 2015 general election. The programmes of the two Governments since then, together with the proposals in the 2017 Conservative election manifesto, are assessed in Chapter Seven.

Information and transparency

The very first requirement – which in a sense underpins all the others – is for greater information and transparency. It appears that the last serious official attempt to obtain and publish information about inequality was the Report of the National Equality Panel in 2010 (Government Equalities Office, 2010). Yet, just as child poverty became a major focus of political attention after 1997, so it should now be a national policy objective to collect and publish information about economic inequality, possibly disaggregated on a geographical, generational and/or minority basis. And, as with child poverty, there should be multi-year targets for reducing it. These should be given statutory force so that the importance of achieving them is recognised and it is harder for subsequent governments or parliaments to ignore them.[1]

In the meantime, policies that could increase inequality should be accepted only if there are clear compensating benefits, and then only for a specified period. To cover all this, the Government should make an annual statement to Parliament about the measures it has taken to reduce inequality, and their effectiveness. Separately, the OBR or another independent agency should be tasked with evaluating progress against the targets. In parallel, there should be a state-funded research programme aimed at a better understanding of the causes of inequality, its effects and possible remedies.

Tax avoidance and rent seeking

One issue that unites economists and commentators of both Left and Right is the need to reduce tax avoidance and rent seeking. In what follows the term 'tax avoidance' is used to cover all the ways in which individuals or companies seek to escape paying tax. In theory, 'avoidance' is sometimes used to describe the use of legal means to avoid paying tax, whereas 'evasion' involves actually breaking the law; in practice, the distinction is often fuzzy.

Tax avoidance

Brooks (2013) provided an overview of the various ways in which big companies and wealthy individuals manage to avoid paying tax. He referred to estimates of the lost direct tax revenue alone of up to £40bn (reflecting the amount of black economy activity that HMRC may be missing). Houlder (2014) referred to official estimates of £34bn, which slightly exceeded the total reductions in public expenditure planned by the Coalition Government. Both Brooks and Houlder quoted various Government ministers about the need for a tougher approach to tax collection, mainly on the basis of protecting the revenue and thus keeping tax rates lower than they would otherwise have been. The Government claims (HM Treasury, 2016a) that the gap of £34bn is among the lowest in the world. But several experts (for example, Murphy, 2014) think that the true figure is much higher, perhaps as much as £120bn if one takes into account profit shifting between jurisdictions by companies such as Google and Microsoft. Yet even the official estimate means that every UK adult pays an additional £1,000 a year in taxes to cover it.

There are in fact various fairly obvious ways in which eliminating or, more realistically, reducing tax avoidance can lower inequality.

- Since it is mostly the wealthy who are able to find ways of avoiding taxes – and indeed this is one of the problems in using tax records to measure income and wealth – **reducing tax avoidance would narrow the economic differentials between the wealthier members of society and everyone else**.
- **Ensuring that everybody pays their taxes has the effect of increasing or protecting the revenues available for redistribution** (and/or targeted public expenditure) to reduce inequality, without increasing tax levels by more than would otherwise be the case. Reducing corporate tax avoidance would also diminish the amounts of money available for excessive executive remuneration.
- **Seeing that everyone pays their share of taxes contributes to a greater sense of fairness and justice,** and thus to a greater degree of social cohesion, which is one of the main underlying aims in reducing inequality. Per contra, if some people are able to avoid paying their taxes, and they are mainly the better-off, this not only shifts the burden onto those less well placed to pay but also makes them less willing to contribute, so further weakening both the tax base and society generally.

Of course, it is necessary to distinguish between the different forms of tax avoidance. We should also note the objection that the room for reducing tax avoidance – as well as expanding the tax base and increasing taxes on personal and corporate income and wealth – is limited by global competition. There is a good discussion in Atkinson (2015, Chapter 10), where the author acknowledges the constraints but argues that these still leave plenty of room for local choices:

> Countries are themselves partly responsible for the terms on which they engage with the world economy. The impact on the extent of inequality depends on domestic policy, and this is one of the reasons we have seen larger increases in inequality in some countries than in others, even though they are faced with similar external challenges. (Atkinson, 2015, p 280)

There are in fact many steps that can be taken by the UK Government to reduce tax avoidance.[2]

First, the tax authorities must be given the necessary resources. As Sikka et al (2016) point out, HMRC's budget has been cut from £4.4bn in 2005/06 to £3.2bn in 2015/16. Staff numbers have been reduced from 100,000 (at the time of the merger of Inland Revenue and HM Customs and Excise in 2004) to 60,000 in March 2016; there are further plans to reduce numbers to 50,000, and possibly 41,000. The issue is not only numbers. The large and increasing pay disparities with the private sector, on top of increased staff turnover and poor morale, have led to a loss of experienced staff, often to accountancy, law and financial services firms. Hence, HMRC lacks the resources for investigations and prosecutions. In February 2016 HMRC had 81 specialists in transfer-pricing (the process whereby multi-entity companies settle the prices on which sub-divisions trade with each other), yet an investigation into just one major company uses up between 10 and 30 specialists; in contrast, the Big Four accounting firms alone have four times as many transfer-pricing specialists (Sikka et al, 2016, p 14).

Sikka (2015a) pointed out that there is a strong economic argument alone for this. For every £1 spent in 2013/14 by HMRC's large business service, an additional £97 was recovered; the local compliance unit, which deals with smaller firms and wealthy individuals, collected an additional £18 for every £1 spent in the same year. Sikka also (2015b) drew attention to the contrast between the authorities' treatment of tax avoidance on the one hand, and benefits fraud, on the other. The losses officially attributed to tax avoidance, are many times greater than those due to benefits fraud (which amount to less than 1% of total benefits expenditure). Yet in 2012/13 nearly 9,000 cases of benefits fraud were prosecuted, as against less than 500 cases of tax avoidance (in 2011/12). Moreover, HMRC's report for 2013/14 stated that during the year 421 individuals had been detained after arrest by HMRC officers, but not one had been charged. Brooks (2013, p 12) published a table showing the number of prosecutions for each £1bn of fraud for each category of tax/benefit. The numbers ranged from 9,000 (benefits such as unemployment or disability) to five (direct taxes such as income tax). As a former tax inspector, Brooks argued that the whole approach of HMRC to tax avoidance had changed from chasing companies and their advisers to helping them to manage their tax relationship with the authorities.[3]

Finally there is HMRC's closeness to corporate interests. The board is heavily populated with people with close links to major corporations, law and accounting firms. The Executive Chair, Edward Troup, is a former tax adviser to companies who is on record as saying that 'taxation is legalised extortion'. Troup is a former partner of a firm whose clients included the Panama-registered fund created by David Cameron's father (see below, Chapter Seven).[4]

Second, the Government could decline to contract for the supply of goods or services with companies that avoid UK taxes. In April 2013 the Coalition Government introduced rules to ban companies and individuals who took part in failed tax avoidance schemes from being awarded central government contracts of £5m and over (HM Treasury, 2013). So far, no such business has been barred (Sikka, 2015a). Similarly, state honours and membership of state agencies and boards could be denied to individuals who are tax avoiders or who are associated with companies that avoid tax. The Government could also decline to employ or seek advice from firms associated with avoidance schemes that had been found to be unlawful, as some have.

Yet Brooks (2013) quoted a number of cases where advisory committees had members drawn from firms that were found guilty of questionable practices. It was reported in 2015 (Boffey, 2015) that several of the private companies bidding for NHS contracts, including Virgin Care, make use of tax havens to shelter profits from tax on a regular basis.

Third, the Government could introduce legislation to make directors personally liable for tax payments (and the associated legal and other costs) where the company's avoidance scheme has been declared unlawful. Those designing and marketing the scheme should be fined a multiple of the tax foregone. Where the individuals belong to a professional body, their membership of that body should be terminated or suspended. In February 2015 the House of Commons Committee of Public Accounts (2015a) accused PricewaterhouseCoopers (PwC) of promoting tax avoidance 'on an industrial scale', helping hundreds of clients to cut their corporation tax bills by setting up bases in Luxembourg (PwC disagreed with the Committee's conclusions). The Committee recommended that HMRC should take a more active role in challenging the advice given by accountancy firms to their multinational clients, and that the Government should introduce a code of conduct for all tax advisers and consult on enforcement of such a code, including through financial sanctions in the event of non-compliance. However, Sikka (2016b) notes that to date no accountancy firm has ever been fined or disciplined by any professional body or government agency for promoting unlawful avoidance schemes.

Fourth, the Government could introduce legislation to require companies to publish the details (name, date of birth, nationality) of all the individuals who own or control shares in a company. The current threshold is 25%, which can easily be got round (Sikka, 2016a). Similarly, the process by which a company can be a director of another company should be banned.

Fifth, the Government could require all firms operating in the UK to publish what they pay in tax each year alongside their annual accounts; ideally, this would form part of an internationally agreed reporting standard. Tax payments would become as routine a part of company reporting as profits or sales figures. Similarly, and as well as the requirement to disclose them to HMRC, the Government could require the promoters to publish full details of any tax avoidance schemes, whether executed by individuals or by corporations.

Sixth, the Government could introduce into Parliament legislation to create a blanket ban on avoidance that would enable a court to strike out any tax avoidance scheme if its intention or effect was to avoid tax: Brooks (2013, p 56) described how the Chancellor, Denis Healey, rejected such a proposal at the time of the 1978 Budget. Since July 2013 there has been a General Anti-Abuse Rule to discourage organised tax avoidance by focusing on the economic substance rather than just the legal form of a transaction. But the definitions involved are too narrow to catch all but the most abusive forms of avoidance (Sikka, 2013).

Seventh, the Government could legislate to require individuals' tax records to be available for public scrutiny, as in the Nordic countries. The making of money is facilitated by the opportunities and rules that society provides. What anyone earns is therefore of legitimate interest in a democratic society, especially where tax avoidance leads to the withholding of revenues that could be spent on new schools and hospitals. Similarly, there should be a public register of trusts, including full details of the beneficiaries. As several newspapers reported at the time (for example, Garside, 2016b), following the Duke of Westminster's death in August 2016, his heir will pay no Inheritance Tax (IHT) on the £9bn that his estate is worth because of the system of trusts in which the estate is held.

Finally, the Government could abolish the 'non-domiciled' status that effectively enables some wealthy individuals who are not fully resident in the UK to exempt their offshore income from UK tax. The number of such individuals was estimated to have risen from 83,000 in 1999 to 123,000 in 2013 (Savage, 2015). In return, 'non-doms' pay an annual fee to the Chancellor of between £30,000 and £90,000. Many of these individuals make no real contribution to the UK economy; if anything, their investment in property inflates house prices and helps to shut out first-time buyers in the major cities. But, irrespective of whether or not they are a net benefit to the UK economy, terminating what is a very obvious relic of empire would send a very clear signal internationally about the British authorities' attitude to tax dodging. Brooks (2013, p 157) noted that a sizeable proportion of these individuals were running hedge funds or private equity funds, some of which make a substantial financial contribution to the Conservative Party (as we saw in Chapter Four).

This takes us to what is surely the central point in the whole tax avoidance debate: the need for a complete change of approach on the part of successive British Governments towards tax and tax avoidance. Brooks (2013) described in painful detail how – whatever the rhetoric about 'all being in this together', and in spite of the often-proclaimed and apparently overriding need to reduce the public fiscal deficit – recent Governments have (a) been ambivalent about the role of taxation in funding the services needed for a civilised society, and (b) connived at, or at least turned a blind eye to, tax avoidance, apparently on the basis that this is one area where Britain can still be economically competitive and 'punch above our weight'. However, the outcome has been tax avoidance on an Olympian scale by large companies and wealthy individuals alike.

Rent seeking

As with tax avoidance, there are many different forms of rent seeking. We noted in Chapter Four Weeden and Grunsky's distinction between four kinds of 'top end' rents: occupational, educational, capitalistic and managerial. In economic terms, all are in effect transfers or redistributions from the rest of society to the rent seekers. Some of these would disappear or be moderated as a result of actions to reform labour market institutions (capitalistic rents) and corporate governance and incentives (managerial rents). But even in those cases, consideration should be given to whether the rents fulfil a public purpose that is sufficient to outweigh the detriments to equality. For example, occupational rents – controls on access to a profession – are surely justified on grounds of public protection: do we really want anyone to be able to set themselves up as a doctor, or even a lawyer, without any prior qualifications? Similarly, do we want anyone to be able to enrol at a university without any evidence about their capacity to benefit from the experience?

However, many of the rents that contribute to rising inequality – for instance, farm subsidies to wealthy landowners or the exemption of sporting estates from business rates – are not of this kind. And, as with tax avoidance, reducing or repatriating avoidable rents would in itself increase or protect the revenues available for redistribution or targeted public expenditure to reduce inequality. In the meantime, it would be helpful if HMRC were more effective in policing existing tax reliefs. A March 2014 National Audit Office report (NAO, 2014a) found that one in five of Britain's largest companies paid no Corporation Tax in 2011/12, while more than half paid less than £10m. The Office calculated that the cost of tax reliefs had risen from 16% to 21% of GDP since 2005. A further report in November 2014 (NAO, 2014b) contained wide-ranging criticisms of HMRC's approach to managing tax reliefs (which HMRC did not accept). The House of Commons Public Accounts Committee's most recent report (2016c) expresses continuing concern that HMRC does not scrutinise effectively whether tax reliefs are being used as intended, or provide Parliament with sufficient information on the costs of reliefs and their effectiveness.

Similarly, neither HMRC nor the Charity Commission monitors the use made by charities of the tax reliefs through Gift Aid and other schemes. Webb (2015b) estimated that the total cost of the charitable sector to the taxpayer was at least £6.5bn (the Government pays a further £11.1bn to charities for some of the services they provide). The issues here – as with other tax reliefs – are (a) who polices these benefits and (b) who ensures that the moneys are used for purposes of which taxpayers, through the Government and Parliament, would approve?[5]

Taxes, transfers and social expenditure

Overview

Widening the tax base by removing or reducing tax reliefs would be a good start on inequality but we also need to look at tax rates.

Foerster et al (2014, p 10) suggested that the OECD-wide average top statutory personal income tax rate declined from 66% in 1981 to 42% in 2010. Similarly, the statutory corporate income tax rate declined from 47% in 1981 to 25% in 2012; taxes on dividend income for the distribution of domestic-source profits fell from 75% to 42% in the same period. In the UK, the top marginal rate was cut in 1980 from 83% to 60%; it is now (January 2017) 45%. In the earlier period there was also an investment income surcharge of 15%.

We also noted in Chapter One the strong (inverse) association between changes in top income tax rates and changes in the pre-tax shares of top incomes. The evolution of top tax rates is a good predictor of changes in income concentration. So one way of reducing the income gap – and, indirectly, the wealth gap – would be to raise the marginal tax rates on top incomes, as well as ending the arrangement whereby capital gains are taxed at a lower rate than other forms of income. However, given the even greater concentration of wealth already noted, and the greatly increased significance of inherited wealth in particular, there is also a case for taxing wealth more directly in some way. It is also desirable to look at the balance between direct and indirect taxes, and at the taxation of companies.

In its review of the relationship between income inequality and growth, the OECD (2012) argued that large and/or progressive tax and transfer systems all reduce income inequality. It noted that taxes accounted for only a quarter of the overall redistributive impact, with the remaining three-quarters due to cash transfers such as pensions, unemployment and child benefits. It nevertheless recommended reassessing tax expenditures that mainly benefit high-income groups (such as tax relief on mortgage interest); reducing distortions in taxing capital incomes (such as reduced taxation for capital gains from the sale of a principal or secondary residence); and shifting the weight of taxation from income to wealth or inheritance because property taxes are among the least distortionary taxes.

One obvious tax expenditure that particularly benefits wealthier taxpayers is pension contributions. In March 2015, in order to pay for a reduction in full-time undergraduate tuition fees, the Leader of the Opposition, Ed Miliband, proposed reductions in the lifetime and annual contributions that could attract tax relief. This is currently worth about £48bn annually (HM Treasury, 2016b), and will rise further as more and more workers enrol automatically in pension schemes (to put it into perspective, this is about half of the annual cost of the NHS). Around two-thirds of this goes to higher earners: in effect, top-rate taxpayers (those earning over £150,000) contribute 55p for every pound saved, basic-rate taxpayers contribute 80p. While it may be right to use the tax system to encourage pension savings, there is no obvious reason why basic-rate taxpayers should contribute extra money towards the pensions of those who are already better off. Yet, to date, the idea of a single, common rate of relief – perhaps 30% – has been eschewed.[6]

Taxes on top incomes

We noted in Chapters One and Four the argument that bargaining effects are the link between top incomes and top tax rates. Piketty et al (2011) estimated that top marginal rates could be as high as 83% before affecting earners' motivation or economic efficiency (see also, Saez and Piketty, 2013). Atkinson (2014, p 628) suggested a top rate of 65% on the basis that even the Coalition Government accepted that the 'poverty trap' faced by many people in the lower part of the income distribution was unfair because people keep so little of their extra earnings, so that the new Universal Credit has a maximum withdrawal rate of 65% (now reduced to 63% under the 2016 Autumn Statement). If a marginal rate of 63% is good enough for those who are scraping by, why is it not good enough for those who are so much richer? Similar issues arise with NI, which is now just another tax and no longer counts solely towards pensions and a small range of allowances. In 2016/17 employees earning less than £155 a week (just over £8,000) pay no NI (to be quite accurate, employers make no NI deductions from their pay). Between £155 and £827 a week, the deduction rate is 12%. But above that (£43,000 a year) the deduction rate is only 2%. This is very clearly regressive.

A 2013 IMF study compared actual top marginal income tax rates to revenue-maximising rates for a number of OECD countries. It concluded that potential revenue-maximising rates averaged about 60%, well above the actual rates in nearly every jurisdiction, and especially the US and the UK. But even if the top rates on only the top 1% were returned to pre-1980 levels, it would not make much of a dent in overall income inequality, so that the increased rates would also have to apply further down the income scale. Nevertheless, as the study made clear, raising top marginal tax rates would not only help to reduce inequality but would also bring in substantial additional revenues. For a range of advanced countries, the richest 10% accounted for between 30% and 50% of all revenue from personal income tax and social contributions, with the top 1% alone accounting for about 8%. The authors noted that whether the increase in the top 10% tax share has exceeded the increase in the income share varies from country to country (IMF, 2013, pp 34–5). An even more radical approach would be to index tax rates to rates of inequality, so that rates automatically become more progressive as inequality rises and become less progressive when it falls, as proposed by Robert Shiller (2003; see also, Burman et al, 2006). This would insure, at least partially, against future increases in after-tax inequality.

Foerster et al (2014, p 68) suggested that there were a number of ways in which the average tax rate paid by top income earners could be increased without necessarily raising top marginal rates. These included abolishing or scaling back a wide range of those tax deductions, credits and exemptions that benefit high-income recipients disproportionately; taxing as ordinary income all remuneration, including fringe benefits, 'carried interest'[7] arrangements and stock options; shifting the tax mix towards a greater reliance on recurrent taxes on immovable property; reviewing other forms of wealth tax, such as inheritance taxes; and examining ways of harmonising capital and income taxation.

Taxes on wealth

As well as leading to huge increases in top remuneration, the fall in the top marginal rates of income tax has contributed to the growing concentration of wealth because the higher-income groups are able to retain a greater share of their incomes. This makes it easier for them to accumulate wealth, leading in turn to further increases in their capital income. Moreover, inheritances and gifts tend to be highly concentrated, which again contributes to increased inequality.

A very recent IFS analysis (Hood and Joyce, 2017) quantifies the growing importance of inheritances. Of those born in the 1970s, three-quarters have or will receive an inheritance, compared with 61% born in the 1950s and 40% born in the 1930s. In the richest fifth of households, an estimated 87% born in the 1970s will receive an inheritance, as against 58% of the poorest fifth. Both among current pensioners and in younger generations, the bigger your income, the more likely you are to receive an inheritance and the larger your inheritance is likely to be. These differentials are likely to grow, not least because younger people today find it harder to accumulate wealth. In short, inheritances will do more to exacerbate inequality in future than they have in the past (Tetlow, 2017).

Generally, wealth is a better indicator of ability to pay than annual income, and indeed taxes on wealth have historically been a major source of revenue. Yet they now yield very little: according to the 2013 IMF study, slightly under 2% of GDP on average across the OECD. As noted in Chapter Three, Piketty (2014a) proposed a progressive global tax on wealth, with a rate of 0.5% on wealth between €200,000 and €1m; 1% between €1m and €5m; 2% above €5m; and 10% above €1bn. It would be levied on physical property, financial and business assets, art treasures and vintage cars, with no exemptions. It would affect only 2.5% of Europe's population and bring in the equivalent of 2% of the EU's annual GDP. Such progressive capital taxation would also help to improve corporate governance by bringing greater transparency to company assets and accounts (Piketty, 2014b).

A recent Fabian Society report (Donovan, 2016) notes that much of the wealth of the super-rich is held as financial assets such as shares, bonds and derivatives. Some of this wealth is routed through tax-avoidance vehicles and tax havens and will have been under-taxed. A recurrent wealth tax might have a number of distortionary effects, such as increased avoidance. But a one-off levy on long-term UK residents with net wealth over £10m (with a second, higher rate on wealth over £20m) would avoid these effects while raising substantial amounts of revenue, perhaps equal to the recent reductions in tax credits (for these, see Chapter Seven).

Foerster et al (2014, p 55) identified three approaches to taxing wealth: taxing the base, asset transfers and increases in value. All could be found within the OECD. But there was a general problem in identifying and valuing many forms of wealth, as well as the risk that some assets might be moved to other jurisdictions (hence the need for Piketty's wealth tax to be global). However, these difficulties did not arise to the same extent with physical property: land and buildings.

Taxes on property

In Britain, as in a number of other wealthy Western countries, property generally, and residential property in particular, benefits from a more favourable tax regime – the exemption of gains in the value of the principal residence when sold, and no effective mechanism for capturing increases in land values (Minton, 2015). Even with the increases introduced in 2014, the existing national tax on property – Stamp Duty – recoups only a small proportion of the property's value when averaged across the years of ownership, takes no account of any increases in value and is anyway imposed on the buyer rather than the seller. So there is a clear case for charging Capital Gains Tax (CGT) on the gains on main residences. Kate Barker (2014) proposed that an individual's or a couple's CGT bill should be rolled up over their lifetime and charged on the death of the second partner, as with IHT. The amount charged would be subtracted from the estate for IHT purposes. By increasing the effective tax rate on owner occupation this would lower the rate of housing inflation. It would also reduce the incentive to hold housing assets for investment purposes, one of the many failures in the housing market (Meek, 2014).

A further consideration is the fact that imputed rents – the rent a homeowner would receive if they did not live in their own home – are exempted from tax, although they are not exempted in a number of EU countries and indeed are included in the definition of income for the national indicator of income inequality in the Netherlands (Bogliacino and Maestri, 2014, p 26). The UK used to tax such 'income' under Schedule A. The OECD recommended in 2011 that imputed rents should be taxed so that housing and alternative investments are treated in the same way (OECD, 2011b; see also, Bartlett, 2013).

In Britain, tax rates on capital gains are still lower than rates on personal income.[8] There is a strong case for taxing capital gains at the same rate as other forms of personal income, not least to discourage wealthier individuals from converting part of their income into capital gains in order to reduce their tax liability. Atkinson (2014, pp 629–31) argued that capital income should actually be taxed at a *higher* rate than earned income, through the reintroduction of earned income relief in personal income tax, so that earnings are taxed at a lower rate over an initial range. Given the role that inheritances play in inequalities of capital income, their value to the beneficiary should be reduced. This could be done either under a lifetime capital receipts tax or under the personal income tax, with appropriate averaging provisions and thresholds. Under both versions, the tax would cover all gifts 'inter vivos', above an additional modest annual exemption.

As Thomas Piketty (2015) noted in his review of Atkinson (2015), Council Tax is now nearly as regressive as the hated 'poll tax' that it replaced. This has led to proposals for a 'mansion tax' on properties worth £2m or more. However, the same objective – of gaining some public benefit from the huge increases in the value of property since the late 1980s – could be more effectively secured through new upper bands in Council Tax, for which the current maximum is £320,000, together with a revaluation of property from 1991 land values. As well as reducing inequality this would take some of the heat out of the housing market: it never ceases to astonish that while significant inflation generally is usually considered a bad thing, house price inflation often appears to be seen as good. Even better would be a tax on increases in the value of land, as advocated by the Land Value Taxation Campaign. As well as being more progressive than existing property taxes, this would discourage the extensive accumulation of land by developers and housebuilders that is one of the principal causes of the chronic imbalance between housing supply and demand (Meek, 2014).

Finally, the IFS (Adam, 2014) has proposed that a progressive tax on the consumption of housing services (a 'housing services tax') should replace both Stamp Duty and Council Tax. All of these proposals rest on the principle that whereas landowners benefit from the various public services paid for by taxpayers generally, the public does not obtain an equivalent benefit from increases in the value of the land that are in part due to the provision of those services in the first place (see also, Chick, 2015).[9]

Direct and indirect taxes

Next under personal taxation, there is the balance between direct and indirect taxes. By definition, direct taxes take account of the ability to pay, whereas indirect taxes do not. Since 1979 in Britain there has been a major shift from direct to indirect taxes: mainly VAT, but also such things as excise taxes. In 1979 the standard rate of VAT was 8%, with a higher rate of 12%. The incoming Government increased the standard rate to 15%, to pay for reductions in the basic and higher rates of income tax. The rate was increased to 17.5% in 1991, to pay for a reduction in the community charge (the 'poll tax'), and then again to 20% in 2011 as part of the Government's deficit-reduction package. This means that indirect taxes in the UK are now raising more revenue than income and capital taxes together.

The *Guardian* and the Press Association (2014) reported a Taxpayers Alliance analysis of ONS figures which showed that in 2012/13 direct and indirect taxes together accounted for an average of 47% of the gross income of the poorest decile, with VAT accounting for the biggest share of the bill. Average gross income, including benefits, was £9,743, but after tax it was £5,132. By contrast, the wealthiest 10% of households paid an average of 35% of their gross income in taxes, £37,287 a year, with income tax accounting for 19.1%.

An ONS report (2016a, p 9) notes:

> Cash benefits have the largest impact on reducing inequality, in 2014/15 reducing the Gini coefficient from 50% for original income to 35.8% for gross

income ... Direct taxes act to further reduce it, to 32.6% in 2014/15. However, indirect taxes have the opposite effect and in 2014/15 the Gini for post-tax income was 36.4%, meaning that overall, taxes have a negligible effect on income inequality.

It is true that many of the goods that consume a large part of the incomes of low-paid workers and families – such as food and children's clothing – are zero-rated for VAT. But, as the IFS commented in 2011:

> VAT should not be considered in isolation from the rest of the tax and welfare system. Since the UK Government is able to levy a progressive income tax and pay welfare benefits that vary according to people's needs and characteristics, this will generally prove a much more effective means of meeting its equity objectives – although the better-off spend a smaller proportion of their incomes on these goods, they spend larger amounts of money and are therefore the main cash beneficiaries of zero rates of VAT. (Adam and Browne, 2011, p 50)

The IFS also referred to the fact that the Mirrlees Review of the UK tax system (Mirrlees et al, 2011) had shown that it was possible to apply a uniform VAT rate with a revenue-neutral compensation package that ensured that the overall reform was broadly distributionally neutral and did not significantly weaken work incentives.

Finally, there is no reason why VAT should not be levied on financial services. In the past the tax authorities may have found it hard to assess exactly how much a bank customer, for example, was paying to open an account or use an automated teller machine. But the Mirrlees Committee thought it would be possible to construct a system capable of making the necessary assessments and produced a rough estimate that it could yield around £7bn annually.[10]

Taxing consumption

VAT is of course a regressive tax on consumption. In Chapters Two and Three reference was made to increasing inequality leading to increasing (and wasteful) expenditure through status competition. In his latest book, Robert Frank (2016) proposes a progressive consumption tax: a tax on annual income net of in-year savings and a large standard deduction (allowance). The rate would start low but then rise as consumption grew. Such a tax would generate revenues that could be reinvested in physical and social infrastructure at the same time as lowering the bar on conspicuous consumption and reducing the overall volume of socially wasteful expenditure.

Personal taxes and the public deficit

Before we leave personal taxes we should perhaps note the relationship between personal taxes and the public finances. Reducing tax avoidance and reliefs that disproportionately benefit the better-off would not only lower inequality but also reduce the public deficit. At present the Government borrows to finance the deficit, and it does so in part by selling bonds to the better-off, the interest on which is paid by everyone. As well as continuing to reduce tax avoidance, would it not be better to increase tax rates, and especially taxes on wealth, and thus reduce the deficit directly? Similarly, the selling-off of state assets through privatisation has generated cash that has substituted for tax revenues. Off-balance-sheet financing of capital projects through vehicles like PFI is another way in which investors can extract income from governments (Arezki et al, 2016). Surely such practices should be banned.

Boosting personal savings

We noted in Chapter Two the current high levels of domestic borrowing. According to Broughton et al (2015), the UK household saving ratio declined from over 13% of disposable household income in 1997 to just under 7% in 2014; the July 2016 rate was 5.1% (Trading Economics, 2016). Atkinson (2014, p 631) noted that the redistribution of wealth was as much about the encouragement of small savings at the bottom as it was about the restriction of excesses at the top. Given that the high rates of return on financial services are very unequally distributed, measures to reduce the wedge between the rate of return and the rate received by small savers would contribute doubly to reducing inequality. He recommended the following.

- **The Government via National Savings should return to offering a guaranteed positive (and possibly subsidised) real rate of interest on savings** up to a maximum amount per person.[11]
- **Institutions should be encouraged to represent the interests of savers and borrowers**, and to provide alternative outlets for savings not driven by shareholder interests, aided by the establishment of a publicly funded money-advice service providing free independent advice to all savers.[12]
- **The payment of a minimum capital endowment for all**, either at adulthood or at a later date, financed by estate taxes and a more progressive tax structure. Such a scheme was introduced in 2005 in the form of Child Trust Funds, which were a vehicle for saving tax-free with a contribution from the Government, but it was abolished by the Coalition Government (together with the planned Saving Gateway scheme aimed at low-income savers). Together with a lifetime capital receipts tax, this would redistribute endowments in such a way as to overcome imperfections in the capital markets such as obstacles to borrowing to set up a business.

Corporate taxation

The case for a company tax is that firms benefit from (a) access to limited liability, (b) being able to use capital derived from people's pension savings (subsidised by other taxpayers) and (c) taxpayer-funded investment in infrastructure, law and order, education and training, health and so on. The corporate level is the one where capital comes together, acquires a distinct legal character and enjoys privileges such as the limited liability that passes risks from its activities on to others. Companies should therefore make some contribution to the public revenues. Yet the proceeds from Corporation Tax lag far behind the rise in corporate profits. Using official figures, Brooks (2013) estimated that while between 1999 and 2011 British companies' profits rose by 58%, Corporation Tax payments increased by only 5%.

This partly reflects the fact that, as in many countries (OECD, 2016a), rates of corporate tax have been reduced, in this case from 52% in 1979 to 20%, the lowest rate ever, and one of the lowest rates in the Western world. Hutton (2014) estimated that if companies in Britain now paid proportionately as much tax as they had in the late 1980s, the country would have been £30bn better off. Whereas in 1980 Corporation Tax generated about 10% of all tax revenue, by 2018/19 it may have fallen to less than 6%. It is true that the value of many of the deductions has also been reduced, and also that companies pay NI on their employees' earnings, VAT on the goods and services they buy and business rates on the property they occupy. Nevertheless, when one takes account of the exemptions that remain, the amount of corporate tax avoidance (including through tax havens and the like), and the current levels of profitability of many British companies,[13] there is clearly scope for increasing revenue from this source without damaging economic efficiency or innovation. It would also reduce the scope for share buy-backs and top salaries, the levels of which are an important contributor to increased inequality. Finally, the shortfalls in corporate tax mean that personal taxes are higher than they might otherwise be and/ or that publicly funded services are poorer than they might be (OECD, 2015c).[14]

Before we leave corporate taxation we should note the strong case for removing the tax reliefs on debt interest that privilege debt over equity as a means of raising funds. As Andrew McNally (2015, p 3) argues, 'our faith in debt has left ownership of the most productive wealth, shares in companies, in the hands of the few'. At the same time, the need to pay creditors means that companies are less likely to experiment, write off old assets, invest in new technology or let their wages bill expand (Webb, 2015b).

Social expenditure

Alcock (2016) reminds us of the collective benefits of welfare provision. The 2010–15 Coalition Government sought to reduce the public financial deficit through a combination of tax increases and spending cuts, with the latter bearing about three-quarters of the burden. But while some areas of public expenditure were protected (the NHS, schools, 16–19 education), others were not, including adult social care, early-years education, Sure Start and the childcare element of Working Tax Credit. Pensions were protected – and indeed enhanced through the so-called 'triple lock' to ensure that growth in value was at least equal to rises in earnings – but spending on and/or eligibility for most forms of social security and tax credits was reduced.[15]

Marx and Van Rie (2014) noted that there was a well-established (inverse) association between overall levels of public social expenditure and various measures of inequality in 30 advanced countries (see also OECD, 2008). But the relationship at the country level is not just about the direct impact of transfers. High-spending countries typically have other institutional features that contribute, notably high levels of minimum wage protection (not necessarily through a statutory minimum wage) and strong collective bargaining compressing wages. This is in addition to more extensive public and subsidised employment, ALMPs (see below) and higher levels of public spending on education (Denmark is the locus classicus).[16]

A similar review (Marx et al, 2014, p 18) noted that:

> several studies have established a strong empirical relationship at country level between the overall level of social spending and various measures of inequality and inequality reduction, including (relative) poverty. This is arguably one of the more robust findings of comparative poverty research over the past decades … *Notable in these analyses was that no advanced economy achieved a low level of inequality and/or relative income poverty with a low level of social spending, regardless of how well that country performed on other dimensions that matter for poverty, notably employment. Vice versa, countries*

> *with relatively high social spending tended to have lower*
> *inequality and poverty.* (Emphasis added)

These various factors may be mutually reinforcing. Barth and Moene (2009) showed how economic and social equality can multiply through the complementarity between wage determination and welfare spending. A more equal wage distribution fuels welfare 'generosity' via political competition. More wage equality leads a majority of voters to support a more generous welfare state: an 'equality magnifying effect'. On the other hand, a more generous welfare state fuels wage equality further through its support to weak groups in the labour market: the 'wage equalisation' effect. Together, the two effects generate a cumulative process that adds up to a substantial social multiplier of more than 50% for the OECD countries between 1976 and 2002. The authors identified three quite distinct societal models:

1. **social democratic:** above-average welfare state generosity and wage equality (Scandinavia);

2. **conservative:** both welfare state generosity and wage equality are at or close to the OECD average (continental Europe);

3. **liberal:** both welfare state generosity and wage equality are below the OECD average (the major Anglophone countries).

They concluded:

> We find that it is complementarities between institutions – not specific features of the welfare states themselves – that can account for the differences between these three worlds of welfare capitalism. (Barth and Moene, 2009, p 37)

Marx and Van Rie (2014) considered whether well-targeted redistributive efforts such as the US Earned Income Tax Credits (EITC) might be just as effective in tackling income inequality and poverty as high levels of social spending and taxation (the EITC is actually less strongly targeted than earlier provisions and caters to larger sections of the population). There was no conclusive answer, especially as few systems are purely selective or genuinely universal. But the strongest redistributive impact was being achieved by countries that combined moderate (Sweden, Finland) to strong (Denmark) targeting with comparatively high levels of spending. This suggested that the most redistributive systems were characterised by 'targeting within universalism ... systems in which many people get benefits but where the poor get relatively more' (Marx and Van Rie, 2014, p 249).

The authors noted that in spite of pro employment, market-based policies, the near-universal rises in labour market participation had done little to dampen income inequality or reduce relative income poverty. Hence the continuing need for some sort of minimum-income protection. But was such protection both affordable and economically desirable? The authors found that the net incomes of minimum-income (social assistance) recipients in nearly all the countries surveyed fell well below the EU's 'at-risk-of-poverty' threshold of 60% of median equivalent income in each country. However, in most European countries the redistributive effort required to lift all equivalent household incomes to the threshold level amounted to less than 5% of the aggregate equivalent household income that was above the 60% threshold; nowhere was it higher than 9%. As regards the effect on incentives to work, the authors commented that 'generally speaking, long-term dependence on social assistance benefits is not an attractive financial situation relative to a full-time minimum-wage job in most of Europe' (Marx and Van Rie, 2014, p 254).

Finally, Marx and Van Rie considered the argument that we should look at other forms of (targeted) income supplements for households that provide some level of income protection but that are also conducive to labour market participation. Tax credits and negative income tax are examples. The EITC scheme had produced some significant improvements, including marked increases in labour market participation and improvements in living standards among some segments of the population, especially single-parent households. However, this might reflect local circumstances, such as the large number of single-parent households, and might not be replicable elsewhere. Moreover, subsidising low-paid work could drive wages down, shifting the intended transfer towards employers (as we noted in Chapter Four in our discussion of rent seeking). The Minimum Wage is discussed further in Chapter Six.[17]

In a parallel analysis, Marx and Verbist (2014) looked at the relative contributions of boosting employment and social investment in countering inequality. While giving more people access to work was desirable for many reasons, it did not automatically translate into less poverty or inequality. Nor would higher minimum wages be sufficient to eradicate in-work poverty: direct income-support policies were still needed even for those in work. However, more investment in some services would definitely yield benefits to equality, with compulsory education a better bet than either tertiary education or early education and childcare because of its compulsory character (within the relevant age group, almost all children participate, and hence acquire a minimum level of skills). The authors concluded:

> The best performers among the rich countries in terms of economic, employment, social cohesion, and equality outcomes have one thing in common: a large welfare state that does several things at the same time, investing in people, stimulating and supporting them to be active and also adequately protecting them and their children when everything else fails. (Marx and Verbist, 2014, p 293)

As opposed, one might add, to excoriating them for their failures to find or retain employment or to cope with the pressures of flexible labour markets.

Atkinson (2014, pp 633–4) proposed that the state should pay everyone a fixed minimum income. It would replace the personal tax allowance, and existing state transfers in payment would be reduced by the same amount. It would be called a 'participation income' because it would require some contribution to society. For those of working age, this could be achieved through full- or part-time waged employment or self-employment; by education, training or active job search; by home care for infant children or elderly people; by regular voluntary work in a recognised organisation; or by some other evident contribution to society. It would probably need to be introduced at EU level, and it might start as a universal basic income for children (see also Reed and Lansley, 2016).[18]

Finally, we should note that a major contributor to the current cost of the welfare state is the cost of pensions. In effect, more than half of the welfare budget goes to just 17% of the population. It is generally accepted that the generations now in retirement have benefited from a number of things that have been denied successor generations, and especially those born in the last 30 years or so: free higher education, windfall gains in property values, subsidised mortgages and final salary pensions (often index linked). But pensioners have also benefited from state pension and other benefits:

> The average income for a retired household before adding in cash benefits from the taxpayer was just under £11,000. The benefits added up to another £10,882 for a total of £21,812. Cash benefits as a percentage of income? 50 per cent ... And this isn't just about generous benefits at the bottom dragging up the average: the top quintile of retired income receivers (on £42,000) still got 26 per cent of income from the state. The average pensioner also received annual benefit in kind of £5,700 from the NHS. (Webb, 2015a, p.8)

So, there appears to be a good case for (a) means testing a number of the benefits currently received by wealthy pensioners, such as the Winter Fuel Allowance and NHS prescriptions and (b) replacing the 'triple lock' – whereby state pensions rise every year by whichever is the higher figure out of rate of inflation, average earnings or 2.5% – by a link to average wages, as recently proposed (November 2016) by the House of Commons Work and Pensions Committee.[19]

Conclusion

This chapter has reviewed the scope for reducing economic inequality through changes in taxes and transfers and other forms of social expenditure. The main proposals are set out in Box 5.1.

Box 5.1 Reducing inequality through taxes, transfers and social expenditure

Reducing economic inequality should be a national policy priority reflected in a number of changes in how it is taken into account in public policy formation, and regularly monitored by an independent state agency like the OBR.

• Tax avoidance

There should be a fundamental change in how the Government sees the various forms of tax avoidance. This should be seen not only in a tougher attitude towards avoiders and their advisers but also in a reversal of the long-term decline in numbers of tax inspectors. There should be full transparency in the ownership and control of all companies operating in the UK. 'Non-dom' status should be abolished.[20]

• Rent seeking

There should be a systematic review of the main forms of rent seeking to see whether there are public benefits that outweigh the damage to equality. Tax reliefs and exemptions that benefit primarily wealthier taxpayers, such as pension contributions, should be progressively withdrawn.

• Balancing different forms of taxation

There should be a review of the balances between:

(a) direct and indirect taxes,
(b) taxes on income and taxes on wealth and
(c) taxes on earned and unearned income.

NI should be treated as an income tax and harmonised with Income Tax.

• Taxes on top incomes and wealth

In the meantime, top personal income tax rates should progress to the same level as the maximum withdrawal rate in the new Universal Credit (now 63%). The threshold for NI should be the same as for the Income Tax Personal Allowance. Tax rates on capital gains should be raised to the same level as taxes on income. Inheritances should be treated and taxed like any other income. There should be a one-off tax on wealth holdings of £10m or over.

• Property taxes

Main residences should be brought within CGT and imputed rents should be taxed as unearned income. There should be new upper bands in Council Tax to reflect the rise in property values in most parts of the country since the early 1990s. There should be a Land Value Tax to capture windfall gains in property values for the common benefit.

• Taxing consumption

VAT should be extended to financial services, and possibly others. VAT rates should be reduced. The case for a progressive consumption tax should be thoroughly investigated, as should a Financial Transactions Tax.

• Personal savings

The Government should do more to encourage personal savings, with a reintroduction of the Child Trust Funds abolished by the Coalition Government.

• Corporate taxation

The reductions in Corporation Tax should be reversed and brought up to the average level for countries with comparable levels of GDP per capita. Tax reliefs for corporate debt should be abolished.

• Social expenditure

The cuts in social expenditure since 2010 should be progressively reversed, to the point where the UK share of social expenditure in GDP is at least equal to the average of countries with comparable GDP per capita. Serious consideration should be given to a guaranteed minimum income for all, with compensating reductions in personal tax allowances and existing state transfers.

• Pensions benefits

The pension benefits received by wealthy pensioners should be means tested. The triple lock should be replaced by a link to average wages.

Finally the role of taxes in financing the public deficit should be properly reviewed.

6

TACKLING RISING INEQUALITY THROUGH POLICY REFORM

Introduction

Chapter Five outlined reforms to taxes, transfers and social expenditure. However 'pre-distribution' is surely better than redistribution. This chapter proposes reforms in a number of further policy areas: ALMPs; labour market institutions; industrial and competition policy; corporate governance; political party funding; education policy; and macroeconomic policy. A summary of the main proposals put forward in Chapters Five and Six can be found at the end.

Active labour market programmes

Several studies (for example, Causa et al, 2014; OECD, 2014) emphasise the role of ALMPs in countering inequality.

Bassanini and Duval (2006) looked at the effects of labour market policies and institutions on structural unemployment and employment rates across the OECD countries over the previous two decades. They found that high unemployment benefits amplify the unemployment effects of adverse shocks. By contrast, a high degree of 'corporatism' (highly centralised and/or coordinated wage-bargaining systems) appeared to improve labour market resilience. There was more tentative evidence that high expenditures on ALMPs had similar effects, while high rates of homeownership slowed down labour market adjustment. Stringent employment protection legislation and highly regulated (that is, protected) product markets, while mitigating the initial impact of adverse shocks, seemed to make unemployment more persistent. Turning to employment rates, they emphasised the important role of tax incentives. High implicit taxes on continued work embedded in old-age pension schemes and other social transfer programmes deterred older workers from continuing to work beyond certain ages. Similarly, low tax incentives for part-time work were associated with lower female employment rates. Family-friendly policies also mattered, with some evidence that childcare subsidies were preferable to child benefits in raising female labour market participation.

Martin and Grubb (2001) examined the experience of five kinds of ALMPs in the OECD countries between 1985 and 2000: public employment services and administration; labour market training; youth measures aimed at the transition from school to work; subsidised employment; and measures for the disabled. Their main conclusion was that such programmes need very careful design in relation to the groups to be targeted and the labour market outcomes to be sought. Job-search assistance, wage subsidies in the private sector and labour market training worked for some groups, although the impacts were not huge. Reviewing 137 ALMPs in 19 European countries, Kluve (2010) came to a similar conclusion.

In this context, it is interesting that in the Country Note that accompanied its 2015 *Going for Growth* report, the OECD called on the UK to strengthen work incentives and active labour market policies (OECD, 2015a). UK spending on ALMPs was significantly below the OECD average. The share of young people not in employment, education or training (NEET) was relatively high, especially among young people with low education.[1] The OECD recommended the UK to increase spending on ALMPs and to improve their efficiency by fostering competition among contracted providers, better profiling of customers and a performance measurement system. The cost of childcare should be further reduced to increase work incentives for parents. In his recent review of the challenges facing the US economy, and especially the significant proportion of people aged 25–54 who are outside the labour force as we noted in Chapter Three, the Chairman of the President's Council of Economic Advisers, Jason Furman (2016), noted that America spent only 0.1% of GDP on ALMPs like job-search assistance and job training. There is clearly a greater role for active labour market policies to play there too.

Labour market institutions

While reducing inequality through taxes and transfers is appropriate, it would surely be better to create market conditions, and especially labour market conditions, that prevent or constrain inequality in the first place: 'pre-distribution' rather than redistribution. With less inequality in the labour market, there would be less need for redistribution through fiscal measures (as well as greater tax revenues and economic demand). It seems clear from the earlier analysis that the neoliberal reforms of the late 1970s and early 1980s have tilted the balance of power between capital and labour too far in the former's direction. As Atkinson (2014, p 625) put it, the benefits from growth now increasingly accrue through rising profits, rather than wages. There would appear to be three main areas of adjustment.

First, given the association between effective trades unions and wage compression there is clearly scope for seeing how the unions can once again be made genuine partners in the national economic enterprise. At the very least, we should revisit some of the restrictions placed on the unions since the early 1980s to see whether and how far they are still needed, in view of the much higher priority now to be accorded to reducing inequality alongside fostering economic growth (in cases where the two may conflict).[2]

Second, we should explore the extent to which collective bargaining can be strengthened, extended or reintroduced. The 2014 ILO report referred to in Chapter Four suggested that collective bargaining was more effective where it was more inclusive and encompassing (where it takes place at the national, industry and/or branch level in multi-employer settings with coordination across levels) than where it is narrow (taking place only at the company or plant level). In the former, collective agreements tend to cover a larger proportion of workers and top–bottom wage differentials; in the latter, the opposite is the case. The Government could also extend the application of collective agreements to non-signatories, reinforcing the equity-enhancing effects of collective approaches. A start could be made by establishing tripartite bodies for wage bargaining in certain sectors, such as contract cleaning or care homes.

Finally, although the strengthening of collective bargaining might help, and even taking account of the possible distortionary effects, we need to look closely at the Minimum Wage.

In their comprehensive review of different ways of redistributing income to which we referred in Chapter Five, Marx and Van Rie quoted an article in the *OECD Observer* in 2007:

> On balance, the evidence shows that an appropriately-set minimum wage need not have large negative effects on job prospects, especially if wage floors are properly differentiated (e.g. lower rates for young workers) and non-wage labour costs are kept in check. (Martin and Immervoll, 2007, quoted in Marx and Van Rie, 2014, p 256)

Marx and Van Rie themselves commented:

> Concerns about work disincentive effects of social safety nets are legitimate, as are concerns over potential negative employment effects of minimum wages, especially if these were to be set at levels high enough to keep households solely reliant on that wage out of poverty. The fact remains, however, that countries like Denmark or the Netherlands combine what are comparatively among the highest levels of minimum protection for workers and non-workers alike with labour-market outcomes that on various dimensions are also among the best in the industrialized world. (Marx and Van Rie, 2014, p 256)

In both the UK and the US the level of the Minimum Wage should be brought closer to the median. This would have several benefits, beyond helping to reduce inequality.

As noted in Chapter Four, a significant proportion of the social budget effectively subsidises low-paying employers through things like tax credits and child credits, boosting their profits by lowering their labour costs. It is particularly objectionable that the transfer to employers is borne in part by low-skilled workers who may not themselves be eligible for tax credits (Rothstein, 2010). Surely it would be better for the state to save this outlay in the first place, rather than try to recoup it through corporate taxes. As well as helping to increase aggregate demand (and tax revenues), this would also boost household – as distinct from corporate – savings rates. Finally, it would improve employee motivation and productivity, as several sets of studies (for example, Coulson and Bonner, 2015) have shown.

In Chapter Three we noted the argument of Buchanan et al (2014) that public sector employment can and should play a larger part in influencing employment conditions more generally. Atkinson (2014, p 628) recommended that the Government should also act as 'employer of last resort' (present author's wording). The state should offer guaranteed public employment at the Living Wage for a minimum number of hours to anyone seeking it. As well as boosting employment (especially among the young), this would tackle the in-work poverty problem: according to Marx and Verbist (2014, p 272), 'as many as a quarter to a third of working-age Europeans living in poverty are actually already in work'. Atkinson recognised that to some readers this might seem outlandish and infeasible on fiscal grounds, 'but for many it may appear no more outlandish or fiscally irresponsible than the policy that financial institutions are too big to fail'.

Industrial and competition policy

This leads naturally to the whole question of the role of government in relation to industrial and commercial development. Mazzucato (2013) and others have drawn attention to the crucial role that the state has played in paving the way for many major technological advances through its support for research, development and innovation. Given the amount of rent seeking that has accompanied the neoliberal reforms, especially but not only in the financial sector, it seems clear that if inequality is to be reversed, halted or slowed, the Government will have to adopt a much more critical approach to the regulation, functioning and outcomes of the various markets than it has in recent years (the May Government's industrial strategy is discussed in Chapter Seven).

Atkinson (2014, p 626) noted that there was a bias to capital when decisions are taken on whether to replace workers with technology. The direction of technological change should be an explicit concern of public policy makers, encouraging innovation that increases employability, notably by emphasising the human dimension of service provision. Of course, a rise in the labour share does not necessarily reduce inequality of household disposable incomes; and one has to trace through the implications (Brandolini, 2010). Nevertheless, Atkinson recommended that public policy should aim to reduce market power in consumer markets as well as rebalancing bargaining power between employers and workers; Furman (2016) makes similar suggestions. The benefits of greater competition for poorer households in particular were one of the main themes of the OECD's (2014) review of responses to inequality. This has two main aspects.

First, facilitation of market exit and entry results in lower prices as well as increased availability and/or better quality of goods and services, all of which are disproportionately valuable to poorer households, enhancing their purchasing power. Second, several studies show that monopoly and other forms of market power are particularly injurious to poorer households. An Australian study (Creedy and Dixon, 1997) of household demand for 14 commodity groups found that the welfare loss associated with monopoly power was greater for low-income households than for high-income ones. A 2004 US study (Hausman and Sidak) established that even allowing for differences in usage, poorer and less-educated families paid more for long-distance phone calls than wealthier and better-educated ones. An OECD study in Mexico (Urzua, 2013) concluded that the relative negative effect of monopoly power was greatest on poor households (see also Causa et al, 2014, and Jaumotte and Koske, 2014).

All this suggests that the Government should adopt a much more proactive stance on market competition where the necessary conditions are in place (especially, reliable and accessible information about product quality), and that it should add to the existing tests for allowing major corporate restructurings the question of whether the proposals would lead to a fairer set of outcomes for all those associated with the companies concerned, not only managers and shareholders but also the workers, local communities and everyone else with a stake in the company.

Corporate governance, behaviour and incentives

One area where Government-led market reforms are certainly needed is corporate governance, something highlighted by the recent shareholder revolts over board decisions on executive pay.[3] There should surely be a fundamental rethink about the nature of the corporation, its social obligations and its accountability. What responsibilities does a company have to the various groups, beyond its owners, who have an interest in its performance, behaviour and impact? Are these responsibilities limited to paying taxes in full and otherwise keeping within the law, or do they go wider? How should these responsibilities be discharged? Who should monitor the discharge of those responsibilities?

There has been a succession of codes of corporate governance, but compliance is voluntary and there are no penalties on corporations or their executives for predatory practices, even if the shareholders were prepared to take the necessary action. Most shareholders are traders and speculators rather than owners. They often hold shares for short periods and have little interest in the companies whose shares they own. Many are based abroad. They have repeatedly failed to curb top salaries and bonuses. We noted in Chapter Three the High Pay Centre's recent estimate that CEO pay in the UK is now 150 times the average worker's pay (the multiple is even higher in the US). Even some conservative commentators (for instance, Smithers, 2013) now feel that many companies – or at least their top executives – have lost all sense of accountability to anyone other than themselves. What is surely needed is a fundamental reform of corporate governance, so that all companies, and especially the larger ones, really do take account of a wider range of interests than just the board and the shareholders.[4]

It is true that the Companies Act 2006 requires company directors to have regard to a range of interests. But apart from various ambiguities in the wording, the only people who can enforce this are the shareholders, and they are very unlikely to do so. There is a further problem that once individual or concerted shareholdings reach 50%, the company in effect becomes the private property of those shareholders. It would certainly be useful to clarify the duties of directors to work for the long-term interests of their companies rather than just the exclusive (and often, immediate) interests of the shareholders. But a better solution might be to require all major companies (and organisations that are legally private but receive large amounts of direct or indirect public funding) to adopt a two-tier structure, where all the main stakeholders, including employees, would be represented on the upper-tier supervisory board. As exemplified in Germany and a number of other successful economies, this would, among other responsibilities, appoint the lower-tier management board and approve its remuneration.

Beyond these reforms and the tax changes already recommended, there are a number of measures that could be taken to bring top executive salaries closer to average salaries, set out in Box 6.1.

Box 6.1 Additional measures to reduce gap between executive and average salaries

• Shareholder votes on pay packages could be made legally binding.

• Companies could be required to report on salary ratios, top to bottom or CEO to median, as is being introduced for public companies in America (Securities Exchange Commission, 2015).

• Remuneration in the form of shares or share options could be abolished or severely limited.

- Bonuses could be confined to a small share of overall remuneration and/or linked to growth in output or investment, rather than to profits, share price or earnings per share.

- Executives could be paid in cash and shares that could be clawed back over a long period, including after they have left the company.

- Employees should be represented on remuneration committees.

- The tax system could be used to punish companies that exceed certain executive levels or ratios.[5]

More generally, there needs to be a complete change of approach, so that company boards are encouraged and supported not only in taking account of a much wider range of interests in the company, but also in taking a longer-term view of what is needed for the company's growth and development. This in turn requires fundamental reforms to the capital markets in order to restore them to their original function of providing capital for companies: as Will Hutton has said, the stock market has become more a vehicle for getting money out of companies than for putting it into them (Hutton, 2015a). This would take us somewhat away from inequality.[6]

Finally, we should note that there is also a strong case for a review of the whole principle of limited liability, on the basis that the detriments may now outweigh the benefits. The introduction of limited liability in the mid-19th century enabled companies to raise large amounts of capital without the problems associated with partnerships. But the combination of limited liability and the separate legal identity of all companies has since been used to protect questionable or illegitimate practices (Corporate Reform Collective, 2014, p 28). Perhaps in future companies should receive the protection of limited liability only if they undertake to look after the interests of all stakeholders: the workers they employ, the customers they serve, the companies with whom they do business, the communities where they operate and the taxpayers who pay for the transport infrastructure and the education system that they rely on.

Another, similar proposal – based on the principle that corporate big business exists under a tacit 'social contract' where the right to do business is balanced by social obligations (Berle, 1962) – is that companies should require a licence to trade, which would be granted only if they committed themselves to certain social goals such as paying their workers a minimum or living wage, recognising trades unions, environmental sustainability and so on (Bowman et al, 2014, pp 136–9). Finally, there is a case for arguing that where a company has received significant amounts of public funding, the Government should be represented on its board (Lazonick, 2014).

The funding of political parties

It seems clear that already in the US, and potentially in Britain, inequality risks being made permanent as a result of the increasing influence that capital is having over the political process. In the UK a number of reforms to limit the role of private interests in public policy making have been discussed in recent years. The most promising of these appears to be the proposal that the political parties should receive state subsidies, alongside subscriptions from individual party members in the UK. There would also be full transparency. There would need to be limits on the subsidy levels.

In 2011 the House of Commons Committee on Standards in Public Life recommended the following.

1. **There should be annual limit of £10,000 on donations from any individual or organisation to any party with two or more MPs** at Westminster or in the devolved legislatures. This should apply to all individuals and organisations, including trades unions.

2. **The limits on campaign spending before an election should be cut by 15%** (as we saw in Chapter Two, the present limits were actually increased by the Coalition Government).

3. **Every party with two or more MPs should receive public funding in proportion to the number of votes received at the previous election.** This would be at a rate of £3 a vote in Westminster elections. Income tax relief should be available on donations up to £1,000 and on membership fees to political parties.

These recommendations were rejected by the main parties but the former Conservative Chancellor of the Exchequer, Kenneth Clarke, has repeated the call for limits to donations and for public party funding (Boffey and Syal, 2015). This would seem to be essential if we are to avoid the plutocratic domination of politics by corporations and wealthy individuals that is now so evident in the US. It would also force the political parties to make greater efforts to reconnect with the electorate by expanding their membership. And it would remove the temptation to accept donations in return for life peerages that we noted in Chapter Two. The costs – about £25m – are small compared with the hundreds of millions of pounds needed to run Parliament and other elected bodies, not to mention the longer-term benefits to democracy.

Ownership of the media

We noted in Chapter Two the evidence of the Media Reform Coalition (2015) about the concentration of newspaper ownership in the UK. The Coalition Government called for urgent reform, including clear ownership thresholds, so that no individual or entity has a controlling share in an organisation with a dominant position in any news market, as well as greater safeguards for journalistic and editorial autonomy. This would indeed seem essential if policies that involve a significant degree of redistribution, or a curb on the ability of the wealthy to exercise disproportionate political and cultural power, are even to be discussed, never mind implemented.[7]

Education policy

> [T]he English educational system will never be one
> worthy of a civilised society until the children of all
> classes in the nation attend the same schools. (Tawney,
> 1964, p 144, quoted in Reay, 2012, p 5)

In Chapter Two we noted that rising economic inequality feeds
through into growing gaps in educational participation and
achievement between pupils from different households, and
that these gaps are in turn harmful to economic growth. It has
indeed been accepted for some time that there are limits to what
schools and colleges can do to compensate for the socioeconomic
backgrounds of their charges (for instance, Thrupp, 1999). But
there are also changes in education policy that could reduce or
limit the differential impact of economic inequality, and therefore
increase growth and efficiency as well as social justice. It is to
these changes that we now turn.[8]

Historically, Britain has had both a large range of school types
and a significant portion of schools that were subject to no, or
very little, state control or coordination.

On the first, the 1944 Education Act established a three-part
system of grammar, secondary technical and secondary modern
schools. By the 1970s most schools had become comprehensives
but a substantial number of grammar schools remained. But
beginning with the creation of Grant Maintained Schools and
City Technology Colleges in 1988 there has been a proliferation
of school types: specialist schools, academies, foundation schools,
trust schools, beacon schools, academies again, free schools,
studio schools, university technical colleges and teaching schools.
In parallel, there has been a proliferation of owners or sponsors.
The private schools always educated a small but significant
share of the school population (7% in England currently). The
churches ran a large number of schools as 'voluntary aided' or
'voluntary controlled' under the 1944 legislation. With the
advent of academies and so-called 'free schools' we now have
an increasing number of schools that are owned and controlled
by external, non-state bodies. So we now have two sorts of

fragmentation: by school type (often corresponding to selectivity of intake) and by ownership and control. Does this matter?

The OECD has estimated that in PISA (Programme for International Student Assessment) 2009, social intake accounted for over 77% of the performance differences between British schools; only Luxembourg had a higher figure (the OECD average was 55% across the OECD as a whole) (OECD, 2010a; see also Thrupp, 1999; Jenkins et al, 2006; Cheng and Gorard, 2010; Centre for Learning and Life Chances in Knowledge Economics and Societies, 2011; Clifton and Cook, 2013).[9] It is clear that in terms of both overall educational performance and equity the most successful countries are those that have integrated, comprehensive systems where between-school differences are minimised (Finland, Canada, Japan, Korea). Countries with traditional selective systems: 'tracking' (Germany, Austria, Hungary), or which emphasise competition and choice (America, Australia, Britain), do significantly worse on both these dimensions (Hanushek and Woessmann, 2006; Alegre and Ferrer, 2010; Glatter, 2010; Clifton, 2011; Bol and van de Werfhorst, 2013). In other words, so far from being seen as antithetical, equity and excellence can actually be combined if a fully comprehensive approach to school organisation is adopted.

The case of Sweden illustrates this very well. It used to be a good performer but has slipped in the rankings. This is almost certainly due, at least in part, to the introduction of 'independent' schools within the state sector (Bangs, 2009; Sharma, 2010; Weale, 2015). This in turn was part of the wider set of neoliberal reforms in the late 1990s/early 2000s that we noted at the end of Chapter Four. Similarly, Finland abolished private and selective schools and gradually incorporated them into a comprehensive system as a means of improving results (Vasagar, 2010). But even Finland's halo has begun to slip. One Finnish researcher has suggested that this may be the result of increasing parental choice since the mid-1990s, again a by-product of deregulation (Nolan et al, 2014). This has created a growing 'tail' of underachievers concentrated in less-advantaged schools, something with which Britain is of course very familiar (Shaw, 2013).

Several studies show how the organisation of schooling is linked to social segregation. A major OECD review of more than 250 separate studies (Waslander et al, 2010) found that the introduction of market mechanisms into schools increased social segregation by creating local school hierarchies that were not subject to the demand and supply pressures of conventional markets. Gorard (2013) looked at national data in England to see how far children living in poverty were clustered within particular schools, and the factors associated with social segregation. He estimated that to create a national system with a properly balanced intake – all schools having the same proportion of poor children – around a third of poor children would have to change school, to one with a lower level of free school meals (FSM). Even beyond the social composition of the area around each school (and local transport facilities), the most important cause of this clustering was the diversity of local schools: areas with grammar schools, faith-based schools and academies had much higher rates of segregation than those that had retained community comprehensives as the dominant type. As we shall see in Chapter Seven, the May Government's proposals for creating new grammar schools would make such clustering even more common.

Finally, a literature review by Allen et al (2014) found that schools are more segregated than neighbourhoods in most parts of England, and that the additional sorting is highest with higher population density and larger proportions of autonomous schools. As Glatter, commenting on this evidence, said: 'Findings such as these question the rhetoric claiming that school structure is unimportant in comparison with teaching quality and leadership' (Glatter, 2014, p 359).

So, if we want to reduce or limit the part that education plays in reproducing or reinforcing inequality, it is imperative to end the segregation of pupils by socioeconomic status and to create a more integrated school system. The underlying principle should be that all schools that are publicly funded should be as alike as possible in pupil intake and resources, so that a student's background and/or where they live makes little difference to the kind of school they attend or the education they receive. This in turn means that there needs to be much greater control and regulation of key aspects of schools, especially intakes and resourcing, but also management and governance. This suggests the following reform programme for the compulsory sector.

All schools and colleges in receipt of public financial support – whether direct (grants to institutions) or indirect (tax breaks) – should be part of the national education system. This would have three levels.

1. **The Secretary of State would remain responsible for the overall funding and performance of the system.** Standards and quality should be monitored by a genuinely independent inspection agency, successor to Ofsted and directly accountable to Parliament. Another independent agency should be responsible for the National Curriculum: a curriculum for all children in all schools that receive public financial support. Both agencies would be required to have regard to the levels of resourcing available to institutions, and how those resources are allocated and used, as well as to the composition of their intakes.

2. **Local middle-tier educational commissions would be responsible for strategic planning.** This would ensure a sufficiency of school places, home-to-school transport (local travel-to-learn patterns would largely determine the commissions' boundaries), support for special needs pupils and school improvement. The commissions should be run by a combination of people with relevant experience and expertise, directly elected members and representatives of other groupings such as employers, trades unions and faith communities.

3. **All schools should become 'trust' or 'voluntary aided' schools with governing bodies appointed by foundations that would own their premises.** Foundations could be responsible for one or more schools. None would be profit making. Changes in school ownership would require the approval of the Secretary of State with the advice of the local commission (for proposals along these lines, see Parker, 2015). The Secretary of State would also

be responsible for ensuring that governing bodies acted in accordance with government regulations and guidance.

As well as organisation and resourcing, creating greater parity between schools means radically changing the whole basis on which pupil places are allocated. The 2014 Annual Report of the Office of the Schools Adjudicator warned that too many schools were flouting local admissions rules and local authorities were often failing to carry out adequate checks. There were particular criticisms of schools that had become their own admissions authorities as academies, and of some schools with a religious character (see next section).

We noted in Chapter Two the links between educational participation and achievement, and economic and social capital. Choice of school is far more critical to the life chances of those who are falling behind academically than it is even for other children. But it is precisely those children whose families often struggle to negotiate our very complex school choice processes, which the increasing fragmentation of the system between many different types and providers has exacerbated (Allen, 2013). Hence no school or college should be able to choose its pupils. School and college admissions should be administered by the local education commissions, who would ensure, so far as possible, that each institution has an intake that is balanced in terms of students' backgrounds, aspirations and abilities.[10]

There should be no selection at age 11. Beyond the general evidence in favour of more inclusive, less segregated systems, and in spite of the common belief that grammar schools provide a 'ladder of opportunity' for bright children from poorer backgrounds, research confirms that grammar schools are nearly always more socially selective than comprehensive ones. For example, a study for the Sutton Trust in 2013 (Cribb et al, 2013) showed that only 2.7% of entrants to grammar schools were entitled to FSM, whereas 12.7% came from outside the state sector altogether, mostly from independent schools. By contrast, around 16% of pupils were eligible for FSM in state secondary schools in England, and just over 6% (now 7%) of English 10-year-olds were enrolled in independent fee-paying schools. The research also showed that in those local authorities that operate a grammar system, children who are not eligible for FSM have a much higher chance of attending a grammar school than similarly high-achieving children (as measured by their Key Stage 2 test scores) who are eligible.[11] Burgess et al (2014) found that selective school systems increased adult wage dispersion by significant amounts.

As well as reducing inequality and raising achievement levels, a more socially integrated school system would have many other benefits. In particular, it would increase the sense of everyone being a part of a wider society: 'we're all in this together'. And it could also lead to lower levels of violent crime (Curtis, 2008). Ideally, such a system should include the private schools (see below).

Faith schools

It has been estimated (Fair Admissions Campaign, 2013) that more than 1.2 million places at state schools are subject to religious selection (16% of all places). That number will have increased since, although there is no more up-to-date figure. Using information from a number of sources as well as schools' admissions directories, the Campaign constructed a map detailing the proportion of pupils that each school was allowed to religiously select in its oversubscription criteria; how many pupils at the school were eligible for FSM by comparison with its local area; and how many spoke English as an additional language. There was a clear correlation between the degree of religious selection and the amount of socioeconomic segregation. Comprehensive secondary schools with no religious character admitted 11% more pupils eligible for FSM than lived in the area. But comprehensive Church of England secondaries admitted 10% fewer, Roman Catholic secondaries 24% fewer, Muslim secondaries 25% fewer and Jewish secondaries 61% fewer. A more recent survey (Johnes and Andrews, 2016) found that faith schools take on 28.4% of pupils who achieve high scores at Key Stage 2, compared with 23.7% for non-faith schools. They also educate lower proportions of disadvantaged pupils and children with special educational needs than other state schools. One in ten faith schools is actually more selective than the average grammar school.

Overall, faith schools clearly promote social segregation. At a minimum, if they wish to continue to receive state support, then they should remain in the state system on the fairer basis proposed for other national schools; if not, they should go private. The issue is not whether or not parents should be able to choose a religious education for their children, but whether the state (taxpayers of other faiths or none, in effect) should subsidise them to discriminate: the same issue indeed as with the private schools.[12]

The private schools

The existence and influence of the English private schools is at the heart of inequality in Britain, as has often been recognised (for example, Social Mobility and Child Poverty Commission, 2014b). If we are even remotely serious about reducing inequality, these schools should at least lose the various economic benefits they currently receive through their charitable status. They would become commercial providers of educational services, which is what they effectively are already. The longer-term aim should be to integrate the remaining private schools into the national system.

Although private schools derive most of their income from tuition fees and endowments, they also derive considerable economic benefits from their charitable status. These benefits are both direct (fiscal savings) and indirect (charitable status helps with reputation and fund raising). As regards the former, the Independent Schools Council (ISC) has given an estimate of £88m annually: the value of rates relief, exemption from tax on investment income, tax relief on Gift Aid for donors and relief from Corporation Tax. As regards the latter, it has been reported that the private school sector is now raising over £100m annually, up from £40m in 2003 (Barker, 2013; see also Barker, 2012).

In addition, the state is subsidising the pensions of private school teachers, an amount estimated at £131m per annum several years ago (Howson, 2010; Shepherd, 2010). There is in fact a net inflow of teachers from the state to the private sector:

the current (2016) ISC Census records, in Table 22, 2,525 full-time state school teachers entering the private sector, against 681 going in the reverse direction (the comparable figure in 1993 was 400 entering the private sector). Surely publicly trained teachers, or the schools that employ them, should be required to repay all or some of their financial support if they move to the private sector, especially if they remain in the state-funded Teachers Pensions Scheme. After all, the additional productivity of the newly transferred teacher represents an additional redistribution towards the new employer and its pupils (Green et al, 2008, p 22).

It is ironic that in spite of these financial advantages – with day school fees about double, on average, state school costs – in PISA 2009 UK state schools outscored private schools by 20 points once the socioeconomic backgrounds of students and schools were accounted for; this compared with an average state school advantage across the OECD of 7 points (OECD, 2010b, p 13.). This raises the issue of whether, beyond the obvious and serious detriments to inequality and social mobility, the problem with the independent schools is not simply value for money (Brown, R., unpublished, *Do We Really Want a Private School Sector?*).[13]

Macroeconomic policy

In the Preface we referred to *The Global Auction* (Brown et al, 2011) and the thesis that globalisation and technological change had together undermined the 'opportunity bargain' or 'contract' whereby personal and social investment in education and higher-level technical training would be rewarded by secure, fulfilling and well-remunerated employment. They and other commentators (for example, Goldin and Katz, 2008; Rajan, 2010; OECD, 2011a, 2015b) nevertheless recommend increased effort in education and training. But what if the jobs are not there?

There seems to be some agreement that, other things being equal, economic growth is positive for equality: of course, the 'other things' are not equal, as we have seen. The reforms recommended here will reduce or moderate inequality, and this in itself will be positive for growth if the recent IMF and OECD economists' analyses that we discussed in Chapter Two are at all to be believed. But is more needed, and what should that 'more' be?

There can be little doubt that while the macroeconomic policies pursued in most Western countries since the late 1970s/early 1980s have lowered general price inflation, they have also reduced economic growth (and increased the value of assets). The same is true of the austerity measures adopted by many Western governments in response to the economic crisis. Most experts are pessimistic about the current prospects for growth, especially as the chances of technological change leading to radical improvements in productivity, at least in the short term, seem small, as we saw in Chapter Three. But a switch to more expansionary policies focused on growth and employment rather than inflation and wages might also be problematic, at least without structural changes.

King (2013) argued that the economic crisis the West now faces – of semi-permanent 'secular stagnation' – is susceptible to neither Keynesian nor monetarist remedies:

> we have ended up with colossal failure, so much so that no longer do we trust either capital markets or, for that matter, each other. We don't trust our banks, our politicians, our foreign neighbours, our central banks or even, in at least one case, our comedians. Societies have become increasingly polarized. There are haves and have-nots. There are generational strains. There is growing mistrust between creditors and debtors. These schisms make macroeconomic success all the less likely because, ultimately, they undermine the functioning of markets upon which macroeconomic success ultimately depends. (King, 2013, p 208)

King recommended a series of structural reforms. We should see creditor nations as being as culpable for debt and its consequences as the debtor nations. Monetary unions – the eurozone – should be accompanied by fiscal unions; recognising the political difficulties with this, King suggests a fiscal 'club' whereby countries unable to access capital markets would automatically receive support from other members without having to pay excessively painful interest rates but would lose their fiscal autonomy during the ensuing bail-out. High levels of government debt could be reduced by economic 'circuit breakers': governments would announce a process that would automatically reduce the deficit year by year, with an automatic suspension in years of economic contraction (effectively what the Gramm-Rudman-Hollings Act did in the US in the late 1980s/early 1990s). We noted in Chapters Two and Four the links between the ending of capital controls, financial bubbles, structural imbalances and economic inequality.

To avoid policy choices being dominated by, and favouring, the 'baby boomers', King argued for a 'social contract' between current and future generations under which there would be continued support for education, infrastructure and children's health, but a serious reduction in expenditure elsewhere, including on defence spending or social benefits (a large proportion of which is spent on pensions). Instead of an inflation target, governments should commit to an acceptable growth rate for nominal GDP, as suggested by Samuel Brittan in the *Financial Times* many years ago, and more recently by Lawrence Summers (2016). To head off protectionist calls to limit capital mobility, enhanced mobility of labour both within and between countries should be encouraged. Confidence in the financial system needed to be restored through:

1. **using macroprudential rules and other devices** to prevent banks from pursuing short-run profit at the expense of long-run stability;

2. where a banking union (where banks are regulated by a group of countries together) is ruled out, **treating national branches of international banks as subsidiaries,** not branches of a global entity. In this way, the potential liability of taxpayers within that nation would necessarily be reduced;

3. **ruling out cross-subsidisation of banking services**. (King, 2013, pp 231–62)

King acknowledged the political and other difficulties of this prescription, but his analysis of the current state of the Western economy is persuasive (for an even more dystopian view, see Shutt, 2014).

Despite their very different starting points, King's prescription has a number of points in common with what Hein and Mundt (2013) called a 'Global Keynesian New Deal'. They argued that under financialisation two distinct types of capitalism have developed: 'debt-led consumption booms' (the US, the UK, Australia, Mexico) and 'strongly export-led mercantilists' (Germany, Japan, China, Korea). Neither type was sustainable. Along with the re-regulation of the financial markets, macroeconomic policies should be reoriented. To avoid unfavourable cost and redistribution effects on firms and workers that favour rentiers, central banks should target real interest rates (rather than unemployment or inflation). Fiscal policies should take responsibility for real stabilisation, full employment and a more equal distribution of disposable income, and wages policies should take over responsibility for nominal stabilisation (stabilising inflation at some target that contributes to the maintenance of a balanced current account). These targets for current account balances should be included in international policy coordination at both regional and global levels. For this purpose, Keynes' 1942 proposal for an International Clearing Union, with incentives and penalties for both debtor and creditor nations, should be revisited. In this way we can avoid the whole burden of adjustment being borne by the debtors and world aggregate demand can be boosted (see also Pettifor, 2006, pp 174–6).

The balance between fiscal and monetary policy

In its 2014 review of responses to inequality the OECD stated:

> *Fiscal policy has played a crucial role in mitigating income inequality in advanced countries.* This has been achieved essentially through the tax–benefit system, which relies on progressive taxation to finance redistributive transfers to poorer individuals and households, as well

as the provision of public goods and services, which creates ... better opportunities for individuals to participate in economic life. Fiscal policy also plays a crucial role in helping to stabilise the economy over the business cycle, which [also] has a bearing on distribution. (OECD, 2014, pp 108–9, original emphasis)

There has in fact been an emerging view that in sustaining the economy too much weight has been placed on monetary policy, especially quantitative easing, and too little on fiscal measures (Davies, 2016a; 2016b; Elliott, 2016; *Financial Times*, 2016; Gross, 2016). The Government should take advantage of record low interest rates to borrow to invest in infrastructure, even at the risk of a (temporary) increase in the deficit (IMF, 2016; Inman, 2016; Kamm, 2016; OECD, 2016b). There is also the argument – made recently by the Governor of the Bank of England (Carney, 2016) – that the heavy reliance on monetary policy has in effect given governments an alibi for avoiding structural reforms (Carney, 2016).

It seems clear that in present circumstances the overriding need is to rebuild demand, which means restoring the link between wage growth and productivity growth. This in turn means controlling corporate globalisation through labour and environmental standards that produce 'upward harmonisation' instead of the current 'race to the bottom' (for example in corporate tax rates), as well as managed exchange rates; strengthening the ability of the Government to produce public goods such as social security, health, education and law and order; re-establishing genuine full employment as the top goal of economic policy; getting a better balance between monetary and fiscal policy; strengthening the regulation of financial markets; reforming corporate governance so that companies are run in the interests of all their stakeholders; and reforming labour markets so that they provide good-quality jobs that pay reasonable wages that grow with productivity. This in turn requires reviving trades unions so that workers can bargain effectively for a share of productivity gains; implementing a proper living wage to provide a true wage floor; and increasing worker protections and social security so that workers have the confidence to press their wage claims and exercise their rights as workers. There will also need to be greater redistribution of wealth through the tax system. This may seem an extreme programme but it is no more extreme than the neoliberal policies put forward by Milton Friedman and others for many years before they finally gained the ear of policy makers.

Summary and conclusions

Commenting on the pressure for healthcare reform in the US, the distinguished doctor and long-standing editor of *New England Journal of Medicine*, Arnold Relman, wrote:

> The US currently wastes vastly more resources on a dysfunctional medical care system than it would ever consider spending on social welfare. (Relman, 2014, p 33)

As we have seen, inequality is almost as much about the misallocation of resources as it is about fairness and social justice. It therefore requires a wide range of complementary responses, as summarised in Box 6.2.

Box 6.2 Tackling inequality through policy reform

• Information and transparency
More information and greater transparency would increase awareness of the extent and impact of greater inequality, and would prompt a better-informed discussion about possible responses. Just as with child poverty, it should be a national policy objective to reduce economic inequality, and the Government should account annually to Parliament on the progress made.

• Reducing tax avoidance and rent seeking
Reducing tax avoidance and rent seeking would reduce inequality because it is mainly the wealthy and the better-off who benefit from these activities. It would also increase the revenues available for the

---

social expenditure that is needed to limit inequality and its effects. All exemptions and tax reliefs that favour the better-off should be withdrawn.

- **Increasing marginal income tax rates and introducing heavier taxes on wealth**

This would also have a positive effect on inequality, as would raising CGT rates, taxing inheritances as income and shifting from indirect to direct taxes. All this should and can be done without any serious damage to economic growth, motivation or innovation.

- **Council tax**

Creating new upper bands and revaluing properties to current levels would make Council Tax more progressive.

- **Supporting saving**

Increased Government support for small savers and the reintroduction of Child Trust funds would also help with inequality.

- **Basic income**

A basic, fixed minimum income would reduce inequality and poverty, but by being linked to a contribution to society through work in the market and/or service to the public it would also contribute to greater social cohesion.

- **Pensions**

Abolishing the pensions triple lock and linking future pensions increases to average wages would begin to address intergenerational inequalities as well as generating savings that could be used for redistribution or public expenditure.

- **Labour market institutions**

Greater use of ALMPs and reforms to labour market institutions, if carefully done, would reduce pre-distribution inequalities by creating a better and fairer balance between labour and capital.

- **State role in market monitoring and regulation**

A stronger state role in monitoring and regulating product and service markets would also help to ensure a better balance between capital and labour factors, which would again assist with inequality.

- **Living Wage**

Raising the Minimum Wage to a genuine Living Wage would improve productivity as well as reducing expenditure on working tax credits.

- **Corporate governance reforms**

Reforms to corporate governance and incentives to better align executives' decisions and actions with the company's longer-term development would reduce inequality towards the top of the income distribution, although they would probably need to be accompanied by tighter regulation of the financial markets if they were to be fully effective (a tax on financial transactions or value added would be a good start).

- **Funding of political parties**

State funding of the political parties, alongside subscriptions from individual members, together with strict overall limits on campaign spending, would help to reduce inequality by limiting the extent to which the very wealthy can determine policies that create or facilitate greater inequality and can resist those with the opposite intentions or effects.

- **Media ownership**

There should be much stricter limits on the ownership of media organisations by wealthy individuals and corporate entities.

- **Education policy**

Although existing educational inequalities are largely a reflection of wider economic and social disparities, policies can be adopted that reduce them still further, the main one being to limit or reduce all forms of segregation in primary and secondary education, while limiting parental choice and promoting greater collaboration through local education commissions.

• Macroeconomic policy

Adopting macroeconomic policies that use the full range of available instruments (fiscal policy, monetary policy and structural reforms) to focus on wage and employment growth (rather than inflation or the share of public expenditure in GDP) would create sustainable economic growth as well as reducing the relative importance of capital that is a major contributor to inequality. But to be fully effective they would require international collaboration over financial flows and corporate taxation as well as on tax avoidance and evasion.

The costs of the reforms

No costings are offered for this programme. There would clearly be 'savings' from reduced tax avoidance and rent seeking. There would also be bigger tax revenues from the higher rates of tax on personal incomes and wealth and on companies, as well as from higher demand and economic growth generally. These increased public revenues should be sufficient for higher rates of expenditure on ALMPs, social protection, social housing and education and training without necessarily increasing the share of public expenditure within GDP. But as well as boosting domestic demand through these measures, GDP should be increased by the reforms to the capital and property markets, corporate governance and education.[14]

7

LOOKING AHEAD

My government will legislate in the interests of everyone in our country. It will adopt a one nation approach, helping working people get on, supporting aspiration, giving new opportunities to the most disadvantaged, and bringing different parts of our country together. (Cabinet Office and Her Majesty the Queen, 2015)

I want to explain what a country that works for everyone means. I want to set our party and our country on the path towards the new centre ground of British politics ... built on the values of fairness and opportunity ... where everyone plays by the same rules and where every single person – regardless of their background or that of their parents – is given the chance to be all they want to be.... Yet within our society today, we see division and unfairness all around.... But perhaps most of all, between the rich, the successful and the powerful – and their fellow citizens. (May, 2016d)

Conservatism is not and never has been the philosophy described by caricaturists. We do not believe in untrammelled free markets. We reject the cult of selfish individualism. We abhor social division, injustice, unfairness and inequality. We see rigid dogma and ideology not just as needless but dangerous. (Conservative Party, 2017, p 9)

Introduction

Previous chapters reviewed recent trends in economic inequality, assessed the various impacts, discussed the causes, and outlined a reform programme. Using broadly the same headings as in Chapters Five and Six, this final chapter considers how the policies of the Cameron and May governments since May 2015 and the proposals in the Conservative Party's May 2017 election manifesto will affect matters. The discussion includes the announcement in October 2016 of the Government's intention to trigger Article 50 of the Lisbon Treaty to enable Brexit and the subsequent Parliamentary vote. In most cases we begin with the Conservative Party's May 2015 election manifesto before considering what has happened since. The overall conclusion is that while there is an increased (and very welcome) recognition of the need to tackle inequality, most of what has been done or announced up to the time of writing (mid-June 2017) will either not make a significant difference, or will actually make things worse. This is particularly unhelpful when most independent commentators expect inequality to increase even further in the next few years if current policies continue unchanged (see discussion of 'just managing' families, pp 188–9).

Tackling inequality as a policy priority: information and transparency

> Our belief in equality of opportunity, as opposed to equality of outcome ... not everyone ending up with the same exam results, the same salary, the same house – but everyone having the same shot at them ... you can't have true opportunity without real equality. (Cameron, 2015a)

> That's why I believe that … the central challenge
> of our times is to overcome division and bring our
> country together by ensuring everyone has the chance
> to share in the wealth and opportunity on offer in
> Britain today. And that starts by building something
> that I call the shared society. (May, 2017a, p 2)

The first issue is the priority actually being accorded to the reduction of inequality.

In an article in *The Guardian* in October 2015 (Cameron, 2015b), the Prime Minister[1] pointed to a number of measures designed to increase equality:

> We're not just the party of the first Jewish prime
> minister and the first female prime minister; we're the
> party that introduced the Disability Discrimination
> Act, legalised gay marriage and reduced stop-and-
> search, and that today is forcing companies to publish
> the gap between men and women's pay, and making
> police record Islamophobia as a separate hate crime.

He also referred to government pressure on major companies to anonymise job applications and a plan for name-blind applications to university (rejected by most universities but subsequently piloted in four institutions). But for all the mentions of equality of opportunity, there were no commitments to tackle inequality, and indeed the word failed to appear in the Prime Minister's article, his 2015 party conference speech, the Queen's Speech setting out the new Government's legislative programme, or the 2015 election manifesto. As the above quotations indicate, Mrs May has made tackling inequality a much higher priority. But there is so far no sign of a reversal of the Treasury's previous refusal to issue any kind of distributional analysis of the Government's various economic decisions, so that this role has passed to independent thinktanks like the IFS and the Resolution Foundation (the Office for Budgetary Responsibility is barred from such analysis).

Tax avoidance

The 2015 manifesto (p 8) spoke of raising 'at least £5bn from continuing to tackle tax evasion, and aggressive tax avoidance and tax planning, building on the £7bn of annual savings delivered in the previous Parliament'. The Government would increase the annual tax charges paid by those with non-domiciled status, 'ensuring they make a fair contribution to reducing the deficit' (p 11), and continue to tackle abuses of this status. The Government would continue to lead international efforts to ensure global companies paid their fair share in tax. The Government would also make it a crime if companies failed to put in place measures to stop economic crime, such as tax evasion, in their organisations, and would ensure that the penalties were large enough to punish and deter (p 11). This last ('failure to prevent') had actually been announced in the March Budget; a consultation document was issued in April 2016 (HMRC, 2016a).

In the post-election July 2015 Budget the Government announced a series of reforms to non-domicile tax status. In particular, a 'deemed domicile' rule would be introduced so that long-term UK residents could no longer claim to be non-domiciled for tax purposes. This meant that non-doms who had lived in the UK for at least 15 of the previous 20 years would lose their special status. The new rules would also ensure that individuals who were born in the UK and who were UK-domiciled at birth would not be able to claim that they were not domiciled for tax purposes while they were living in the UK (HM Treasury, 2015a). The Government also brought all UK residential property within the scope of inheritance tax, irrespective of the ownership structure or the domicile and residence of the beneficial owner. These provisions would now be extended to loans from non-dom parents to children to help them to get onto the property ladder (HM Treasury, 2016c). However, the non-dom clauses in the Finance Bill were dropped in the final Parliamentary proceedings that enabled the Bill to become law just before Parliament was dissolved on 3 May 2017. This means that none of these reforms have been enacted.

Tax avoidance was highlighted by the publication in April 2016 by the International Consortium of Investigative Journalists of the Panama Papers, some 11.5 million leaked documents. These showed how large numbers of wealthy individuals, including the Prime Minister's father, were using one Panamanian law firm (Mossack Fonseca) to shield money from prying eyes. The investigation was subsequently awarded a Pulitzer Prize. Following the revelations in *The Guardian* and other newspapers, the Government announced the creation of a cross-agency task force to analyse the information. In November 2016 the Chancellor confirmed that 22 individuals were facing civil and criminal investigations and a further 43 people were under review while their links to the offshore files were investigated further (Watt and Pegg, 2016).

Tougher action against tax avoiders was one of the main themes of Mrs May's pitch for the Conservative Party leadership:

> And tax. We need to talk about tax. Because we're Conservatives, and of course we believe in a low tax economy, in which British businesses are more competitive and families get to keep more of what they earn – but we also understand that tax is the price we pay for living in a civilised society. No individual and no business, however rich, has succeeded all on their own. Their goods are transported by road, their workers are educated in schools, their customers are part of sophisticated networks taking in the private sector, the public sector and charities. It doesn't matter to me whether you're Amazon, Google or Starbucks, you have a duty to put something back, you have a debt to your fellow citizens, you have a responsibility to pay your taxes. So as Prime Minister, I will crack down on individual and corporate tax avoidance and evasion. (May, 2016a)

In August 2016 the Government issued two consultative papers, one that could mean tax advisers having to pay fines of up to 100% of the tax avoided if the scheme was found by the court to be unlawful, the other ('requirement to correct') proposing to punish offshore tax evaders who failed to come clean about their finances before September 2018 (HMRC, 2016b, 2016c).

The 2017 election manifesto stated:

> We have taken vigorous action against tax avoidance and evasion, closing the tax gap – the difference between the amount of tax due and the amount collected – to one of the lowest in the world. We will now go further. We will legislate for tougher regulation of tax advisory firms. We will take a more proactive approach to transparency and misuse of trusts. We will improve HMRC's capabilities to stamp down on smuggling, including by improving our policing of the border as we leave the European Union. We will also take further measures to reduce online fraud in Value Added Tax. (Conservative Party, 2017, pp 16–17)

However, there are a number of ways in which this statement might be challenged.

Box 7.1 Action against tax avoidance in the UK: reality check

• **Reduction of HMRC resources**

There is no sign of the longstanding reduction in HMRC resources being reversed. The November 2015 Autumn Statement (HM Treasury, 2015b) envisaged a further 18% cut in the Revenue's budget, HMRC not being one of the small group of departments whose budgets were to be 'protected'.[2]

• **Limited progress of tax avoidance investigations**

In November 2016 the National Audit Office reported (NAO, 2016a) that a specialist HMRC unit was investigating outstanding receipts of £1.9bn from 6,500 super-rich taxpayers. Most of the receipts involved aggressive avoidance schemes. However only two of the individuals had been criminally investigated. As an indication of the scale of the task facing the unit, the report disclosed that the 6,500 had on average four serious tax issues each, and around 4,000 of these inquiries had been open for more than three years. In January 2017 the Public Accounts Committee observed that the amount of tax paid by such taxpayers had actually fallen since the unit was established in 2009 even though tax receipts generally had risen to £23bn (House of Commons Committee of Public Accounts, 2017).

More generally, the Committee has continued to criticise the Revenue's performance on tax avoidance, noting in particular the paucity of prosecutions of individuals for offshore tax evasion (House of Commons Committee of Public Accounts, 2015b, 2016a, 2016c).

• No action on government contracts
The Government has still not declined to contract for the supply of goods and services with companies that avoid UK taxes.

• No action on personal liability of company directors
There are no plans to introduce legislation to make directors personally liable for tax payments or the associated legal and other costs where the company's avoidance scheme has been declared unlawful.

• No action on publication of shareholder details
Nor is there yet any commitment to require companies to publish the details (name, date of birth, nationality) of all the individuals who own or control shares in a company (as opposed to just those who own 25% or more). Similarly, there are no plans to ban the process by which a company can be a director of another company.

• No action on trust registration
There are no plans to require the registration of all trusts.

• No action on publication of companies' tax payments
There are no plans to require all firms operating in the UK to publish what they pay in tax each year alongside their annual accounts.

• No blanket ban on tax avoidance schemes
There is no proposal to introduce legislation to create a blanket ban on avoidance that would enable a court to strike out any tax avoidance scheme if its intention or effect was to avoid tax.

It also appears that HMRC will have to repay large firms some £55bn of tax due to discrepancies between UK and EU tax law going back to 1973 (Lawrence, 2017).

As regards international action, in June 2015 the UK was reported (Bowers, 2015a) to have rejected an EU proposal for a Consolidated Common Corporate Tax Base which would see countries adopting a common set of rules on where company profits arise. In November 2015 the UK was reported (Bowers, 2015b) to have joined Luxembourg, the Netherlands and Belgium in blocking attempts by MEPs to gain access to secret European archives detailing some of the most controversial tax policies tailored for multinational corporations over two decades. More recently, the UK was reported (Rankin, 2016) to have contested the EU's proposal that Guernsey, Jersey and the British Overseas Territories should be put on a blacklist of tax havens. Yet the Overseas Territories (and the Crown Dependencies) are central to international attempts to curb tax evasion. As Richard Brooks observed in April 2016, more than half of the 200,000 secret companies set up by Mossack Fonseca were registered in the British Virgin Islands (BVI), where details of company ownership do not have to be filed with the authorities, never mind be made public. Similarly, *The Observer* in May 2015 (Doward and Stevens, 2015) reported the US Justice Department's allegation that the BVI, together with the Cayman Islands and the Turks and Caicos, had played an important part in masking kickbacks between FIFA officials and executives.

Zucman (2013) estimated that in 2008, 8% of the global wealth of households was held in tax havens, of which three quarters ($4.5tn) was unrecorded. However, this estimate may be far too low (Murphy, 2015; Christensen and Henry, 2016). In a major study, Harrington (2016) sheds light on the ways in which wealth managers, many of them members of the London-based Society of Trust and Estate Practitioners, created the BVI trust laws where wealth in trusts can now be held in perpetuity, out of reach even of those who are meant to inherit it. A very recent study of the tax paid by the richest 0.01% of households in Scandinavia (Alstadsaeter et al, 2017) finds that the main reason why the very wealthy are able to evade tax – about 30%

of the tax due, compared to a national household average of 3% – is the extensive use of offshore accounts to hide their wealth. According to Sikka (2017b), between 2010 and 2015 there were only 11 British prosecutions for offshore tax evasion. This figure includes just one from the voluminous inside information provided by a former HSBC employee showing that the bank may have aided 3,600 individuals to dodge taxes. Yet in January 2016 HMRC told the Public Accounts Committee that it had quietly abandoned its criminal investigation into the bank's role in alleged illegal activities.

Of course, Brexit will make it harder for the UK to protect its overseas territories from harsher EU rules on money laundering and information disclosure (Murphy, 2017). Money laundering was further highlighted by a recent *Guardian* investigation (Hopkins et al, 2017) which alleged that several British banks were involved in processing large amounts of money from Russian criminals, seemingly without their knowledge.

So, in spite of strong words by the new Prime Minister, the question raised in Chapter Five – whether there has been a real change of heart on the Government's part on the whole approach to tax avoidance – remains open.[3]

Rent seeking

The March 2017 Budget (HM Treasury, 2017) stated that 'the Government will shortly bring forward a green paper to examine markets that are not working efficiently or fairly' (p 48), but nothing had appeared by the time the election was called. The 2017 election manifesto stated:

> We will … commission an independent review into the Cost of Energy, which will be asked to make recommendations as to how we can ensure UK energy costs are as low as possible, while ensuring a reliable supply and allowing us to meet our 2050 carbon reduction objective. Our ambition is that the UK should have the lowest energy costs in Europe, both for households and businesses. (Conservative Party, 2017, p 22)

In the interim, there would be a safeguard tariff cap to extend the price protection currently in place for some customers on the poorest value tariffs (Conservative Party, 2017, p 60). This appears to fall well short of the cap on the standard variable cap for all consumers trailed in the media in the run-up to the release of the manifesto. This may reflect successful lobbying by the major energy companies (Vaughan, 2017). On page 16, the manifesto stated that a new Conservative Government would 'examine ways in which the regulation of utilities and transport infrastructure can be improved to deliver a better deal for customers and sharper incentives for investment efficiency'. Elsewhere, on pages 59–60, there were promises that a future Conservative Government would be more active in protecting consumers from market abuses. However, it is not clear whether and how far this will address the major corporate abuses described in Chapter Four (see also Sikka, 2017a).

Taxation of income

In Chapter Five it was argued that one important way of reducing the income gap would be to raise top marginal income tax rates. This would also indirectly reduce the wealth gap because the better paid are able to save a bigger portion of their income. However, the 2015 manifesto promised no increases in tax rates (VAT, Income Tax, National Insurance) in the next Parliament. The personal allowance would be increased to £12,500 and the 40p higher rate threshold increased to £50,000 (both by 2020). The top rate of income tax would remain at 45%. Hence the July 2015 Budget increased the personal allowance to £11,500 from 2016/17 and the higher rate threshold to £43,000 (this was further increased to £45,000 in the March 2016 Budget).

These plans were endorsed in the November 2016 Autumn Statement (HM Treasury, 2016a), in the March 2017 Budget (HM Treasury, 2017), and in the 2017 election manifesto (although increases in income tax and National Insurance were not ruled out). However, tax savings through 'salary sacrifices' (where employees accept cuts in pay in return for benefits) and benefits in kind will be stopped, with exceptions for ultra-low emissions cars, pensions, childcare and cycling. Together, these changes will mean the less well-paid paying less tax, but the better-paid also paying less; those whose income is below the level of the personal allowance – some 23 million adults - will of course receive no benefit at all. People earning between £8,000 and £11,000 and below the state pension age will still have to pay NI contributions. This means that the opportunity to relieve some pressure on low-paid employees by raising the NI threshold to the same level as the Income Tax Personal Allowance has not been taken.

The March 2017 Budget (HM Treasury, 2017) confirmed these decisions. But the Chancellor also proposed to increase NI contributions for the self-employed from 8% to 10% in 2018, and 11% in 2019. This was to take account of the fact that, because of changes to state pension entitlements in 2016 to include the self-employed, their more favourable NI treatment could no longer be justified. It would also prevent firms offering self-employment-only contracts from undercutting those that continue to offer conventional employment contracts. But following strong opposition from within the Conservative Party and the conservative press, the Government agreed to delay implementation until Matthew Taylor's report on the gig economy (due autumn 2017; see note 3) was received. It should be noted that under the Chancellor's proposals, self-employed workers earning under £16,250 (54% of all self-employed workers) would actually have been better off. So once again the main concern has been for those towards the upper end of the income spectrum.

Taxation of wealth

The 2015 manifesto was silent on Capital Gains Tax. However, the March 2016 Budget cut the higher rate from 28% to 20%, and the basic rate from 18% to 10%, except for residential property and carried interest (see Chapter Five, note 7). This will actually increase the differential with income tax. Eley (2016) observes that since its creation in 1965, the maximum rate of CGT has varied between 18% and 40%. He also notes that it is a tax paid overwhelmingly by the better-off: the latest figures (for 2013/14) show that 65% of the £4.3bn raised from individuals (as opposed to trusts) arose on chargeable gains of more than £500,000.

We noted in Chapters Three and Five the key role which the accumulation of wealth plays in causing or exacerbating inequality, with inheritances and gifts being highly concentrated, so that there is a strong case for some form of wealth tax. However, the 2015 election manifesto committed the next Conservative Government to *increase* the effective inheritance tax (IHT) threshold for married couples and civil partners to £1m by 2020, the aim being to 'take the family home out of tax for all but the richest' (Conservative Party, 2015, p 65). This was duly included in the July 2015 Summer Budget. The increase in the threshold is being phased in over three years from April 2017 and is being funded by introducing a taper to the annual allowance for pension tax relief for those with a total annual income over £150,000. According to figures from the House of Commons Library, it amounts to a tax reduction of £38,400 for each of the £650,000 estates affected (Asthana, 2017).

Of course, IHT is only a shadow of its predecessors, starting with Estate Duty in 1894. Collinson (2015) quoted estimates by Harvey Cole (former Leader of Winchester City Council) that in 1938/39 more than 150,000 estates were liable to estate duty, which was almost 30% of all deaths, compared to just 16,000 today. Just before the Second World War, with rearmament consuming vast government revenues, it contributed nearly 15% of all tax raised, compared to less than 2% today. This diminution also reflects the numerous ways in which IHT can be reduced through investment reliefs and gifts (Cumbo, 2016b). In a further article, Collinson (2016b) reports research by Prudential suggesting that fewer than three in ten people will leave any kind of inheritance, and those who do so will average just £191,000, well below the existing rates of £325,000 for a single person and twice that for a married couple, let alone the new effective rate of £1m. An analysis by Rachel Reeves (2017) finds that in 2015/16, 96 of the 100 parliamentary constituencies with the highest number of property sales over £650,000, were in London or the South East (and most have Conservative MPs).[4]

Savings

Collinson (2016a) also shows how many of the allowances and savings incentives – all of which represent forgone tax revenues – benefit a small number of mostly wealthy people, and yet the national household savings ratio is again at a very low level, as we saw in Chapter Five. The March 2016 Budget introduced two new schemes to boost savings. First, a 'Help to Save' scheme aimed at people on low incomes able to save up to £50 a month (to a maximum of £1,800 over three years). Second, a new Lifetime Individual Savings Account (ISA, in which any gains are tax-free), allowing 18- to 40-year-olds to save up to £4,000 a year and receive a 25% bonus for every pound they put in, although the money can be withdrawn without penalty only (a) to buy a first property or (b) after the age of 60. A number of independent commentators (for example, Cumbo, 2016a) have pointed out that given the amounts involved it is young people from wealthier families who will benefit most.

Prem Sikka (personal communication) notes that when the Minimum Wage was introduced only 1 in 50 workers stood to benefit, the proportion now is 1 in 20. So many families are just not in a position to save, especially as many companies are also abandoning defined benefit pension schemes (this is partly due to continued quantitative easing: see Altmann, 2017). In the March 2017 Budget (HM Treasury, 2017), the Chancellor stated that raising the annual Individual Savings Allowance (ISA) to £20,000 would 'help everyone'. Yet, as a letter in *The Guardian* on 10 March 2017 from Wendy Ekberg pointed out, with average household debt close to £13,000 and so many incomes below the tax threshold, investing in an ISA is only for the better-off. Indeed, they can invest every year and pay no tax on the gains, so increasing inequality further.

Corporate taxation

We noted in Chapter Five that in Britain, as in many other Western countries, company taxes now represent a much smaller share of tax revenues. This reflects the reductions in tax rates as well as the many exemptions. Under the Coalition Government the rate of Corporation Tax was cut from 28% to 20%, the joint lowest in the OECD and the lowest in the G7. The Cameron Government planned to reduce it still further, to 17% by 2020, although this would be partly financed by larger companies being obliged to pay their tax earlier. The May Government confirmed this policy (HM Treasury, 2016a, p 3), as did the 2017 election manifesto. There have also been reductions in business rates for smaller firms. Osborne (2016a) quotes a survey by the accountants UHY Hacker Young that indicates that FTSE100 companies paid tax equal to 23% of their profits in 2014/15, almost a quarter less than in 2010. The main reasons were falling tax rates and the use of allowances, including the ability of companies since 2013 under Patent Box legislation to apply a lower rate of Corporation Tax to profits from their own patented inventions. Property and real estate firms had the lowest effective rate because as real estate investment trusts they do not face Corporation Tax. Lower corporate taxes are often held to be vital for attracting inward investment, yet many comparable European countries – France, Germany, Scandinavia – manage to combine healthy inward investment and much higher rates of corporate tax.

Jobs and income

The 2015 manifesto spoke of 'helping business to create two million new jobs, giving business the most competitive taxes of any major economy, and supporting three million new apprenticeships' (p 17). At the same time, the Conservative Party 'strongly support[ed]' the National Minimum Wage and wanted to see further real-terms increases in the next Parliament. It also supported the Living Wage and would continue to encourage businesses and other organisations to pay it 'wherever they can afford it'. The 2015 manifesto committed the new Government to taking 'further steps in eradicating abuses of workers, such as non-payment of the Minimum Wage, exclusivity in zero-hours contracts, and exploitation of migrant workers' (pp 19–21).

As the Resolution Foundation noted in its June 2015 review of Universal Credit (UC) (Finch, 2015), one in five UK workers is low paid, with the UK ranking among the worst performers in the OECD.[5] Moreover, the proportion of workers paid below the Living Wage has increased in recent years (Osborne and Gayle, 2015). The proposal in the July 2015 Budget for an increased minimum wage of £7.20 an hour for those aged over 25 from April 2016 (rising to 60% of the median wage by 2020) was therefore welcome. As well as helping to reduce inequality this will improve employee motivation and productivity, as noted in Chapter Six (for definitions of the Minimum and Living Wages, see Chapter Four, note 6).

However, the new minimum wage – the National Living Wage (NLW) – falls well below the real Living Wage of £8.45 nationally, £9.75 in London. Moreover, its impact in reducing inequality will be offset for many low income households by the planned welfare cuts (see next section), as has been widely recognised (for example, Hirsch, 2015). Nevertheless, the Resolution Foundation (D'Arcy et al, 2015) has estimated that up to a third of workers in the top low-wage 'hotspots' (all outside London) would be getting a pay rise; those who have been on the Minimum Wage for the past five years would be getting a 10.8% increase, five times as fast as the current rise in annual average earnings. At current rates of profitability, service companies in particular should be well placed to pay these increases.[6]

In the 2016 Autumn Statement the Chancellor announced that the NLW would be further increased to £7.50 from April 2017. Proposals to double the fines for non-payment, and to punish repeated failure to pay by disqualification as a company director, are also welcome, although how effectively the NLW will be enforced remains unclear given both the big increase in the number of workers covered and the pressures on HMRC. In September 2016 it was reported (Booth, 2016b) that only three employers had been prosecuted for paying workers below the Minimum Wage despite HMRC finding some 700 who had broken the law over the past two-and-a-half years. The following month it was announced that HMRC was establishing a special unit to investigate firms that avoid giving workers employment protections by using agency staff or calling them self-employed (Booth, 2016b). Of course, if the Government demanded that all of its contractors and suppliers paid the Living Wage, national pay norms would rise immediately.[7]

Finally, the plan to make large employers bear the cost of increased numbers of apprenticeships – confirmed in the 2015 Autumn Statement and being implemented from April 2017 – is a long overdue recognition that much more needs to be done on the demand side if our longstanding skills shortages are ever to be overcome (although a targeted scheme would have been preferable: Brown, 2016). The rationale, as the *Financial Times* pointed out in a Leader on 10 July 2015, is that with the state out of funds and the business world flush, companies should pay up for the Government's priorities (the levy is intended to raise nearly £3bn by 2020). However, there remain concerns about the risk that employers will game the system by artificially routing other forms of training into apprenticeships or hiring apprentices as a means of avoiding the Minimum Wage (Committee of Public Accounts, 2016b).

Social expenditure

We noted in Chapter Five that cuts in public expenditure were the main way in which the Coalition Government aimed to reduce the public deficit following the 2008 crisis, and that cuts in social expenditure (other than on pensions) were a key part of that, with the welfare state being seen primarily as a means of promoting employment. The Cameron and May Governments and the 2017 election manifesto all continued this policy.

Accordingly, the 2015 election manifesto committed the new Government to cap overall welfare spending, to lower from £26,000 to £23,000 the total amount of benefits any individual household could receive ('so as to reward work'), and to continue to roll out UC. In addition, the Conservative Party would introduce tax-free childcare for parents in work and give working parents of 3- and 4-year-olds 30 hours of free childcare a week (compared to the existing 15 hours). A new Conservative Government would freeze working-age benefits for two years from April 2016, with exemptions for disability and pensioner benefits (as already), as well as for maternity allowance, statutory maternity pay, statutory paternity pay, statutory adoption pay, and statutory sick pay. The manifesto added: 'We will work to eliminate child poverty and introduce better measures to drive real change' (p 28). Pensioner benefits would continue to be protected, including the free bus pass, TV licence and Winter Fuel Payment (p 65).

The post-election July 2015 Budget stated that to achieve a budget surplus by 2019–20, around £37bn of 'further consolidation measures' would be needed. Of this, £12bn a year was to be found through 'welfare reform'. The measures proposed included the freezing of working-age benefits, tax credits and Local Housing Allowances for four years, reducing rents in social housing by 1% a year for four years, lowering the benefit cap, and reforming tax credits and UC, with support 'focused on those with lower incomes'. It should be noted that whilst the reduction in social rents saves money in housing benefits, it is not actually a welfare cut but an increased subsidy to social tenants, the cost of which falls on local authorities and housing associations rather than the Government.

In the event there was considerable opposition to the reforms to tax credits, with Government defeats in the House of Lords. The IFS (Elming et al, 2015) showed that under the Government's proposals, working families with children and eligible for tax credits would be on average £737 a year worse off by 2020. For these families, the tax credit cuts dwarfed the gains from the NLW. Other independent analyses came to similar conclusions. In the 2015 Autumn Statement the Chancellor announced that the tax credit taper rate and thresholds would after all remain unchanged. Tax credits were anyway being phased out as UC was introduced. There would be no further changes to the UC taper or to work allowances beyond those already approved by Parliament. Annual welfare savings of £12bn would still be achieved. Nevertheless, because the cuts to working allowances in the July 2015 Budget were still being carried through, most of those eligible for UC from April 2016 would be worse off. To quote the Director of the IFS:

> the long term generosity of the welfare system will be cut just as much as was ever intended as new claimants will receive significantly lower benefits than they would have done before the July changes. (Johnson, 2015b, p 3)

The 2015 Autumn Statement also incorporated the outcome of the post-election Spending Review, covering the period to 2020. Even though departmental spending was planned to fall at less than half the rate in the previous five years, total managed expenditure would fall from 39.7% of national income in 2015/16 to 36.4% in 2020/21 (HM Treasury, 2015b, Table 1.6). This would be the lowest share since 2000. Health, schools, international development and defence would continue to be protected (we shall shortly see what this means for schools).

The tax cuts in the March 2016 Budget, especially the cuts in the rate of CGT, again focused attention on the distributional effects of the Cameron Government's tax and benefits policies, as did the resignation of the Work and Pensions Secretary, Iain Duncan Smith, on 18 March 2016 (ostensibly over cuts to disability benefits). In a widely quoted analysis, the IFS (Hood and Johnson, 2016) found that whilst the new Government's tax and benefit reforms would have little impact on pensioners, poorer working households would be hit hard, especially those with children. This was the result of a combination of continued protection of pensioner benefits (especially the triple lock), and the further deep cuts in welfare spending (especially the freezing of most working-age benefits and the lower benefits cap). By contrast, households in the upper half of the distribution would see little change, with some benefits cuts and small tax rises being offset by the further increases in the personal income tax allowance and the raising of the higher rate income tax threshold. The Resolution Foundation's *Autumn Statement Response* (2016) came to a similar conclusion: the totality of tax and benefit changes due in the current Parliament would leave the poorer half of households £375 a year worse off on average by 2020/21, while the richer half would be £235 a year better off.

'Just managing' families

One of the strongest themes in Mrs May's early speeches as Prime Minister was the need for greater recognition of the problems of what she called 'just managing' low- to middle-income families (for example, May, 2016b). This was also one of the main themes in the 2017 election manifesto:

As Theresa May said when she first became prime minister, the work of the government under her leadership will be driven not for the benefit of a privileged few but by the interests of ordinary working families: people who have a job but do not always have job security; people who own their own home but worry about paying the mortgage; people who can just about manage but worry about the cost of living and getting their children into a good school. (Conservative Party, 2017, pp 7–8)

No official definition of 'just managing' families has been offered. The Resolution Foundation (Finch, 2016) has described them as low- to middle-income households in the bottom half of the distribution who are above the bottom 10% and who receive less than a fifth of their income from means-tested benefits. This covers around six million working households and ten million adults. In spite of five in six of these families having at least one member in full-time work, nearly four-fifths of these individuals earn less than £21,000 (the median gross wage). A research study of 187,000 households across the UK by the consultancy Policy in Practice in November 2016 (Ghelani, 2016) estimated that the cuts to UC and the four-year benefit freeze, coupled with rising rents and inflation, would see low-income working families typically losing £48.90 a week by 2020; out-of-work households would be £33.54 a week worse off.

So there was considerable speculation that more support would be given to such households in the November 2016 Autumn Statement. In the event such help was limited. The Chancellor announced that the UC taper rate – the rate at which the benefit is withdrawn as recipients' earnings rise – would be reduced from 65% to 63% from April 2017. This would enable recipients to hold on to an additional 2p in every pound they earn in employment. There would be no further welfare savings during the course of the Parliament. Nevertheless, tax credits will remain frozen for the rest of the decade, and the additional costs of the taper (about £1bn over 5 years) are much less than the £3bn-a-year reduction in the Work Allowance made by the previous Chancellor. To quote the Resolution Foundation's verdict:

overall the rhetorical commitment to just managing families has not been delivered upon, with the giveaway from that reduced taper being wiped out more than twice over by just the additional takeaway from higher inflation combining with a freeze on benefits over the next three years. When set against all other policy changes announced since the 2015 election, the Autumn Statement only undoes 7 per cent of the hit from benefit cuts to the bottom half of the income distribution. (Corlett et al, 2016, p 3)

Analysing the distributional impact of the 2016 Autumn Statement on top of the changes introduced since May 2015, the Resolution Foundation estimated that by 2020 all working families entitled to UC would be £1,200 a year worse off in current prices (using the Consumer Prices Index deflator). The sum increases to £1,400 for working families with children. This results from a combination of the Cameron Government's benefits freeze and cuts to work allowances, and in spite of gains from income tax cuts, the NLW, additional hours of free childcare and the new reduction in the UC taper. By contrast, four-fifths of the gains from the tax changes will go to the richest half of households. This share of the gains is equivalent to £1bn of expenditure in 2020, greater than the £0.6bn to be spent in the same year to reduce the UC taper. The IFS distributional analysis (Waters, 2016) reaches a similar conclusion.

It is therefore clear that the tax and benefit changes announced since May 2015 will hurt those in the bottom half of the income distribution (especially the poorest decile), while the tax changes favour the richest decile. A February 2016 Fabian Society report (Harrop and Reed, 2016) reckoned that if the undertakings in the Conservative 2015 manifesto were fully delivered, households in the top fifth of the distribution would be receiving an average of £9,400 a year in tax allowances and welfare payments; the poorest fifth (for whom benefits might be their only income source) would receive only £800 more (see also Browne and Hood, 2016). A January 2017 Resolution Foundation report (Corlett and Clarke, 2017) argues that the £12bn cuts in working-age welfare are the main reasons for expecting in the next few years the sharpest increases in inequality since the 1980s. While almost the entire bottom half of the working-age distribution will suffer falling living standards, incomes in the top half of the working-age distribution are projected to grow by 4%, largely comprising 'unimpressive' pay growth and a slight boost from income tax cuts.

An even more recent report by the Foundation states:

> The real inequity lies with the fact that the combination of low pay growth and regressive benefits cuts means, all told, *the next four years (2016–17 to 2020–21) are on course to be even worse for the poorest third of households than the four years following the financial crisis (2007–08 to 2011–12)*. (Clarke et al, 2017, p 3; original authors' emphasis)

The IFS reaches a similar conclusion:

> We also project increases in inequality: both because forecast growth in average real earnings would benefit higher income households more than lower income ones, and because cuts in the real value of benefits will reduce incomes among poorer working households. Real incomes are projected to fall among the poorest 20% of households over the next five years, with households with children being particularly affected. (Hood and Waters, 2017, pp 1-2; see also Equality Trust, 2017)

The same analysis projects a rise in child poverty, taking it back to around the level of the early 2000s (about 1 in 3 children). This is explained by the planned changes to working-age benefits, which are a major source of income for households with children (see also End Child Poverty, 2017).

The 2017 Conservative election manifesto said nothing about the welfare budget, but did propose that from 2020 the triple lock (see Chapter Five) should be replaced by a new 'double lock', so that pensions will rise 'in line with the earnings that pay for them, or in line with inflation – whichever is highest' (Conservative

Party, 2017, p 64). In future, the Winter Fuel Payment would be means-tested; all other pensioner benefits – including free bus passes, eye tests, prescriptions and TV licences – would be maintained for the duration of the present Parliament.

Labour market institutions

As we saw in Chapter Four, the reduction in trade union membership and activities in most Western countries, in parallel with a decline in collective bargaining arrangements, has contributed to the compression in wages that is one of the main causes of increased inequality. However, Conservative Party policy has been to weaken the unions even further. The 2015 election manifesto stated:

> Strikes should only ever be the result of a clear positive decision based on a ballot in which at least half the workforce has voted. This turnout threshold will be an important and fair step to rebalance the interests of employers, employees, the public and the rights of trade unions. We will, in addition, tackle the disproportionate impact of strikes in essential public services by introducing a tougher threshold in health, education, fire and transport. Industrial action in these essential services would require the support of at least 40 per cent of all those entitled to take part in strike ballots – as well as a majority of those who actually turn out to vote. We will also repeal nonsensical restrictions banning employers from hiring agency staff to provide essential cover during strikes; and ensure strikes cannot be called on the basis of ballots conducted years before. (pp 18–19)

Accordingly, the Trade Union Act 2016 requires 50% of union members to turn out in a vote for strike action for the action to be legal. For essential public service workers, a strike will also have to have the support of 40% of workers eligible to vote. Notice of industrial action to the employer is doubled to 14 days and there is now a time limit on how long after a ballot action can be taken. We noted in Chapter Four the long-term decline in union membership. Whereas 24 million working days in 1984 were lost to strikes, in the 12 months to the end of October 2016 the figure was 304,000 (ONS, 2016c). Previous employment laws have all but halted widespread wildcat strikes, secondary picketing and public ballots, all of which were distinctive features of the 1970s disputes. Finally, there have been no moves to reduce the much higher fees for access to employment tribunals introduced by the Coalition Government in 2013 which, according to official figures (Ministry of Justice, 2017), have led to a 70% fall in the number of tribunal cases.[8]

Industrial strategy

One area where the May Government clearly differed from the Cameron Government is industrial policy. In January 2017 the Government published a Green Paper *Building our Industrial Strategy* (Department for Business, Energy and Industrial Strategy, 2017b), setting out a strategy with ten 'pillars': investing in science, research and innovation; developing skills; upgrading infrastructure; supporting businesses to start and grow; improving procurement; encouraging trade and inward investment; delivering affordable energy and clean growth; cultivating world-leading sectors; driving growth across the whole country; and creating the right institutions to bring together sectors and places. The paper is light on resourcing although it speaks of an additional £4.7bn investment in R&D by 2020/21 and a £175m network of 'prestigious new Institutes of Technology' to deliver higher-level technical education. Whilst most commentators have welcomed a more active Government stance, there is actually very little in the paper that is new.

The passage on industrial strategy in the 2017 election manifesto also contains familiar material. There is a commitment to achieve the current OECD average of spending 2.4% of GDP on R&D 'within ten years, with a longer-term goal of 3%' (Conservative Party, 2017, p 19). The document goes on to say that a future Conservative Government would increase the number of scientists working in the UK and enable leading scientists from around the world to work here. Yet, on pages 20–21, it speaks of doubling the Immigration Skills Charge levied on companies employing migrant workers to £2,000 by the end of the Parliament. Finally, the manifesto promises to create UK sovereign wealth funds, to be known as 'Future Britain Funds', 'to hold in trust the investments of the British people, backing British infrastructure and the British economy'. In the first instance these will be created out of revenues from shale gas extraction, 'dormant assets' and receipts from the sale of some public assets (Conservative Party, 2017, p 20). However, the UK does not yet have any commercial shale gas production and it will be many years before there are substantial tax revenues from this source; and after the many sell-offs over the years there cannot be many worthwhile public assets still to be disposed of. Finally, the manifesto signals (pp 17–18) that a future Conservative Government will scrutinise company takeovers and mergers more closely, especially those affecting national infrastructure.

Corporate governance and financialisation

As noted in Chapters Three and Four, one of the major contributors to the concentration of high incomes has been the acceleration in the remuneration of top executives, especially (but not only) in financial services. This reflects the wider problems with corporate governance which we also discussed. However the Conservatives' 2015 election manifesto contained only a small number of proposals, all aimed at trying to avoid a repetition of the circumstances in the financial markets that led to the economic crisis, but none on corporate governance.

In contrast, one of Mrs May's earliest declared priorities was for shareholders and other stakeholders to have more control over company boards and their decisions:

> The people who run big businesses are supposed to be accountable to outsiders, to non-executive directors, who are supposed to ask the difficult questions, think about the long-term and defend the interests of shareholders. In practice, they are often drawn from the same narrow social and professional circles as the executive team and the scrutiny they

provide is often limited. If I'm prime minister, we're going to change that – and we're going to have not just consumers represented on company boards, but employees as well.

I want to make shareholder votes on corporate pay not just advisory but binding. I want to see more transparency, including the full disclosure of bonus targets and the publication of 'pay multiple' data: that is, the ratio between the CEO's pay and the average company worker's pay. And I want to simplify the way bonuses are paid so that the bosses' incentives are better aligned with the long-term interests of the company and its shareholders. (May, 2016b)

In the event, the Green Paper that appeared at the end of November 2016 (Department for Business, Energy and Industrial Strategy, 2016) was something of a damp squib. What had previously been commitments, or at least statements of intent, on these issues were now just options for consultation. This is a particular pity because in talking about the groups from which most City and corporate actors are drawn, Mrs May put her finger on one of the main reasons for the misalignment between individual and corporate (and indeed national) interests which is a major contributor to increased inequality.

In the light of the Philip Green/BHS/Arcadia brouhaha in 2016 – where Sir Philip Green and his family were found to have extracted huge sums of money from BHS but left it with losses and a large pension deficit that eventually led to its demise – the consultative paper proposed extending to large private companies the requirement on public companies to explain any non-compliance with corporate governance codes, although without including any sanctions (for a forensic analysis of how BHS was 'milked', see Sikka, 2016b). Separately, the Treasury has commissioned a review of 'patient capital' by Sir Damon Buffini to see how to break down the barriers to getting long-term investment into innovative firms (May, 2016e). It is not clear why or how this will come to different conclusions than the very similar review commissioned by Sir Vince Cable as Business Secretary in the Coalition Government (Cable, 2014).

The 2017 election manifesto stated:

> The next Conservative government will legislate to make executive pay packages subject to strict annual votes by shareholders and listed companies will have to publish the ratio of executive pay to broader workforce pay. Companies will have to explain their pay policies, particularly complex incentive schemes, better. We will commission an examination of the use of share buybacks, with a view to ensuring these cannot be used artificially to hit performance targets and inflate executive pay. (Conservative Party, 2017, p 18)

It went on to propose that 'to ensure employees' interests are represented at board level', the law would be changed to ensure that listed companies will have to nominate a director from the workforce, create a formal employee advisory council, or assign responsibility for employee representation to a designated non-executive director. As several commentators have pointed out, this falls well short of a requirement that workers should be directly represented on all major company boards, something which is commonplace in much of the rest of Western Europe. It is hard to disagree with what Peter Wilby (2015) wrote in his review of Will Hutton's 2015 book *How Good We Can Be?* (Hutton, 2015b):

> leaders of the corporate sector, particularly those providing 'financial services', are doing so well out of short-termist capitalism that they resist even modest attempts to ameliorate its negative long-term effects, and portray such policies as 'anti-business'.

Education

> The greatest injustice in Britain today is that your life is still largely determined not by your efforts and talents but by where you come from, who your

parents are and what schools you attend. This is wrong. We want to make Britain the world's Great Meritocracy: a country where everyone has a fair chance to go as far as their talent and their hard work will allow, where advantage is based on merit not privilege. To succeed, we must redouble our efforts to ensure that everyone, no matter who they are or where they are from, can have a world-class education. (Conservative Party, 2017, p 49, original author's emphasis)

The 2015 election manifesto committed the party to ensuring 'a good primary school place for your child, turning every failing and coasting secondary school into an academy, and delivering free schools for parents and communities that want them, helping teachers to make Britain the best country in the world for developing maths, engineering, science and computing skills, and making sure there is no cap on university places, so we have aspiration for all' (p 33). The amount of money following each child into school would be protected, as would the Pupil Premium for disadvantaged pupils. Schools funding would be made fairer: funding for the 69 least well-funded local authorities in the country had already been increased and this was to be the baseline for their funding in the next Parliament. State schools would not be allowed to make a profit. The Education and Adoption Bill would turn round underperforming schools and improve adoption services. Powers would be created to speed up the process of changing a failing school's leadership and turning it into an academy, and schools deemed to be 'coasting' would also face being taken over. The Bill was enacted as the Education and Adoption Act in February 2016.

In the March 2016 Budget, however, the Chancellor announced that the Government would be seeking powers to compel *all* state schools to become academies, and a White Paper to this effect was published immediately afterwards (Department for Education, 2016a). But there was strong and widespread opposition and the legislation was eventually dropped in October 2016. Nevertheless, the Government continues to promote conversions through the National and Regional Schools Commissioners.

In September 2016, in a speech at the British Academy (May, 2016b), the new Prime Minister announced four changes in education that would realise her vision of 'a truly meritocratic Britain that puts the interests of ordinary, working class people first':

1. **Universities wishing to charge above the standard fee of £6,000 would have to sponsor or support schools.**

2. **Faith schools would be allowed to select all of their pupils on religious grounds**, and not just half, as at present.

3. **To justify their charitable status, private schools would have to sponsor or support state schools** or fund a number of places at their own expense for pupils from lower income backgrounds who cannot afford the fees.

4. **The existing restrictions on selective schools expanding, new selective schools being opened and non-selective schools becoming selective (that is, grammar schools) would be removed.** Such provision must 'contribute meaningfully to raising outcomes for all pupils in every part of the system'. A £50m capital fund would be established for this purpose.

A consultation paper was issued shortly afterwards (Department for Education, 2016b). The March 2017 Budget (HM Treasury, 2017, p 42) confirmed the Government's intention to extend the free schools programme with investment of £320m up to 2020 to help fund 140 schools 'including independent-led, faith, selective, university-led and specialist maths schools'. The 2017 election manifesto confirmed this and the other proposals in the September 2016 speech.[9]

In Chapter Six we reviewed the very strong evidence that all forms of educational selection – whether by location, religious faith, wealth or social status – contribute to social segregation and inequality, and Mrs May's proposals have prompted even more such evidence (for example, Andrews et al, 2016). If implemented, they will exacerbate the fragmentation of the system that is in itself a major obstacle to fairness of opportunity as well as educational effectiveness. They are also a huge distraction from the real problems facing the state school system as funding per pupil is reduced, so that many schools are planning to lay off staff, there are worsening teacher shortages, class sizes are increasing, and there are insufficient places in many areas. There are also to be major cuts in council-funded ancillary services. And while there is certainly a case for some equalisation in the levels of funding received by state schools in different parts of the country, there are no proposals to close the huge funding gap between state and private schools, which is in itself a major contributor to inequality.[10]

Finally, there is the issue of whether academisation is not the Government's ultimate objective in education but merely a means to the end of privatisation. At the moment this can only be speculation (Turner, 2015). What is less speculative is the observation that academisation has created – with academy sponsors and their friends – a whole new sub-group of political party donors, as well as fresh opportunities for private interests to make money from public funding.[11]

Macroeconomic policy

> Monetary activism to keep interest rates low and stimulate the economy. Fiscal responsibility to restore confidence and rebuild our battered public finances.
> (George Osborne, quoted in Wren-Lewis, 2015b, p R6)

The overall thrust of the 2015 election manifesto and the associated legislative programme was to improve incentives to work by controlling or reducing taxes. This required substantial further reductions in public expenditure and welfare benefits. The manifesto (pp 8–9) spoke of a further £30bn of 'fiscal consolidation'; £13bn would be found from departmental savings, £12bn from welfare savings:

> This £30 billion of further consolidation is necessary
> to ensure that [public] debt keeps falling as a share
> of GDP and to deliver a balanced structural current
> budget in 2017–18.

Together with greater incentives for business, this would produce such a strong economic performance that in 2018/19 the Government would be 'set to move into surplus' (p 9). However, in the March 2016 Budget the date for achieving the surplus was put back to 2019/20 and this target in turn was abandoned in July 2016 in the wake of the Brexit vote, like the previous targets set by the Coalition Government (by 2014/15 in 2010, by 2016/17 in 2012). In the March 2017 Budget the target for removing the deficit was 'as soon as possible in the new Parliament' (HM Treasury, 2017, p 1). The 2017 election manifesto spoke of achieving a balanced budget 'by the middle of the next decade' (Conservative Party, 2017, p 14). Given the scale of the public expenditure cuts, as well as the treatment of personal and corporate taxes, it is impossible to avoid the conclusion that it is not the elimination of the deficit but lower taxes and a permanent shrinkage in the size of the state that has been the real priority of all the Governments since 2010, as Peter Taylor-Gooby and Gerry Straker suggested in 2011. For all the references to the need for a stronger state role in future – for example, on pages 8–9 – this will also be the effect of the policies in the 2017 election manifesto.[12]

In Chapter Six it was argued that in current circumstances the most important objective of economic policy is to increase growth. This means rebuilding demand, which means restoring the link between wage growth and productivity growth, which in turn will require a number of major structural reforms, especially in the labour market. We also noted and endorsed the views of those – including the Governor of the Bank of England in his Liverpool speech (Carney, 2016) – who felt that too much was being asked of monetary policy, and that, within fiscal policy, too much was being expected of expenditure cuts, and too little of targeted tax increases for those able to bear them.

Ahead of the 2016 Autumn Statement there were predictions in the press of some loosening of fiscal policy, as urged by the

OECD, the IMF and others (for example, Wolf, 2016). There is indeed to be increased spending on infrastructure, including a new National Productivity Investment Fund of £23bn from 2017/18 to 2021/22, targeted at transport, digital communications, R&D and housing (HM Treasury, 2016a, p 2). However, this is pretty small beer in a £1.8tn economy, and incidentally smaller than the Coalition's capital spending cuts in 2010 (£30bn). It is particularly disappointing in view of the OECD's estimate (2016b) that the amount of 'fiscal space' – the room for more Government debt – has risen more in the UK than in any other developed country (a view it has just reiterated in its June 2017 Economic Forecast: OECD, 2017). The departmental spending plans set out in the Spending Review 2015, which will 'deliver £3.5bn of additional savings in 2019–20' (HM Treasury, 2016a, p 14), remain in place.

Brexit

> I want this United Kingdom to emerge from this period of change stronger, fairer, more united and more outward-looking than ever before. I want us to be a secure, prosperous, tolerant country – a magnet for talent and a home to the pioneers and innovators who will shape the world ahead. (May, 2017b).

In line with the Prime Minister's January 2013 announcement (Cameron, 2013), the 2015 manifesto stated (p 72) that a new Conservative Government would negotiate 'a new settlement for Britain in Europe', and then hold an 'in-out' referendum before the end of 2017. Crucial to this would be new rules linking EU immigrants' benefits to prior earnings (pp 29–30). The Prime Minister subsequently obtained agreement to some limits being placed on EU migrants' in-work benefits, the so called 'emergency brake'. Implementing these rules would have been subject to the agreement of the other member states. But in any case the new settlement was rejected in the June 2016 referendum by 51.9% to 48.1%, and the Prime Minister announced his intention to step down as soon as his successor was appointed. On 3 October 2016 the new Prime Minister announced that the Government would trigger the Article 50 process for leaving the EU by the end of March 2017 (May, 2016d). In a further speech in January 2017 – the 'Brexit speech' – Mrs May set out the Government's negotiating objectives (May, 2017b). On 13 March 2017 Parliament voted to commence the Article 50 process.

Several studies of the Brexit vote (for example, Bell and Machin, 2016) have highlighted economic inequality as a major causal factor. Perhaps the clearest evidence to date comes from the study by the Legatum Institute and the Centre for Social Justice (2016). This found that the AB social grade was the only one in which a majority voted Remain; in all the other social grades, the majority was for Leave. Of people living in households earning more than £60,000 a year, 65% supported Remain; among those earning less than £20,000, 62% voted Leave.

As indicated in the Preface, any comments now on how Brexit will affect inequality must inevitably be speculative. But one of this book's main arguments is that reversing, halting or even slowing the rise in inequality through greater redistribution will be less difficult with a healthy level of economic growth than without it (of course, that growth also has to be shared out much more evenly). Yet most independent commentators – most recently, the EY ITEM Club (2017) – think that departure from the EU will damage growth, and have reduced their long-term forecasts accordingly (the main reasons are the impacts on investment, competition and consumers' costs). So it is difficult not to conclude that almost any form of Brexit will be a major setback for any serious effort to address inequality, always assuming the latter to be forthcoming from the Government (see Conclusion).

Finally, there is the question of whether, even if the Government has a clear and credible agenda for tackling inequality, the focus and resources will be available for delivering it, both within Parliament and within Whitehall, given the overriding demands of Brexit. The independent Institute for Government has issued repeated warnings (for example, 2017) about the need for greater realism about the amount of resources that will be needed both for the Brexit negotiations and for implementation. It appears to be the view of most commentators that Brexit will absorb nearly all the Government's time and energy, especially since the Conservative Party lost its overall Commons majority. This means that time and effort that might have been devoted to domestic policy design and implementation will now be needed for cobbling together support on a measure-by-measure basis.

The political system

In Chapter Two we noted the important part that external funding (funding other than through party members' subscriptions) was playing in US politics and, increasingly, in Britain. The issue has been highlighted by what has emerged to date about the possible role of 'dark money' in influencing the Brexit vote, and in particular the confirmation by the Electoral Commission in April 2017 that it is investigating spending by the Leave.EU campaign (and especially whether work done for Leave.EU by Cambridge Analytica constituted an undeclared donation from an impermissible foreign source: Watt, 2017; see also Cadwalladr, 2017).

At the time of writing (mid-June 2017) the outcomes of the investigation are not known. But it is already clear from a May 2017 report in *The Sunday Times* (McCall and Watts, 2017) that the great bulk of funding for both sides in the referendum campaign came from a small number of sources, with nearly two-thirds of the money that bankrolled the Leave campaign coming from just five rich businessmen (all but one of them in financial services). However, neither of the main parties' election manifestos contained any proposals for controlling the role of money in British politics.[13]

In Chapter Four we referred to the 'path dependency' theory of Monica Prasad and her contrast between the 'adversarial' politics of the US and the UK and the more consensual politics of France and Germany. In fact, anyone who doubts the adversarial character of modern British politics need only refer to what has been said both during the Brexit campaign and subsequently by partisans on all sides. However ,the 2017 Conservative election manifesto proposed (p 43) not only to continue with a 'first past the post' system of voting for Parliamentary elections but actually to extend it to police and crime commissioner and mayoral elections (replacing proportional representation). Yet without some more representative system, 'elective dictatorships' can be established on the basis of a minority vote (the vote to leave the EU received the support of just under 38% of those eligible to vote).[14]

Conclusion: the future for inequality

> We are a government that is not afraid to act to ensure the benefits of economic growth are shared by all. (May, 2016e)

So what impact will the measures introduced or announced by the Cameron and May Governments since May 2015 and those contained in the 2017 Conservative election manifesto have on economic inequality?

The stronger stance on tax avoidance is welcome but there appear to be no plans to reverse the long-term reduction in the number of tax officials. The increased Minimum Wage is also welcome, although the proposed increase to £7.50 implies that the 2020 figure will fall short of the previous target of £9. The Government could do more to promote the real Living Wage, for example, by making it a pre-condition for public subsidies or contracts, or even tax breaks. Increases in the personal income tax allowance benefit low-income households if they have enough income to be taxed, but help the top half of earners more (especially as the allowance covers both earned and unearned income). Similarly, the introduction of Help to Save is offset by the new Lifetime ISA (it is anyway arguable that if low-income savers have any spare cash they should invest it in a pension). If carried through, abandoning the triple lock and means-testing the Winter Fuel Allowance would begin to reduce the share of social expenditure taken up by pensions. The recognition of the need for government to be active in promoting industrial competitiveness is also welcome, but what it will mean in practice is less clear (the same can be said of the approach to market abuses and competition policy).

The increases in free childcare for 3- and 4-year-olds will be helpful where both parents are working for at least 16 hours a week, and provided the necessary funding is forthcoming. The present 15 hours a week (term-time only) is underfunded, so that nurseries are forced to cross-subsidise it by charging fees for additional hours (there may also be capacity issues). In any case, it only covers part of the costs of childcare. Moreover, a recent IFS analysis based on what happened after the 15-hours regime was introduced suggests that the overall effect on labour supply will be quite small (Brewer et al, 2016). There have also been extensive cuts to children's centres and other services across the country, and more are anticipated. A recent parliamentary question elicited the information that the numbers of Sure Start centres closing had increased each year from 12 in 2011 to 156 in 2015 (Walker, 2016). There are also continuing concerns about the funding of nursery schools, a third of state nursery schools having closed since 1980 (Weale, 2017). The increased number of apprenticeships will be a step forward but it is still not clear how this will be achieved, especially if quality is also to be improved, or even maintained (Amin-Smith et al, 2017).

However, these mostly small positives are heavily outweighed by the negatives:

Box 7.2 Summary of the negative effects of the Cameron and May government reforms, and 2017 Conservative election manifesto proposals

• **The continuing reductions in public expenditure, together with increased usage charges, will hit the public services** (and jobs) on which the poorer and less advantaged members of society especially rely, the scale, accessibility and quality of which were already reduced in the last Parliament (Crewe, 2016).

• **The freezing of the top marginal rate of income tax has done nothing to reduce inequality,** while the freezing of the VAT rate (and the failure to reform Council Tax) has meant that the poorest households continue to pay a bigger share of their income in taxes than the wealthiest.

- **The raising of the IHT threshold increases still further the value of inherited wealth**, as well as reducing the incentive to 'trade down' to help housing supply. The cuts in the tax allowance for pension contributions for people with higher earnings which are intended to pay for this could have been used to soften welfare cuts (as noted in Chapter Five, current arrangements for tax relief on pension contributions cost the Exchequer £49bn in 'lost' tax, about half the annual cost of the NHS). No action is being taken to introduce a flat rate of tax relief on pension contributions. Similarly, the cuts in Capital Gains Tax will mostly benefit the better off.

- **There have been no moves to tax property more fairly.** [15]

- **The reduced rates of Corporation Tax will deprive HMRC of revenue** whilst transferring wealth to a sector that already has record levels of savings, as we saw in Chapter Three.[16]

- **The welfare reforms compound the cutbacks under the Coalition Government.** They are bound to increase child poverty as well as inequality, as an official assessment leaked to *The Guardian* in 2015 (Butler and Malik, 2015) made clear.[17]

- **The industrial relations reforms will further weaken the ability of the unions to act as a moderating force on inequality.** There are no parallel constraints on the movement or withdrawal of capital by companies.

- **The proposed corporate governance reforms barely scratch the surface of what is needed to make companies serve a wider set of stakeholders** than just senior management.

- **The fragmentation of the school system will increase still further with additional academies and free schools**, whilst any expansion of grammar schools will increase social segregation yet further. The chaotic system of local oversight – academy chains, local authorities, Regional Schools Commissioners, Ofsted – will continue.

- **The macroeconomic policies of the two post-2015 Governments and confirmed in the 2017 manifesto have done very little to tackle the chronic imbalances in the UK economy:**

  - between London and the South East, and the rest of the country;
  - between finance and the rest of the economy;
  - between consumer spending and the other major components of demand;
  - between imports and exports;
  - between investment in housing and other forms of investment;
  - between 'world-class' universities and internationally poor youth and adult skill levels;
  - between the economic and political power of those at or nearing retirement and those born after 1980; or
  - between Westminster and Whitehall and the regions and localities.

- **Brexit will almost certainly increase inequality** through its impact on economic growth and efficiency.

- **There are no proposals to make our politics more representative or less adversarial, in fact quite the opposite.**[18]

Finally, and following the Conservatives' loss of their overall Commons majority, there is the issue of whether there is sufficient support within the Parliamentary Party for any of the more positive inequality measures. As Martin Kettle wrote in a perceptive article in *The Guardian* in May (Kettle, 2017), even if the Government is able to give sufficient attention to its domestic agenda, Conservative MPs who share Mrs May's approach to social issues are fairly thin on the ground. The Party's decision after the election to seek the support of the Democratic Unionist Party (DUP), a socially conservative group, will also not help the reformist cause (and indeed the manifesto commitment to review the pensions triple lock and means–test the Winter Fuel

Allowance, both of which are strongly opposed by the DUP, have already been jettisoned).

Taken as a whole, not only will the policies of the Cameron and May Governments and the Conservative 2017 election manifesto not reduce inequality, they will actually increase it. Upward redistribution will continue. This is hardly surprising. For all the rhetoric of 'a one nation approach', 'a country that works for everyone', and 'a shared society', these are essentially the continuation of the neoliberal policies, pursued or endorsed by different governments of all persuasions in Britain since the 1980s, which were one of the main contributors to increasing inequality in the first place, and which have now with the Brexit vote finally come home to roost.

So what will be the future for inequality? Quite apart from the implications for social justice, it is clear that:

- the present degree of economic inequality in Britain and most Western societies generates a wide and substantial range of social, economic, educational, environmental and political costs and detriments;
- these costs and detriments outweigh any presumed benefits; and
- without significant remediation, such inequality and the associated costs and detriments will increase even further.

It also seems apparent that:

- these remedial actions will need to cover a wide range of areas including, but going well beyond, redistribution through taxes and transfers, urgent and necessary as that is
- many of them will be, or at least appear to be, quite radical in terms of the prevailing political discourse (at least in the UK and the US); and
- they will require a strong state role if they are to be even minimally effective.

But the literature, evidence and argument in this book show quite clearly that there is no alternative to such measures if economic inequality is not to go on rising. It is up to us.

SUGGESTIONS FOR FURTHER READING

There has been a huge outpouring of books on inequality even in the period since mid-2014 when work on this book began. Here are some suggestions for further reading (all are included in the References).

Several books focus on the *impact* of rising inequality, and especially the non-economic aspects. They include Wilkinson and Pickett's *The Spirit Level* (2009), Danny Dorling's *Inequality and the 1%* (2014) and Michael Marmot's *The Health Gap* (2015). Joseph Stiglitz's *The Price of Inequality* (2013a) deals with the economic and political effects of inequality in the US; his more recent book *The Great Divide* (2015) is a selection of articles and essays about inequality, rather than a systematic treatment. Robert Reich's latest book, *Saving Capitalism* (2016), is also good on the impact of inequality, although again mainly written for an American audience.

There is then a group of books that essentially espouse one main factor in the causes of increased inequality. These include Thomas Piketty's *Capital in the Twenty-First Century* (2014a: inequality rises because in normal times the return on capital exceeds economic growth); Brynjolfsson and McAfee's *The Second Machine Age* (2014: computerisation and smart machines); Richard Baldwin's *The Great Convergence* (2016: globalisation and IT reinforcing one another); Frank and Cook's *The Winner-Take-All-Society* (2010: the ability of 'superstars' to corner the market for talent); and Andrew Kliman's *The Failure of Capitalist Production* (2012: capitalism's inevitable tendency to self-destruct). Stewart Lansley's *The Cost of Inequality* (2011: blaming rising inequality on neoliberalism), also falls into this category, as does Jamie Galbraith's latest book, *Inequality: What Everyone Needs to Know* (2016: changes in the control of world financial systems).

There are then several books that survey inequality in a *wider historical and global perspective*. Angus Deaton's *The Great Escape* (2013) provides an account of the changing relationship between economic progress, on the one hand, and poverty and ill-health, on the other, over the past 250 years. Walter Scheidel's *The Great Leveler: Violence and the History of Inequality from the Stone Age to the Twenty-First Century* (2017) argues that, historically, economic development has always led to inequality, which has been halted only through the destruction of capital. Branko Milanovic's *Global Inequality: A New Approach for the Age of Globalization* (2016) and Francois Bourguignon's *The Globalization of Inequality* (2015) also look at world-wide trends, covering both between- and within-society inequality. All these books give a good general picture, as does the OECD's latest (2015b) report *In It Together: Why Less Inequality Benefits All*. The very recent *The Inclusive Growth and Development Report 2017* (2017) by the World Economic Forum covers similar territory: its 'inclusive development index' identifies those wealthy countries that manage to combine growth with some degree of fairness (neither the UK nor the US is in the top 20).

Finally, there are some books that it is hard to categorise. The contributors to *Rethinking Capitalism* (2016: edited by Jacobs and Mazzucato) outline a number of ways in which the current capitalist model might be reformed to produce sustainable and shared growth. Robert Frank's latest book, *Success and Luck: Good Fortune and the Myth of Meritocracy* (2016), shows how our societies are even less 'meritocratic' than they used to be. Robert J. Gordon's *The Rise and Fall of American Growth* (2016) is a tour de force and a 'must read' for anyone interested in the development of the US economy. The late Tony Atkinson's *Inequality: What Can Be Done* (2015) reflects a lifetime of studying and thinking about inequality that it would be very difficult for anyone to emulate. If there is one more book you should read on the subject, this is the one.

NOTES

Chapter One

[1] Salverda et al (2009), Atkinson (2015) and Galbraith (2016) all provide useful introductions to the relevant economics literature.

[2] Posen (2014) argues that, conceptually, we should distinguish inequality from injustice, insecurity and inclusion, even if practically they are often interrelated. We should always try to specify who is harmed by inequality and how.

[3] For recent surveys of global trends in inequality, see Bourguignon (2015) and Milanovic (2016).

[4] Surveying 15 OECD countries, Atkinson (2015, p 25) noted that only Switzerland had managed to combine below-median poverty with above-median top income shares. Higher poverty tends to go with larger top shares (see also Oxfam, 2016).

[5] For a discussion of the merits and demerits of the various inequality measures, see Charles-Coll (2011), Salverda et al (2014) and Galbraith (2016).

[6] It should be noted that while in the US income inequality has increased fairly gradually over the period, in the UK income inequality rose sharply in the 1980s but has more or less plateaued since. These are of course aggregate figures.

[7] The source is the Top Incomes Database http://topincomes.g-mond. parisschoolofeconomics.eu/#Database. The UK data to 1986 represent the share taken by married couples and single adults, whereas the post-1992 data are for all adults (there is a break between 1987 and 1992). The US data are for all adults.

[8] Leigh (2007) argued that within-country changes in top income shares can be a useful proxy for changes in other inequality measures, such as the Gini coefficient. Indeed, the relationship between the top 10% share and several other inequality measures remained statistically significant even with both country and year fixed effects.

[9] To make these figures more concrete, the former US Treasury Secretary Lawrence Summers (2015) estimated that if the US had the same income distribution today as in 1979, the bottom 80% of the population would have $11,000 more per family while the top 1% would have $750,000 less.

[10] See also Piketty et al (2011) and Atkinson (2015, pp 179–83). Atkinson has a figure (7.2 on page 182) showing the strong association between percentage changes in (a) the top marginal after-tax retention rate and (b) the share of income going to the top 1% in 18 rich Western countries. The values are highest for the US and the UK, and lowest for Denmark, Switzerland and Germany. He also notes (page 61) that as well as the reductions in tax rates after 1979 there was the erosion of the tax base owing to tax avoidance and other activities. Hence the effective tax rate was considerably lower than the nominal rate. Tax avoidance is looked at more closely in Chapters Five and Seven.

[11] Furman (2016) and Haldane (2016a) provide up-to-date and authoritative surveys of the effect of the recession on economic inequality in America and Britain respectively.

[12] For the UK, the data source is https://www.ons.gov.uk/economy/grossdomesticproduct/gdp-analysed-by-income-category. For the US, https://fred.stlouisfed.org/series/A4002E1A156NBEA. According to Reed and Himmelweit (2012), the decline in the UK wage share is the largest of any major OECD country other than Australia.

Chapter Two

[1] For further reading on social mobility, see Performance and Innovation Unit (2001), Bloodworth (2016), Calder (2016) and Social Mobility Commission (2016).

[2] For the US, the Standard and Poor's survey (Maguire, 2014) remains a good summary of increasing socioeconomic differentials (see also Mettler, 2014, and Goldrick-Rab, 2016). The tertiary differential in the UK is less acute but the same stratification by income and class is apparent, especially for access to the more selective ('high tariff') institutions (Office for Fair Access, 2014; see also Boliver, 2011; Crawford, 2014; Crawford et al, 2014b; Antonucci, 2016). There is also the issue of how sustained even the current position will be, given the role of public expenditure in fuelling improvements in state school results (Dorling, 2012, pp 170–86) and the poor current outlook for such spending (see Chapter Seven). Reardon and Waldvogel (2016) provide a good recent summary of international evidence about inequalities of educational achievement.

[3] There have been repeated warnings about the threat to the world economy from existing levels of debt (for instance, Dobbs et al, 2015). In April 2015 the IMF drew attention to high levels of household debt in Britain (IMF, 2015). In November 2016 the Bank of England's Financial Sustainability Report (Bank of England, 2016) noted that the overall ratio of household debt to income in the second quarter of the year was 133%.

The Governor has very recently warned about these levels of debt (Carney, 2017). Moreover, this is the aggregate level. As we saw in Chapter One, real incomes have flatlined, so that many households will have difficulty in repaying their debts, especially if interest rates are increased. It is hardly surprising that the household savings ratio has dropped to one of the lowest figures on record (see Chapter Five).

4   The term 'rent seeking' describes the case where a firm is able to obtain an income over and above its income from the sale of goods and services. The classic instance is where a group of suppliers colludes to fix prices at a higher level than would be produced through normal competition. State subsidies or differential tax breaks would be other examples. 'Financialisation' describes the process whereby, as economies develop, an increasing proportion of economic activity is accounted for by the financial services sector (for a fuller definition, see Epstein, 2005).

5   This is pretty much the story of the public financing of public universities in England, Australia and the US over the past 20 years or so. As direct public funding falls, institutions increasingly plug the revenue gap with tuition fees (which often represent a barrier to wider social participation).

6   Research by the Google Transparency Project found at least 80 such moves in the past decade where the online giant had taken on government employees and European governments took on Google staff (Doward, 2016).

7   It seems par for the course that the only mainstream media coverage of the MRC report was in the *Guardian* and on the BBC.

8   In a study of the manufacture of cotton cloth in three European regions (Northern Italy, South Germany and Lancashire) between 1000 and 1700, Charles F. Foster (2013) showed how wealth distribution, technical and commercial innovation and plural political institutions were linked in enabling those regions to become more prosperous. More equal distribution of wealth meant that more people had capital to invest in innovation, for which commercial competition was also essential. Such equalisation of wealth was protected by political institutions that kept the concentration of wealth in check. But over time wealth became more concentrated as more successful concerns bought up their competitors and/or used their commercial and financial muscle to gain political power. In other instances the traditional authorities – the monarchy, the aristocracy, the church – reasserted themselves. But in all cases the region declined relative to its rivals.

9   The final irony is that, as Deaton (2013, pp 51–6) notes, the evidence is that while poverty certainly generates misery, additional income (beyond about $70,000) does not improve happiness.

Chapter Three

1   In addition, in 2012, 80 million people – around a quarter of the population – reported that during the previous year they had not gone to the doctor

when sick or filled a prescription because of the cost (Claudia Chaufan, Associate Professor at the University of California, San Francisco, quoted in O'Hara, 2014).

[2] Other recent studies that link off-shoring and imports to a weakening of employment, especially of low-skilled workers, include Ashournia et al (2014); Oldenski (2014); Pessoa (2016); Autor et al (2014); Bloom et al (2015); and Autor et al (2016).

[3] In 2012, Aditya Chakrabortty referred to separate surveys by the Centre for Research on Socio-Cultural Change at the University of Manchester for the *Guardian* and by the Asian Development Bank (Xing and Detert, 2010). Both demonstrated that building iPhones would still be hugely profitable even if it was done in the US. Manufacturing iPhones in China (to exacting performance standards) had delivered huge returns for Apple employees and investors as well as enormous cash reserves for the company (as we shall see in Chapter Five, Apple is also very adept at minimising its tax payments). As Merryn Somerset Webb wrote in the *Financial Times* in October 2016: 'Consider the fabulous tailwinds global firms have been working with for 30-odd years. Interest rates have been coming down fast, making debt cheaper. Globalisation has meant that they have been able to move and sell around the world with huge ease, with full political support. It has given them access to vast pools of cheap labour and the ability to structure themselves to pay as little tax as possible to the most competitive jurisdictions on offer. It's been a good – and very profitable combination.'

[4] According to research by Capita Asset Services for the Association of Corporate Treasurers (Percy, 2016), the FTSE 100 companies currently have a cash pile of £166bn, an increase of 34% since the economic downturn in 2008. The rise is due to companies cutting investment and retaining earnings since the crisis. The average FTSE 100 company now (August 2016) has cash and cash equivalents of £1.9bn. The US equivalent total is $1.77tn, most of it held overseas (Moody's, 2016). There is strong political pressure for at least some of these holdings to be repatriated in return for lower corporate tax rates, something to which President Trump is committed.

[5] For productivity, see Chapter Four, note 4.

[6] There is a substantial literature on the (lack of any) relationship between a firm's performance and executive remuneration, with several studies – for example, Bertrand and Mullainathan (2001); Bebchuk and Fried (2004); Bebchuk and Grinstein, 2005; Bebchuk et al (2010) – emphasising the important part played by luck. In his latest book, Robert Frank (2016) argues that winner-take-all-markets (see below) magnify this: there are so many contestants – and they are all talented, highly motivated and hardworking – that luck is what distinguishes the most successful. A very recent study of FTSE 350 businesses by the University of Lancaster Management School for the CFA Society of the UK (Hass et al, 2016) finds that any correlation between pay and performance is 'negligible'. Philip Aldrick (2017) observes that if shareholder value is to be maintained, a

company's return on capital must at least cover its cost of capital. No British bank has achieved this since the crisis, yet their CEOs have continued to receive multi-million-pound bonuses.

[7] Atkinson (2015, p 83) traces this theory back to Tinbergen (1975).

[8] It can hardly be a coincidence that it was the Rust Belt states – from western Pennsylvania through to eastern Iowa – whose votes gave President Trump the White House (Longworth, 2009). There was strong support for Brexit in the 'old' industrial areas of the North and Midlands, and much of the French National Front's support comes from the decaying industrial areas of northern and eastern France.

[9] Similarly, differential university tuition fees in the UK are bound to lead to upward pressures on charges that it will be very difficult to prevent.

[10] Alan B. Krueger (2013) traced the idea of a superstar economy back to Marshall (1890). Jon Bakija and colleagues (2012) classified American taxpayers in the top 0.1% by occupation in 2004. They found that executives, managers, supervisors and financial professionals accounted for about 60% of the group, and for 70% of the increase in the share of national income going to the top 0.1% of the income distribution between 1979 and 2005.

Chapter Four

[1] For similar conclusions, see Bowman et al (2014); Henry (2014); Wren-Lewis (2015a) and (2015b); Beatty and Fothergill (2016); Etherington and Jones (2016).

[2] Dorling has a table (Table 5 on page 176) showing trends in mortality inequality of decile groups by area, the geographical concentration of the national Conservative vote by area and the national income share of the best-off 1%. In each case values fell from 1918 to the mid-1970s and then began to rise again to 2005.

[3] See also Gosling and Lemieux (2001); Lemieux et al (2007); and Atkinson and Voitchovsky (2011). Atkinson (2015, p 92) wondered if the increased pressure for short-term returns to boost shareholder value might have led companies to discount the reputational risks from excessive pay. Another contributory factor could be the transfer of state enterprises to private shareholders and the consequential reduced ability of governments to influence pay levels and relativities through public sector employment.

[4] For a similar argument, see Reed and Himmelweit (2012). There has been a good deal of discussion in recent years about lagging British productivity. Blanchflower (2015) estimated that UK labour productivity remained about 2% below its level prior to the crisis. This was 16% lower than it would have been, had productivity maintained its pre-downturn trend: 'Median wages seem to have become "decoupled" from productivity growth because of rising inequality, which means that a growing share of the value from productivity growth is absorbed by pensions and higher salaries for top earners (Bell and Van Reenen, 2014).' (Blanchflower, 2015, p F79).

The persistence of poor levels of productivity was a major theme of the recent November Autumn Statement (HM Treasury, 2016a) and of the still more recent Green Paper on Industrial Strategy (Department for Business, Energy and Industrial Strategy, 2017b). But with labour so cheap – due to greater labour market flexibility and greater numbers coming on to the labour market because of demography and immigration – it appears that firms have less incentive to invest in innovation, at least pre-Brexit. The Green Paper states (p. 18) that the UK has ranked in the lowest 25% of all OECD countries for investment in 48 of the last 55 years.

5   There is a considerable literature on how means of rewarding employees and shareholders through bonuses, stock options, buy-backs and excessive dividends have damaged long-term company development (for example, Hall and Murphy, 2003; Lazonick, 2013, 2014). French (2016) advocates a new tax, levied at source on companies paying dividends or undertaking share buy-backs. The proceeds could be used to provide generous allowances for capital investment or workforce training.

6   The current National Living Wage (NLW; formerly the Minimum Wage) for those over 25 is £7.20 an hour. The current Living Wage (LW) is £9.75 in London and £8.45 elsewhere. The NLW is set by the Government with the advice (previously) of the Low Pay Commission. The LW is set by the independent Living Wage Commission. For recent developments here and on industrial strategy, see Chapter Seven.

7   A recent post by Heavy (2017) lists four Goldman Sachs alumni with key posts in the new Administration: Steve Bannon (Chief Strategist); Steven Mnuchin (Treasury Secretary); Gary Cohn (Council of Economic Advisers); and Jay Clayton (Securities and Exchange Commission).

8   In the US, the Forbes List of the world's richest billionaires includes four members of the Walton family, the owners of Walmart, in the top 12. They have a combined wealth of $161bn. As well as engaging in large-scale tax avoidance, Walmart pays near-poverty wages, which means the US taxpayer having to give workers massive subsidies in the form of Medicaid and food stamps (letter in the *Guardian,* 17 February 2016, from Steve Quinn).

9   Pettifor (2006, p 7) quotes Keynes (1930, Chapter 35): 'Deflation … involves a transference of wealth from the rest of the community to the rentier class and to all holders of title to money; just as inflation involves the opposite. In particular it involves a transference from all borrowers, that is to say from traders, manufacturers, and farmers, to lenders, from the active to the inactive.' Krippner (2011) argues that financialisation was seen by US policymakers in the late 1970s/early 1980s as a way of staving off the distributional crises of which hyper inflation was leading.

10   Similarly, Marshall (2015) reported that in the past five years the Federal Reserve had pumped more than $3.5tn into bond markets, driving down the benchmark rate and increasing the price of many assets. The windfall gains to corporate executives and intermediaries could have been offset by fiscal measures but were not, no doubt due at least in part to the political strength of Wall Street and its friends in Congress. In a more recent piece

King (2016) proposes that the Bank of England should create a 'gilt purchase fund', its size to be determined by the Bank's Monetary Policy Committee according to the demand shortfall in the economy. This could be used to stimulate spending directly.

[11] 'Kuznets process' refers to the theory of the American economist Simon Kuznets (1955) that within-society economic inequality increases and then falls as countries industrialise (setting up a wedge between agricultural and industrial wages) and then mature as most employment becomes industrial. In their comprehensive review of the literature on inequality, Foerster and Toth (2015, p 1800) find only limited support for sector bias/dualism. However Milanovic (2016, Chapter Two) argues that the post-1980s increase in inequality (a) has historical antecedents and (b) will be repeated again in future (although Milanovic is also unclear how and when the present phase will end). For accounts of the dismantling of Bretton Woods and the subsequent financial liberalisation, see Helleiner (1994) and Pettifor (2006).

[12] In Finland the main cause of growing income inequality was the increase of income among high-income groups, which was mainly driven by increases in capital income. At the same time, the redistributive impact of taxes and benefits fell. This was mainly due to the dual taxation system: differences in taxation between capital and earnings that favoured those with more capital income, that is, the wealthiest. However, poverty and inequality rates remain relatively low, income mobility is high and all this is combined with high levels of subjective well-being (Fritzell et al, 2014, pp 244–5). In Sweden, too, the increase in income inequality has been characterised by a strong rise in top incomes and a growing importance of capital income. And again the dual taxation system that Sweden introduced in connection with major tax reforms in the early 1990s has played an important part. Even so, popular support for a redistributive welfare state remains high, and a clear majority think income differentials are too large (Blomgren et al, 2014, pp 660–2).

[13] Cornia (2012) found that the decline in inequality was mostly due to the reduction in the skill premium (following the rapid expansion of secondary education), a fall in the supply of unskilled labour and a return to collective bargaining and increases in the minimum wage.

Chapter Five

[1] It is interesting that in October 2014 the Government issued guidance to all departments about applying an 'impact on family life' test to all new policy proposals (Department for Work and Pensions, 2014).

[2] The Coalition Government introduced a 'Diverted profits tax' – popularly known as the 'Google tax' – to prevent multinationals from escaping UK tax by moving profits on their UK business abroad. Sikka (2016c) notes that no test cases have yet been brought against Google, Amazon, Apple, Starbucks or any other multinational company for avoiding UK taxes by

shifting profits to other jurisdictions. There has in fact been considerable criticism of government deals with a number of major companies where the details have been disclosed. The then Business Secretary, Sajid Javid, admitted that the £130m tax settlement with Google in January 2016 'was not a glorious moment' (Syal, 2016). According to a recent report in *The Times* (Kington, 2017), the Italian Government has reached a settlement of nearly twice that amount for half the period of tax payments (5 years as against 10). Google's UK turnover is estimated to be 10 times its turnover in Italy.

[3]   In April 2016 the Scottish National Party's leader at Westminster, Angus Robertson, established through a Parliamentary Question that whereas there are nearly 4,000 Department for Work and Pensions benefits investigators, there are only 700 officials in the two HMRC units dealing with the wealthiest half a million people in the UK. Yet benefit fraud costs the UK £1.3bn a year, while even on official estimates the annual tax gap is 26 times bigger (Garside, 2016a).

[4]   Sikka et al (2016) recommend that there should be a Supervisory Board, consisting of stakeholders, to watch over the HMRC board to give it direction and enhance its public accountability. The Board should act as a bulwark against corporate capture and inertia and be accountable to parliamentary committees. It should also support and protect tax whistle-blowers.

[5]   David Craig's (2015) *The Great Charity Scandal* (Bournemouth: Original Book Company) raises some pertinent questions about what British charities do with the £80bn they receive each year from donors.

[6]   In March 2015 the lifetime allowance for pensions tax relief was restricted to £1m (from April 2016); the annual allowance has been reduced to £40,000 for most taxpayers. In March 2015 the Treasury issued a consultative paper *Strengthening the Incentive to Save – Consultation on Pensions Tax Relief*, which had a single flat rate as an option. There were rumours – almost certainly 'market-testing' by the Treasury – that the Chancellor would introduce this in the March 2016 Budget but nothing was done, although the Government has recently (November 2016) announced an intention to reduce the annual allowance for a small sub-section of taxpayers (HM Treasury 2016c). Webb (2015d) reckoned that about 90% of the tax relief goes into investment funds, a boost to the City of about £40m a year.

[7]   Carried interest is income flowing to the general partner of a private investment fund. For tax purposes it is generally treated as a capital gain but there is a strong argument for regarding it as income, as proposed by the Tax Policy Center. Aldrick (2016) notes that the concept dates back to the 12th century, when Italian merchants would earn 20% of the profits made by owners of the cargo carried on their ships.

[8]   The current (January 2017) rates of tax on personal incomes – after a personal allowance of £11,000 for most taxpayers – are 20% on incomes up to £32,000, 40% on incomes between £32,000 and £150,000, and 45% on incomes above £150,000. For capital gains, after an allowance of

£11,000, the rates are 18% for basic rate taxpayers and 28% for higher rate (40%) taxpayers and above. If a basic rate taxpayer has capital gains that together take their income and gains above the £32,000 threshold then they pay the CGT rate on the proportion of gains above the threshold.

[9] The Equality Trust (2014a) found that even with rebates the poorest tenth of households paid almost 6% of their income in Council Tax, against 1.39% for the richest tenth. It argued for extra bands for the most valuable properties and a commitment to regular revaluations. As well as being fairer, this would increase the costs of leaving property empty. The regressive nature of Council Tax was reinforced by the abolition by the Coalition Government of the previous entitlement to Council Tax benefit and the subsequent withdrawal of the transitional government grant for the Discretionary Relief scheme (by local councils) that replaced it. As a result, few local authorities are able to support poorer Council Tax payers to the level of the old benefit entitlement (letter from David Plank in the *Guardian*, 14 December 2016). The policies of the Cameron and May Governments to allow local councils to levy higher Council Tax rates to help fund social care without any revaluations or higher bands makes the position even more unfair (especially as, with the withdrawal of government grants, the differences between what wealthier and poorer areas can raise will increase even more – Smith et al, 2016).

[10] An alternative – bearing in mind the continuing rent seeking of the financial sector, which routinely charges 2% or more for services rendered – would be a tax on financial transactions, or at least on financial value added (Burman et al, 2016, provides a good review of the arguments and means). This would also help to produce greater stability in the financial markets.

[11] In 2015 the Coalition Government introduced 3-year 'guaranteed growth bonds' with an initial interest rate of 4% for pensioners aged 65 and older. In the November 2016 Autumn Statement (HM Treasury, 2016a) the Chancellor announced the Government's intention to introduce in April 2017 a new 'market-leading' 3-year investment bond for those aged 16 and over, with a limit of £3,000 for each investor.

[12] This would seem even more necessary in view of the Coalition Government's partial deregulation of private pension pots in the March 2014 Budget so that people of 55 and over are no longer required to purchase an annuity on retirement. This seems as likely to benefit the City as it is potential pensioners, as the OECD has very recently (December 2016) warned (Cumbo, 2016c).

[13] Corporate profits in the UK reached an all-time high of £102.1bn in the first quarter of 2015; the all-time low of £1,024m was in the first quarter of 1955. Between 1955 and 2016 the quarterly average was £32.9bn (Trading Economics, 2017).

[14] As well as reducing the rates of Corporation Tax, the Coalition Government took an axe to the offshore anti-tax avoidance 'controlled foreign companies' laws, and announced a tax exemption for companies' branches in overseas tax havens. The Treasury estimated that this would cut the largest companies'

tax bills by some £7bn over four years. In spite of much ministerial rhetoric about a 'march of the makers' and an industrial strategy to rebuild Britain's manufacturing base, this was paid for by a reduction in tax allowances for business investment in plant and machinery (Brooks, 2013, p 190). Until the measures announced in the March 2015 budget, banks were even able to claim relief from Corporation Tax on the many millions (in fact, billions) of pounds of compensation they are paying customers for mis-selling products such as Payment Protection Insurance (Pratley, 2015). In the post-election Budget in July 2015 the Chancellor announced phased cuts in the bank levy, which were intended to claw back some of the subsidies received by the banks in the wake of the 2008 crisis. The revenue shortfall was meant to be met by an 8% surcharge on the banks' Corporation Tax. But in December 2015 it was reported (Bowers, 2015c) that, largely because of the large losses sustained in the wake of the 2008 crisis, seven of the largest and most profitable City investment banks had paid no Corporation Tax in the previous year.

[15] Lupton et al (2015) summarise their analysis of the distributional impact of the changes as follows: 'it is poorer population groups who have been most affected by direct tax and benefit changes and in fact … savings made from changes in benefits have been offset by expenditure on direct tax reductions further up the income distribution, meaning that in combination, these changes have made no contribution to reducing the deficit or paying down the debt … modelled estimates suggest that poverty is higher in 2014/15 and will rise further, and there are signs of increasing material deprivation and hardship arising from a combination of rising costs of living, reductions in the value of benefits and short-term benefit sanctions. Real wages have also fallen, as have earnings among the self-employed who, supported by the Coalition Government, now constitute a much larger share of employment.' (Lupton et al, 2015, p 57; for findings along similar lines, see Hills, 2014; Broughton et al, 2015 and De Agostini et al, 2015).

[16] As a share of GDP, UK public social spending is slightly above the OECD average (OECD, 2016d). The position improves when private social spending is included but the UK is still well below the more 'egalitarian' advanced countries. Moreover, such expenditure is planned to fall sharply over the next few years as 'austerity' continues (Alcock, 2016, pp 145–51).

[17] Rothstein (2010) simulated a number of scenarios for the economic incidence of the EITC. In each of the scenarios, a large portion of low-income single mothers' EITC payments was captured through reduced wages. Workers who were EITC-ineligible also saw wage declines. By contrast, a conventional Negative Income Tax (NIT) discouraged work and so induced large transfers from employers to their workers. He estimated that $1 in EITC spending increased after-tax incomes by $0.73, while $1 spent on the NIT yielded $1.39.

[18] Of course, it would have to be set at the correct level. The Joseph Rowntree Foundation (2016) calculates every year the annual pre-tax income people need not only for food, shelter and clothing but also to participate in

society: a 'minimum income threshold'. The latest (July 2016) thresholds are £17,100 for single people and £18,900 each for couples with two children. It has just been reported (Brooks, 2017) that local councils in Fife and Glasgow are investigating a pilot of a basic income for every citizen, taking account of similar projects in Finland, Ontario and Utrecht.

[19] Alternatively, benefits such as the Winter Fuel Allowance could be taxed as income. Using Department for Work and Pensions and ONS data, the pressure group Reform (Mosseri-Marlio, 2016) estimates that the annual cost of the triple lock will have increased from £1.47bn in 2012 to £4.67bn by 2017, and that the cumulative total will exceed £20bn by 2017/18. In an interview with the *Observer* in July 2016 (Boffey, 2016) the former Pensions Minister, Lady Altmann, said that she had urged David Cameron to drop the 2.5% when both inflation and earnings were so low, but that he had declined on political grounds. However, in the November 2016 Autumn Statement (HM Treasury, 2016b), the Chancellor committed the Government to maintaining the lock until the end of the present Parliament although he did not rule out a review before then (see also Johnson, 2015a, and King, I., 2016). This issue is discussed further in Chapter Seven.

[20] In Chapter Seven it is proposed that the British Overseas Territories and Crown Dependencies should be brought within the UK tax and regulatory regime.

Chapter Six

[1] There is a particular issue for young people. Dorling (2015) noted that according to official figures about 750,000 young people (17% of 16- to 24-year-olds) were unemployed. Many others were under-employed, working part-time or on zero-hours contracts, or even claiming to be self-employed to avoid the stigma of unemployment. The few jobs on offer to young adults were mostly precarious, and almost all were low-paid, at least by North European standards. In fact, the largest real-terms falls in hourly wages between 2008 and 2014 were for the youngest employees in Britain. At the same time, and in spite of the Government's espousal of them, there were far fewer apprenticeships available than there were young people out of work. Moreover, many apprenticeships were of short duration and/or of dubious quality. A more recent analysis by the Learning and Work Institute for the educational charity Impetus-PEF found that an average of 1.3m (17%) of 16- to 24-year-olds spend at least six months out of education, employment or training, a much higher number than the Government's estimate. Only a fifth of young people who are NEETS manage to get a job or enter education and stay there for a year (Impetus-PEF, 2016) The Government's plan to create three million apprenticeships by 2020 through a levy on major employers is referred to in Chapter Seven.

[2] Atkinson (2015, p 130) has a useful list of the main restrictions placed on the trade unions between 1980 and 1993. For more recent trades union legislation, see Chapter Seven.

3   In April 2016 59% of BP shareholders voted against the Board's pay award to the Chief Executive, Bob Dudley. The Board had agreed to a 20% increase, to £14m, in a year when staff generally were subject to a pay freeze, 7,000 jobs were lost, the share price fell by 13% and the firm lost $6.5bn. Other recent revolts have involved Weir, Smith and Nephew, and WPP (whose Chief Executive, Sir Martin Sorrell, receives annual pay of £70m). A number of fund management companies – for example, BlackRock, Hermes and L&G Investment Management – have vowed to be more critical of top pay packages. And several major City voices – the star fund manager Neil Woodford, the outgoing Director General of the Institute of Directors, Sir Simon Walker and the former City Minister Lord Myners – have called for change. However, the reported response of the Chair of WPP's remuneration committee, Sir John Hood, shows why self-regulation here is very unlikely to be effective: 'Sir Martin doesn't have a superstar salary. He has a salary that is in the range of other chief executives in the UK. What Sorrell has is an incentive programme that rewards him highly for value creation, for increasing shareholder wealth. His remuneration is highly levered towards that' (Sweney, 2016). However Sorrell's pay has been reduced to £48m for 2016 (Sweney, 2017).

4   Mitchell and Sikka (2014) even contest the notion that the shareholders are actually the owners of a company: 'Shareholders own a piece of paper that entitles them to receive income from a company. They do not own its assets, cannot personally access them or use them. They have powers to appoint directors but cannot direct them to use any particular business strategy. They cannot force directors to pay a dividend or demand a higher one. They cannot demand to see a company's books, or personally audit them. They can sit back and receive dividends, but are not responsible for the harmful use of the resources generating those dividends.' This view of the limits of shareholder control has been consistently upheld by the courts. It means that our major corporations are effectively ownerless. Sikka (2014b) noted that it was hard to find a FTSE 100 company where shareholders provided even 50% of total capital. At Barclays, shareholders provided just 4.9%. This compared with 5.1% at Lloyds Banking Group, 5.8% at RBS, 6.9% at HSBC and 7.2% at Santander. The remainder was provided by savers and other creditors, who, whatever their other input, have no right to elect directors or direct business.

5   In December 2016 the *New York Times* reported (Morgenson, 2016) that Portland, Oregon, City Council had voted to impose a surtax on companies whose CEO earned more than 100 times the median pay of their rank-and-file workers. The May Government's corporate governance reform proposals are discussed in Chapter Seven.

6   There is a particular problem with the banks because of their role as creators of money and credit. One possibility would be to adopt Professor Colin Mayer's suggestion (2013) that banks should be required to become 'public benefit companies' so that their shareholders would have to accept that banks had wider responsibilities and make lower returns; they could also

become mutuals or cooperatives. More radical still would be to nationalise them, or at least increase the state stake in their 'ownership', something quite common in continental Europe. However, the state would need to be quite an active shareholder: its recent part-ownership of HBOS, Lloyds and RBS has not prevented various abuses, although its record in holding the management to account is certainly no worse than that of the other shareholders.

[7] The report of the Leveson Inquiry (Leveson, 2012) noted that while plurality was to some extent safeguarded through competition policy, including limits on cross-ownership of different forms of media, there needed to be some way of protecting it from 'organic change'. In November 2015 Ofcom published a 'framework' for measuring media plurality through three metrics: the availability of news sources, consumption and impact. Ownership is not covered directly but by aggregating availability and consumption by owner (separately for retail and wholesale news sources). The Government's response to the December 2016 21st Century Fox bid for the balance of Sky will be a test case for its approach to protecting media plurality.

[8] Before doing so, we should just note that a report for the OECD (2015c) estimated that bringing all pupils to the same minimum level of achievement would increase the UK's national economic output by more than £2tn by 2095, spread over 65 years.

[9] PISA tests 15-year-olds in science and a number of other subjects in over 70 countries, with the results being published every three years by the OECD. In spite of significant methodological flaws, it has an increasing influence on education policy. W. Stewart (2016) provides a good recent critique.

[10] There are various ways in which this can be done, including area-wide banding where students of a wide range of abilities are enrolled at all local schools, as operated successfully in our direct knowledge by the former Inner London Education Authority (see also Sutton Trust, 2009). The commissioners would also provide or validate information about local provision, handle complaints against schools and promote cooperation and collaboration between institutions (which could also be covered in Ofsted inspections).

[11] The Trust has just (December 2016) published a useful summary (Cullinane, 2016) of the evidence about the educational and social impact of grammar schools.

[12] A 2015 British Humanist Association survey found that the great majority of schools breaching Government rules about parental financial contributions were faith schools. Many parents were put under intense pressure, with schools sending out frequent reminders, encouraging parents to set up standing orders, and even (in the case of a Catholic primary) suggesting that parents whose children were on FSM should contribute the amount they were 'saving'.

[13] A recent analysis reported in the *Times Educational Supplement* (Barker, 2016) suggests that nearly all of the superior performance of private school sixth-forms over state ones is accounted for by their students' higher ability on arrival. Yet the average fee per term in the private sector is higher than the average funding *per year* in the state sector (I owe this point to James Kewin). It would appear that a large portion of the fee income is being spent on the private schools' facilities to make them even more attractive to wealthy overseas families (Chu, 2016).

[14] Atkinson (2015, Chapter 11) provides detailed costings for his proposals, which would be revenue-neutral and would produce significant reductions in both inequality and poverty.

Chapter Seven

[1] David Cameron was Prime Minister from the May 2015 election. He was succeeded by Theresa May on 13 July 2016. George Osborne was Chancellor until 14 July 2016 when he was succeeded by Philip Hammond.

[2] The November 2016 Autumn Statement (HM Treasury, 2016a, p 40) said 'The government is investing further in HMRC to increase its activity on countering avoidance and taking cases forward for litigation, which is expected to bring over £450 million in scored revenue by 2021–22', but no details were given. Given what we know about the challenges facing HMRC, a really significant investment, especially in people, will be needed if we are to make a serious dent in tax avoidance.

[3] Before we leave tax avoidance, we should just note the growing concern, voiced in the Chancellor's speech accompanying the 2016 Autumn Statement (HM Treasury, 2016a), about the revenue lost – possibly as much as £11.8bn – through the rapid growth in incorporated small businesses. Incorporation enables those affected, particularly people with temporarily high incomes, to store money in their companies and pay income tax later at lower rates when their earnings are smaller. In October 2016 the Prime Minister asked the Chief Executive of the Royal Society of Arts, Matthew Taylor, to conduct a review of the current regulatory framework in the light of changes in the pattern of employment. Taylor's report is expected in autumn 2017. In the meantime, the 2017 election manifesto states that 'a new Conservative government will act to ensure that the interests of employees on traditional contracts, the self-employed and those working in the "gig" economy are all properly protected' (Conservative Party, 2017, p 16). However, most of the specific pledges on protecting workers' rights are already covered by current legislation or business initiatives.

[4] It should be noted that some opponents of the proposal in the 2017 election manifesto that a person's wealth above £100,000 should be used to pay for their care costs were calling it a 'wealth tax', echoing the Conservatives' successful 2010 branding of Gordon Brown's plan to recoup the costs of social care by remodelling IHT as a 'death tax' (Jack, 2017). The 2017 proposal was subsequently modified by a promise to also cap care costs

(BBC, 2017). A much better way of funding social care would be for pensioners to continue to pay National Insurance, perhaps at a lower rate.

[5] UC replaces Jobseeker's Allowance, Housing Benefit, Working Tax Credit, Child Tax Credit, Income-related Employment and Support Allowance and Income Support. It was first introduced in parts of Greater Manchester and Cheshire in 2013 and is now being rolled out across the country. The aim is to strengthen work incentives but this has partly been undermined by the tax credit cuts. Evidence presented recently to the House of Commons Work and Pensions Committee suggests a multitude of problems with its implementation (Butler, 2017a).

[6] According to the ONS (2016c), the net rate of return in the second quarter of 2016 was 18%; the corresponding figure for manufacturing firms was 13.6%. In the third quarter of 2015 the service return was 23.2%, the highest since the present series began in 1997. We saw in Chapter Five that corporate profits reached an all-time high in the first quarter of 2015.

[7] In January 2017 Sir David Metcalf was named as the first Director of Labour Market Enforcement (Department for Business, Energy and Industrial Strategy, 2017a). A Parliamentary Question in April 2017 elicited the information that no budget had yet been set for the Director. In February 2017 Debenhams headed a list of 360 firms 'named and shamed' for underpaying staff (Butler and Booth, 2017).

[8] Beckett (2015) gives a good overview of the Cameron Government's trade union legislation.

[9] The manifesto contains a passage on page 50 acknowledging that while the proposed changes 'will have a great effect ... alone they cannot overcome the unfairness of selection by house price, where ordinary working class families find it difficult to access the best schools because they cannot afford to live in the catchment area. We will therefore conduct a review of school admissions policy. We will be clear at the outset that we will never introduce a mandatory lottery-based school admission policy.' It is helpful that a future Conservative Government is prepared to look at admissions given the importance of this for dealing with inequality in education as we saw in Chapter Six. It will be very interesting to see what the terms of reference will be, but the immediate ruling out of a lottery suggests that we should not be holding our breath

[10] The NAO (2016b) has estimated that while average per-pupil funding will rise from £5,447 in 2015/16 to £5,519 in 2019/20, cost pressures through pay rises and higher employer contributions to NI and pensions will mean an 8% real terms cut by 2020. Its report criticised the Department for Education for failing to understand or to say how schools will cope with these funding levels. Millions of pounds have, of course, been spent on establishing new academies and free schools, which now absorb more than half of Government funding for new school places (NAO, 2017). The 2017 election manifesto (p 51) commits the Government to increasing the overall schools budget by £4bn by 2022. But this will still be insufficient to compensate schools for rising costs without cutting staff. The IFS (Crawford,

2017) estimates that the £4bn increase will actually represent a 6.9% real terms fall in revenue per pupil between 2015/16 and 2020/21.

[11] A *Times Educational Supplement* scrutiny of academy trusts' 'related party transactions' of over £250,000 in 2014/15 (George, 2017a) established that they had a total value of £53m. Just over half were made to the academy sponsor or to a sister organisation of the school or trust. One academy trust paid nearly £600,000 over two years to a company whose directors included two of the trust's trustees. A second investigation (George, 2017c) found further evidence of conflicts of interest where schools were transferred ('re-brokered') from one academy trust to another by regional headteacher boards. A third investigation (Hazell, 2017) found a near-universal refusal by ten academy trusts (and one federation of maintained schools) to disclose any information about the reasons for the big increases in CEO salaries (the increases – 18% in one case, and between 14.6% and 20% in another – compare with a national 2% cap on teachers' pay in 2015/16 and a 1% cap in 2016/17). George (2017b) reports that more than two dozen academy trusts have refused to comply with government transparency rules about disclosing the salaries of directors and highly paid employees. Finally, George (2017d) finds that three of the Government's Regional Schools Commissioners made key decisions affecting the academy trusts who later employed them.

[12] Emmerson (2017) provides a useful analysis of the economic backdrop to the 2017 general election.

[13] Under the compromise agreed in Parliament to enable the trade union legislation to become law, only new union members will have to opt in to their union's political funds. There has been no parallel proposal to impose similar requirements on companies (as well as overall limits and full transparency). Should companies not be compelled to consult their shareholders if they wish to 'opt in' to political donations, and if they choose to do so, should their contribution to the donation not be deducted from their dividends? What about applying to such votes the same requirements of a 50% turnout and 40% support imposed on the unions?

[14] The manifesto also promises (p 43) to repeal the Fixed-term Parliaments Act 2011, another potential check on the executive.

[15] '... it is a commonplace that the British residential property system is creating surreal house prices and monumental social unfairness. Huge mortgages for the young, the lottery of property inheritance and crazily high rents are becoming permanent parts of our social landscape. But crucial in this story is that property is effectively only taxed when it is bought and sold. There has not been a revaluation of residential property prices, on which the ineffectual council tax is based, since 1991. As a result, the property market is, because of generous inheritance tax thresholds, tax exemption of capital gains on homes and trivial council tax receipts, the world's biggest onshore tax haven creating the world's highest real house prices' (Hutton, 2017).

[16] Martin Wolf (2015) argued that current levels of corporate surpluses (in both Britain and the US) were contributing to the savings glut that we noted in Chapter Three, note 4. He suggested higher taxes on retained corporate earnings with deductions for investment (and dividends). Whatever else our companies are spending their money on, it is not charity. According to Philip Collins (2016), less than a quarter of the charitable donations of £1m or over in 2014 came from firms. Only 23% of FTSE companies gave even 1% of their pre-tax profits to charity.

[17] According to the *Guardian* report, the memorandum sent to the Work and Pensions Secretary two weeks before the May 2015 election stated: 'Around 40,000 more ... children might, in the absence of any behaviour change, find themselves in poverty as a result of reducing the cap to £23,000. If these families respond to the cap by making behaviour change, for example moving into work, they are likely to see themselves and their children move out of relative poverty.' Yet, according to Butler and Malik (2015), the latest official figures showed that 59,000 households had been hit by the £26,000 cap since its introduction in April 2013. Work and Pensions research from December had found that just 11% of households just below the cap level moved into work. This figure rose marginally to 15.7% for households who were capped. A very recent study by Cardiff University (Butler, 2017b) finds that a record 60% of British people in poverty live in a household where at least one person is in work. It is surely time to abandon the pretence that employment is the answer to poverty.

[18] In addition, the 2017 election manifesto states (p 80) that a future Conservative Government will not proceed with the second stage of the Leveson Inquiry into the culture, practices and ethics of the press.

REFERENCES

Acemoglu, D. and Autor, D. (2010) *Skills, Tasks and Technologies: Implications for Employment and Earnings.* NBER Working Paper No. 16082. Cambridge, MA: NBER.

Acemoglu, D. and Robinson, J.A. (2012) *Why Nations Fail: The Origins of Power, Prosperity and Poverty.* London: Profile Books.

Achur, J. (2010) *Trade Union Membership 2010.* London: BIS.

Adam, S. (2014) *Housing Taxation.* Presentation at ESRC–British Academy event 'UK housing: setting out the challenge', London, 29 October. London: IFS and Economic and Social Research Council.

Adam, S. and Browne, J. (2011) *A Survey of UK Tax System.* London: IFS.

Aghion, P., Besley, T., Browne, J., Caselli, F., Lambert, R., Lomax, R., Stern, N. and Van Reenen, J. (2013) *Investing for Prosperity: Report of the LSE Growth Commission.* London: LSE.

Alcock, P. (2016) *Why We Need Welfare.* Bristol: Policy Press.

Aldrick, P. (2016) Globalisation ain't broke, but that doesn't mean it can't be fixed, *The Times,* 28 May: 51.

Aldrick, P. (2017) Company bosses get rich even if they fail to generate genuine wealth, *The Times,* 10 January: 37.

Alegre, M.A. and Ferrer, G. (2010) School regimes and education equity: some insights based on PISA 2000, *British Educational Research Journal,* 36 (3): 433–461.

Alesina, A. and Perotti, R. (1993) *Income Distribution, Political Instability, and Investment.* NBER Working Paper No. w4486. Cambridge, MA: NBER.

Allen, K. (2014) Home buyers left behind in Britain's two-speed housing market, *Financial Times*, 17 January: 3.

Allen, R. (2013) Fair access: Making school choice and admissions work for all, in J. Clifton (ed) *Excellence and Equity: Tackling Educational Disadvantage in England's Secondary Schools*, London: Institute for Public Policy Research, pp 29–36.

Allen, R., Burgess, S. and McKenna, L. (2014) *School Performance and Parental Choice of School: Secondary Data Analysis – Research Report*. Available at https://www.gov.uk/government/publications/school-performance-and-parental-choice-of-school.

Alstadsaeter, A., Johannesen, N. and Zucman, G. (2017) *Tax Evasion and Inequality*, May 28. Available at: https://via.hypothes.is/http://gabriel-zucman.eu/files/AJZ2017.pdf.

Altmann, R. (2017) There is a magic money tree – it's called QE, *Financial Times Money*, 10 June: 7.

Alvaredo, F., Atkinson, A.B., Piketty, T. and Saez, E. (2013) The top 1 percent in international and historical perspective, *Journal of Economic Perspectives*, 27 (3): 3–20.

Alvaredo, F., Atkinson, A.B. and Morelli, S. (2016) The challenge of measuring UK wealth inequality in the 2000s, *Fiscal Studies*, 37 (1): 13–34.

Amin-Smith, N., Cribb, J. and Sibieta, L. (2017) *IFS Green Budget 2017: Reforms to Apprenticeship in England*. Report R 124. Available at https://www.ifs.org.uk/publications/8863.

Andrews, J., Hutchinson, J. and Johnes, R. (2016) *Grammar Schools and Social Mobility*. London: Education Policy Institute.

Antonucci, L. (2016) *Student Lives in Crisis: Deepening Inequality in Times of Austerity*. Bristol: Policy Press.

Arezki, R., Botlon, P., Peters, S., Samama, F. and Stiglitz, J. (2016) *From Global Savings Glut to Financing Infrastructure: The Advent of Investment Platforms*. IMF Working Paper WP/16/18. Washington, DC: IMF.

Arpaia, A., Perez, E. and Pichelmann, K. (2009) *Understanding Labour Income Share Dynamics in Europe*. Munich Personal RePec Archive Paper No. 15649, posted 17 June 2009. Available at http://mpra.ub.uni-muenchen.de/15649.

Ashournia, D., Munch, J. and Nguyen, D. (2014) *The Impact of Chinese Import Penetration on Danish Firms and Workers*. Department of Economics Discussion Paper No. 703. Oxford: Department of Economics.

Asthana, A. (2017) Inheritance tax cut will enrich London elite at expense of north, says MP. *Guardian,* 1 March: 18.

Atkinson, A.B. (2014) After Piketty? *The British Journal of Sociology*, 65 (4): 619–638.

Atkinson, A.B. (2015) *Inequality: What Can Be Done?* Cambridge, MA and London: Harvard University Press.

Atkinson, A.B. and Voitchovsky, S. (2011) The distribution of top earnings in the UK since the Second World War, *Economica*, 78: 440–459.

Atkinson, A.B., Piketty, T. and Saez, E. (2011) Top incomes in the long run of history, *Journal of Economic Literature*, 49 (1): 3–71.

Attanasio, O., Hurst, E. and Pistaferri, L. (2013) *The Evolution of Income, Consumption, and Leisure Inequality in the US, 1980–2010*. Available at web.stanford.edu/Michigan_paper_march13.pdf.

Autor, D.H., Dorn, D. and Hanson, G.H. (2014) *The Labor Market and the Marriage Market: How Adverse Employment Shocks Affect Marriage, Fertility, and Children's Living Circumstances. Preliminary Draft July*. Available at chasp.lbj.utexas.edu/category/initiative-research/files/2015/04/TheLaborMarket-MarriageMarket-July2014.pdf.

Autor, D.H., Dorn, D. and Hanson, G.H. (2016) *The China Shock: Learning from Labor Market Adjustment to Large Changes in Trade*. Discussion Paper No. 9748. Munich: IZA.

Autor, D.H., Katz, L.F. and Kearney, M.S. (2006) *The Polarization of the U.S. Labour Market*. NBER Working Paper No. 11986. Cambridge, MA: NBER.

Autor, D. H., Katz, L. and Krueger, A. (1998) Computing inequalities: have computers changed the labour market? *Quarterly Journal of Economics*, 113: 1169–1214.

Autor, D.H., Levy, F. and Murnane, R.J. (2003) The skill content of recent technological change: an empirical exploration, *The Quarterly Journal of Economics*, 118: 1279 – 1333.

Bailey, J., Coward, J. and Whittaker, M. (2011) *Painful Separation: An International Study of the Weakening Relationship between Economic Growth and the Pay of Ordinary Workers.* London: Resolution Foundation.

Bailey, M.J. and Dynarski, S.M. (2011) Inequality in post-secondary education, in G.J. Duncan and R.J. Murnane (eds) *Whither Opportunity? Rising Inequality, Schools, and Children's Life Chances*, New York: Russell Sage Foundation, pp 117–132.

Bakija, J., Cole, A. and Heim, B. (2012) *Jobs and Income Growth of Top Earners and the Causes of Changing Income Inequality: Evidence from U.S. Tax Return Data.* Department of Economics Working Paper 2010-22 (revised 2012). Williamstown, MA: Williams College.

Baldwin, R. (2016) *The Great Convergence: Information Technology and the New Globalization.* Cambridge, MA and London: The Belknap Press of Harvard University Press.

Ballarino, G., Bratti, M., Filippin, A., Fiorio, C., Leonardi, M. and Scervini, F. (2014) Increasing Educational Inequalities?, in W. Salverda, B. Nolan, D. Checchi, I. Marx, A. McKnight, I.G. Toth, and H. van de Werfhorst (eds) *Changing Inequalities in Rich Countries: Analytical and Comparative Perspectives*, Oxford: University Press, pp 121–145.

Bambra, C. (2016) *Health Divides: Where You Live Can Kill You.* Bristol: Policy Press.

Bangs, J. (2009) Taking the Eden out of Sweden. The Scandinavian 'free schools' system is not the panacea politicians believe it to be, *Times Educational Supplement*, 3 April: 33.

Bank of America Merrill Lynch (2015) *Thematic Investing Robot Revolution – Global Robot and AI Primer.* Available at https://www.bofaml.com/content/dam/boaimages/documents/PDFs/robotics_and_ai_condensed_primer.pdf.

Bank of England (2016) *Financial Stability Report November 2016 Issue No. 40.* London: Bank of England.

Barker, I. (2012) Independent schools benefit from sweet charity. Professional fundraising nets 24 institutions more than 1m each, *Times Educational Supplement*, 8 June: 12–13.

Barker, I. (2013) Elite alma maters inspire the wealthy to dig deep. Haul of £115m as UK private schools step up fundraising efforts, *Times Educational Supplement*, 21 June: 14, 16.

Barker, K. (2014) *Housing: Where's the Plan?* London: London Publishing Partnership and Enlightenment Economics.

Barker, I. (206) From class C to A-grade, state schools are on the rise, *Times Educational Supplement*, 5 February: 8–9.

Barry, B. (2005) *Why Social Justice Matters.* Cambridge: Polity Press.

Bartels, L.M. (2008) *Unequal Democracy: The Political Economy of the New Gilded Age.* New York: Sage.

Barth, E. and Moene, K.O. (2009) *The Equality Multiplier.* NBER Working Paper No. 15076. Cambridge, MA: NBER.

Barth, E., Bryson, A., Davis, J.C. and Freeman, R. (2014) *It's Where You Work: Increases in Earnings Dispersion across Establishments and Individuals in the US.* Centre for Economic Performance Discussion Paper No. 1311. London: LSE.

Bartlett, B. (2013) Taxing homeowners as if they were landlords, *New York Times*, 3 September. Available at http://economix. blogs.nytimes.com/2013/09/03/taxing-homeowners-as-if-they -were-landlords/?r=0.

Bassanini, A. and Duval, R. (2006) *Employment Patterns in OECD Countries: Reassessing the Role of Policies and Institutions.* OECD Social, Employment and Migration Working Paper No. 35. Paris: OECD.

Bazot, G. (2014) *Financial Consumption and the Cost of Finance: Measuring Financial Efficiency in Europe (1950–2007).* Working Paper No. 2014-17. Paris: Paris School of Economics.

BBC (2017) General election: Theresa May changes social care plans. 22 May. Available at: http://www.bbc.co.uk/news/ election-2017-40001221.

Beatty, C. and Fothergill, S. (2016) *Jobs, Welfare and Austerity. How the Destruction of Industrial Britain Casts a Shadow over Present-day Public Finances.* Centre for Regional Economic and Social Research. Sheffield: Sheffield Hallam University.

Bebchuk, L. and Grinstein, Y. (2005) The growth of executive pay, *Oxford Review of Economic Policy*, 21 (2): 283–303.

Bebchuk, L. and Fried, J. (2004) *Pay Without Performance: The Unfulfilled Promise of Executive Compensation.* Cambridge, MA: Harvard University Press.

Bebchuk, L.A., Grinstein, Y. and Peyer, U. (2010) Lucky CEOs and lucky directors, *The Journal of Finance*, 65 (6): 2363–2401.

Beckett, A. (2015) Vuvuzelas unite, *London Review of Books*, 22 October: 25–28.

Belfield, C., Cribb, J., Hood, A. and Joyce, R. (2016) *Living Standards, Poverty and Inequality in the UK: 2016*. London: IFS.

Bell, B. and Machin, S. (2016) *Brexit and Wage Inequality*. London: LSE.

Bell, B. and Van Reenen, J. (2013) *Extreme Wage Inequality: Pay at the Very Top*. Occasional Paper, Centre for Economic Performance. London: LSE.

Belley, P. and Lochner, L. (2007) *The Changing Role of Family Income and Ability in Determining Educational Attainment*. NBER Working Paper No. 13527. Cambridge, MA: NBER.

Bennett, J.E., Guangquan, L., Foreman, K., Best, N. Kontis, V., Pearson, C., Hambly, P. and Ezzati, M. (2016) The future of life expectancy and life expectancy inequalities in England and Wales: Bayesian spatiotemporal forecasting, *The Lancet*, 386, July 11: 163–170.

Berle, A.A. (1962) A new look at management responsibility, *Human Resource Management*, 1 (3): 1–5.

Bertrand, M. and Morse, A. (2013) *Trickle-Down Consumption*. NBER Working Paper No. 18883. Cambridge, MA: NBER.

Bertrand, M. and Mullainathan, S. (2001) Are CEOs rewarded for luck? The ones without principals are, *The Quarterly Journal of Economics*, 116 (3): 901–932.

Besley, T. and Persson, T. (2011) *Pillars of Prosperity: The Political Economics of Development Clusters*. Princeton, NJ, and Oxford: Princeton University Press.

Bhagwati, J.N. (1982) Directly unproductive, profit-seeking (DUP) activities, *Journal of Political Economy*, 90 (5): 988–1002.

BIS (2016) *Trade Union Membership 2015*. Statistical Bulletin. May 2016. London: BIS.

Blanchflower, D. (2015) As good as it gets? The UK labour market in recession and recovery, *National Institute Economic Review*, 231: F76–80.

Blanden, J., Gregg, P. and Machin, S. (2005) Social mobility in Britain: low and falling, *CentrePiece*, Spring 2005, 18–20. Centre for Economic Performance. London: LSE.

Blau, F.D. and Kahn, L.M. (2013) Immigration and the Distribution of Incomes. CESifo Working Paper No. 4561. Munich: Ludwig-Maximilians University Center for Economic Studies and the Ifo Institute.

Blomgren, J., Hiilamo, H., Kangas, O. and Niemala, M. (2014) Finland: growing inequality with contested consequences, in B. Nolan, W. Salverda, D. Checchi, I. Marx, A. McKnight, I.G. Toth and H. van de Werfhorst (eds) *Changing Inequalities and Societal Impacts in Rich Countries: Thirty Countries' Experiences*, Oxford: University Press, pp 222–247.

Bloodworth, J. (2016) *The Myth of Meritocracy*. London: Biteback Publishing.

Bloom, N., Draca, M. and van Reenen, J. (2015) Trade induced technical change? The impact of Chinese imports on innovation, IT and productivity, *Review of Economic Studies, Advanced Access*. Available at https://people.stanford.edu/nbloom/sites/default/files/titc.pdf.

Boffey, D. (2014) Tories 'try to buy election' with huge rise in campaign spending, *Observer*, 14 December: 1, 7.

Boffey, D. (2015) Valuable NHS deals won by firms using tax havens, *Observer*, 22 March: 26.

Boffey, D. (2016) Doubts grow over 'totemic' cash pledge to pensioners, *Observer*, 30 July. Available at https://www.theguardian.com/money/2016/jul/state-pension-triple-lock-doubts.

Boffey, D. and Syal, R. (2015) Tax avoiders and hedge funds. The Tories invited them to the party, *Observer*, 15 February: 28–29.

Bogliacino, F. and Maestri, V. (2014) Increasing economic inequalities? in W. Salverda, B. Nolan, D. Checchi, I. Marx, A. McKnight, I.G. Toth, and H. van de Werfhorst (eds) *Changing Inequalities in Rich Countries: Analytical and Comparative Perspectives,* Oxford: University Press, pp 15–48.

Bol, T. and van de Werfhorst, H. (2013) Educational systems and the trade-off between labor market allocation and equality of opportunity, *Comparative Education Review*, 57 (2): 285–308.

Boliver, V. (2011) Expansion, differentiation, and the persistence of social class inequalities in British higher education, *Higher Education*, 61: 229–242.

Booth, R. (2016a) Edward Troup: from tax haven adviser to leading HMRC's Panama inquiry, *Guardian*, 11 April. Available at http://www.theguardian.com/politics/2016/agr/11/edward-troup-advising-tax-havens-leading-hmrs-panama-papers-inquiry-access.

Booth, R. (2016b) Under-paying bosses escape prosecution, *Guardian*, 28 September: 26.

Boston Consulting Group (2013) Majority of large manufacturers are now planning or considering 'reshoring' from China to the U.S. 24 September. Available at http://www.bcg.com/medica/pressreleasedetails.aspx?id=tcm:12–144944.

Bound, J. and Johnson, G. (1989) *Changes in the Structure of Wages during the 1980s: An Evaluation of Alternative Explanations.* NBER Working Paper No. 2983. Cambridge, MA: NBER.

Bourguignon, F. (2015) *The Globalization of Inequality.* Princeton, NJ and Oxford: Princeton University Press.

Bowers, S. (2015a) Britain rejects plan to fight tax avoidance, *Guardian*, 19 June: 15.

Bowers, S. (2015b) Britain joins move to block MEPs' access to stash of secret tax files, *Guardian*, 5 November: 5.

Bowers, S. (2015c) Anger at City banks paying little or no corporation tax, 22 December. Available at http://www.theguardian.com/business/2015/dec/22/anger-at-city-banks-paying-little-or-no-corporation-tax.

Bowles, S. and Jayadev, A. (2005) *Guard Labor.* Santa Fe Institute Working Paper, 2005-07-30. Available at http://www.santafe.edu/media/workingpapers/05-07-030.pdf.

Bowles, S. and Park, Y. (2005) Emulation, inequality and work hours: Was Thorsten Veblen right? *The Economic Journal*, 115: F397–F412.

Bowman, A., Erturk, I., Froud, J., Johal, S., Law, J., Leaver, A., Moran, M. and Williams, K. (2014) *The End of the Experiment? From Competition to the Foundational Economy.* Manchester: Manchester University Press.

Brandolini, A. (2010) Political economy and the mechanics of politics, *Politics and Society*, 38 (2): 212–226.

Brewer, M., Cattan, S., Crawford, C. and Rabe, B. (2016) *Does Free Childcare Help Parents Work?* London: IFS.

British Humanist Association (2015) Schools requesting financial contributions. Available at https://humanism.org.uk/wp-content/uploads/Schools-requesting -financial-contributions-report-FINAL.pdf.

Brooks, L. (2017) Universal basic income trials being considered in Scotland, *Guardian*, 1 January: 12.

Brooks, R. (2013) *The Great Tax Robbery: How Britain Became a Tax Haven for Fat Cats and Big Business.* London: Oneworld Publications.

Brooks, R. (2016) We don't need to reform tax havens – just get rid of them, *Guardian*, 5 April: 33.

Broughton, N., Kanabar, R. and Martin, N. (2015) *Wealth in the Downturn: Winners and Losers.* Social Market Foundation, March 2015. Available at http://www.smf.co.uk/wp-content/uploads/2015/03/Social-Market-Foundation-Publication-Wealth-in-the-Downturn-Winners-and-losers.pdf.

Brown, P., Lauder, H. and Ashton, D. (2011) *The Global Auction: The Broken Promises of Education, Jobs and Incomes.* Oxford: University Press.

Brown, R. (ed) (2011) *Higher Education and the Market.* New York, NY and London: Routledge.

Brown, R. (2014) The real crisis in higher education, *Higher Education Review*, 46 (3): 4–25.

Brown, R. (2016) The apprenticeship levy is a missed opportunity, *Times Education Supplement*, 18 March: 46–47.

Brown, R. (unpublished) Do we really want a private school sector?

Brown, R. with Carasso, H. (2013) *Everything for Sale? The Marketisation of UK Higher Education.* London and New York, NY: Routledge.

Browne, J. and Hood, A. (2016) *Living Standards, Poverty and Inequality in the UK: 2015–16 to 2020–21.* Report No. 114. London: IFS.

Brynjolfsson, E. and McAfee, A. (2014) *The Second Machine Age: Work, Progress and Prosperity in a Time of Brilliant Technologies.* New York, NY and London: Norton.

Buchanan, J., Dymski, G., Froud, J., Johal, S., Leaver, A. and Williams, K. (2014) Unsustainable employment portfolios, *Work, Employment and Society*, 27 (3): 396–413.

Bukodi, E., Goldthorpe, J.H., Waller, L. and Kuha, J. (2014) The mobility problem in Britain: new findings from the analysis of birth cohort data, *British Journal of Sociology*, 65 (3): 1–25.

Bureau of Economic Analysis (2016) *Corporate profits (gross operating surpluses) before tax. Table 6.17B.* Available at www.bea. gov/national/nipaweb/SS_Data/Section6All_xls.xls.

Bureau of Labor Statistics (2016) *Union Members 2015.* News Release. Available at www.bls.gov/news.release/pdf/union2. pdf.

Burgess, S., Dickson, M. and Macmillan, L. (2014) *Selective Schooling Systems Increase Inequality.* Department of Quantitative Social Science Working Paper No. 14-09. London: UCL Institute of Education.

Burman, L.E., Rohaly, J. and Shiller, R.J. (2006) *The Rising-Tide Tax System: Indexing (at Least Partially) for Changes in Inequality. Draft.* Available at aida.wss.yale.edu/~shiller/ behmacro/2006–11/burman-rohaly-shiller.pdf.

Burman, L.E., Gale, W.G., Gault, S., Kim, B., Nunns, J. and Rosentahl, S. (2016) Financial transaction taxes in theory and practice, *National Tax Journal*, 69 (1): 171–216.

Butler, P. (2017a) Welfare reform is not only cruel but chaotic. May needs to address this, *Guardian,* 3 May: 32.

Butler, P. (2017b) In-work poverty at record high, says study, *Guardian,* 23 May: 4.

Butler, S. and Booth, R. (2017) Record number of firms shamed over pay, *Guardian,* 16 February: 22.

Butler, P. and Malik, S. (2015) Thousands plunged into poverty by benefit cap, *Guardian*, 30 May: 1–2.

Cabinet Office and Her Majesty the Queen (2015) *Queen's Speech 2015.* Available at https://www.gov.uk/government/ speeches/queens-speech-2015.

Cable, V. (2014) *Innovation and the UK's Knowledge Economy.* 22 July. Available at https://www.gov.uk/government/speeches/ innovation-and-the-uks-knowledge-economy.

Cadwalladr, C. (2017) Follow the data: is this the document that connects the Brexit campaigns to a US billionaire – and blows a hole in our democracy? *The Observer*, 14 May: 14-15.

Calder, G. (2016) *How Inequality Runs in Families*. Bristol: Policy Press.

Cameron, D. (2013) *EU Speech at Bloomberg*. 23 January. Available at https://www.gov.uk/government/speeches/eu-speech-at-bloomberg.

Cameron, D. (2015a) *The Prime Minister's Party Conference Speech in full*. 7 October. Available at http://www.conservativehome.com.

Cameron, D. (2015b) Conservatives have become the party of equality, *Guardian*, 26 October.

Card, D. (2009) Immigration and inequality, *American Economic Review: Papers and Proceedings 2009*, 99 (2): 1–21.

Card, D. and DiNardo, J.E. (2002) *Skill Biased Technological Change and Rising Wage Inequality: Some Problems and Puzzles*. NBER Working Paper No. 8769. Cambridge, MA: NBER.

Card, D., Lemieux, T. and Riddell, W.C. (2003) *Unionization and Wage Inequality: A Comparative Study of the US, the UK and Canada*. NBER Working Paper No. 9473. Available at http://www.nber.org/papers/w9473.

Carney, M. (2016) *The Spectre of Monetarism*. Speech at Liverpool John Moores University, 5 December. Available at www.bankofengland.co.uk/publications/Documents/speeches/2106/speech946.pdf.

Carney, M. (2017) *Lambda*. Speech given at the London School of Economics, 16 January. Available at www.bankofengland.co.uk/publications/Documents/speeches/2017/speech954.pdf.

Case, A. and Deaton, A. (2015) *Rising Morbidity and Mortality in Midlife among White Non-Hispanic Americans in the 21st Century*. Available at http://www.pnas.org/cgi/doi/10.1073/pnas.1518393112.

Causa, O., de Serres, A. and Ruiz, N. (2014) *Can Pro-Growth Policies Lift All Boats? An Analysis Based on Household Disposable Income*. Economics Department Working Paper No. 1180. Paris: OECD.

Center for Responsive Politics (2016a) *Federal Election Spending By Donor Industry*. 11 October. Available at https://www.opensecrets.org/outsidespending/summ.php?disp=I.

Center for Responsive Politics (2016b) *Election Overview.* Available at http://www.opensecrets.org/overview.

Centre for Learning and Life Chances in Knowledge Economies and Societies (2011) *Education, Opportunity and Social Cohesion.* London: Institute of Education. Available at http://www. llakes.org/wp-content/uploads/2011/06/Socialcohesion_ webversion.pdf.

Chadwick, L. and Solon, G. (2002) Intergenerational income mobility among daughters, *The American Economic Review*, 92 (1): 335–344.

Chakrabortty, A. (2012) Bad apple? *Guardian*, 24 April: G2, 5–7

Chang, H-J. (2013) The myth of the lazy mob, *Guardian*, 29 January: 26.

Charles, K.K., Hurst, E. and Killewald, A. (2013) Marital sorting and parental wealth, *Demography*, 50: 51–70.

Charles-Coll, J. (2011) Understanding income inequality, *International Journal of Economics and Management Sciences*, 1 (3): 17–28.

Chen, W-H., Foerster, M. and Llena-Nozal, A. (2013) Demographic or labour market trends: What determines the distribution of household earnings in OECD countries? *OECD Journal: Economic Studies*, Volume 2013: 179–207.

Cheng, S.C. and Gorard, S. (2010) Segregation by poverty in secondary schools in England 2006–2009: a research note, *Journal of Education Policy*, 25 (3): 415–418.

Chennells, L. and Van Reenen, J. (2002) Technical change and the structure of employment and wages: a survey of the microeconometric evidence, in N. Greenan, Y. L'Horty, and J. Mairesse (eds) *Productivity, Inequality and the Digital Economy: A Transatlantic Perspective*, Cambridge, MA: MIT Press, pp 175–229.

Chetty, R., Hendren, N., Kline, P. and Saez, E. (2014a) *Where Is the Land of Opportunity? The Geography of Intergenerational Mobility in the United States.* NBER Working Paper No. 19843. Cambridge, MA: NBER.

Chetty, R., Hendren, N., Kline, P., Saez, E. and Turner, N. (2014b) *Is the United States Still a Land of Opportunity? Recent Trends in Intergenerational Mobility.* NBER Working Paper No. 19844. Cambridge, MA: NBER.

Chick, M. (2015) There's better ways to tax wealth than a mansion tax, 13 February. Available at https://www.opendemocracy.net/ourkingdom/martin-chick/there%27s-better-ways-to-tax-wealth-than-mansion-tax.

Chick, V. and Pettifor, A. (2010) *The Economic Consequences of Mr Osborne. Fiscal Consolidation: Lessons from a Century of Macro Economics.* Available at http://www.debtonation.org/wp-content/uploads/2010/06/Fiscal-Consolidation1.pdf.

Christensen, J. and Henry, J. (2016) The offshore trillions. Letter in *New York Review of Books*, 10 March.

Chu, B. (2016) The charts that shows how private school fees have exploded over the past 25 years, *Independent*, 10 May. Available at http://www.independent.co.uk/home-news/the-charts-that-shows-how-private-school-fees-have-exploded-a7023056.html.

Chusseau, N. and Dumont, M. (2012) *Growing Income Inequalities in Advanced Countries.* Society for the Study of Economic Inequality Working Paper 2012-260. Available at www.ecineq.org/milano/wp/ecineq2012-260.pdf.

Chusseau, N., Dumont, M. and Hellier, J. (2008) Explaining rising inequality: skill-biased technical change and North–South trade, *Journal of Economic Surveys*, 22 (3): 409–457.

Cingano, F. (2014) *Trends in Income Inequality and Its Impact on Economic Growth.* OECD Social, Employment and Migration Working Paper No. 163. Paris: OECD.

CIPD (2015) *The View from Below: What Employees Really Think about Their CEO's Pay Packet.* London: CIPD.

Clark, G. and Cummins, N. (2014) Intergenerational wealth mobility in England, 1858–2012: Surnames and Social Mobility, *The Economic Journal*, 125: 61–85.

Clarke, S., Corlett, A., Finch, S., Gardiner, L., Henehan, K., Tomlinson, D. and Whittaker, M. (2017) *Are we nearly there yet? Spring Budget 2017 and the 15 year squeeze on family and public finances.* London: Resolution Foundation.

Clifton, J. (2011) International comparisons can be instructive if used properly – but on this too, England is lagging behind, *Times Educational Supplement*, 15 July: 21.

Clifton, J. and Cook, W. (2013) The achievement gap in context, in J. Clifton (ed) *Excellence and Equity: Tackling Educational Disadvantage in England's Secondary Schools*, London: IPPR, pp 17–28.

Collins, C., Flannery, H. and Hoxie, J. (2016) *Gilded Giving: Top-Heavy Philanthropy in an Age of Extreme Inequality.* Washington, DC: Institute for Policy Studies.

Collins, P. (2016) Businesses are the skinflints of charity giving, *The Times*, 30 December: 25.

Collinson, P. (2015) Inheritance tax just for the super-rich? That's rubbish, *Guardian*, 25 April: 44.

Collinson, P. (2016a) Britain is a savers' paradise – for the few, *Guardian*, 30 April: 46.

Collinson, P. (2016b) Why fear inheritance tax? Your cash will all be gone, *Guardian*, 4 June: 40.

Connelly, R., Sullivan, A. and Jerrim, J. (2014) *Primary and Secondary Education and Poverty Review.* Centre for Longitudinal Studies. London: UCL Institute of Education.

Conservative Party (2015) *The Conservative Party Manifesto 2015.* Available at https://s3-eu-west-1.amazonaws.com/manifesto2015/ConservativeManifesto2015.pdf.

Conservative Party (2017) *Forward, Together: Our Plan for a Stronger Britain and a Prosperous Future.* London: Conservative Party.

Cooper, K. and Stewart, K. (2013) *Does Money Affect Children's Outcomes?* York: Joseph Rowntree Foundation.

Corak, M. (2013) *Income Inequality, Equality of Opportunity and Intergenerational Mobility.* Discussion Paper No. 7520. Munich: IZA.

Corak, M., Curtis, L. and Phipps, S. (2011) Economic mobility, family background and the well-being of children in the United States and Canada, in T. Smeeding, M. Jaentti, and R. Erickson (eds) *Persistence, Privilege and Parenting: The Comparative Study of Intergenerational Mobility*, New York, NY: Russell Sage Foundation, pp 73–108.

Cornia, G.A. (2012) *Inequality Trends and their Determinants: Latin America over 1990–2010.* United Nations University UNU-WIDER Working Paper No. 2012/09. Available at https://www.wider.unu.edu/publication/inequality-trends-and-their-determinants.

Corlett, A., Finch, D., Gardiner, L. and Whittaker, M. (2016) *Bending the Rules: Autumn Statement Response.* London: Resolution Foundation.

Corlett, A. and Clarke, S. (2017) *Living Standards 2017.* London: Resolution Foundation.

Corporate Reform Collective (2014) *Fighting Corporate Abuse: Beyond Predatory Capitalism.* London: Pluto Press.

Coulson, A.B. and Bonner, J. (2015) *Living Wage Employers: Evidence of UK Business Cases.* London: Citizens UK on behalf of the Living Wage Foundation.

Council of Economic Advisers (2016) *The Long-Term Decline in Prime-Age Male Labor Force Participation.* Available at https://www.whitehouse.gov/administration/eop/cea.

Coutts, K. and Gudgin, G. (2015) *The Macroeconomic Impact of Liberal Economic Policies in the UK.* Centre for Business Research. Cambridge: Judge Business School.

Craig, D. (2015) *The Great Charity Scandal.* Bournemouth: Original Book Company.

Crawford, C. (2014) *Socio-Economic Differences in University Outcomes in the UK: Drop-Out, Degree Completion and Degree Class.* London: IFS.

Crawford, R. (2017) *Spending on Public Services.* London: Institute for Fiscal Studies, 26 May. Available at: https://www.ifs.org.uk/uploads/Presentations/Rowena%20Crawford%2C%202017%20General%20Election%2C%20manifesto%20analysis.pdf.

Crawford, C., Innes, D. and O'Dea, C. (2015) *The Evolution of Wealth in Great Britain: 2006–08 to 2010–12.* London: IFS.

Crawford, C., Macmillan, L. and Vignoles, A. (2014) *Progress made by High-Attaining Children from Disadvantaged Backgrounds, Research Report.* London: Social Mobility and Child Poverty Commission.

Creedy, J. and Dixon, R. (1997) The relative burden of monopoly on households with different incomes, *Economica*, 258: 285–293.

Crewe, T. (2016) The strange death of municipal England, *London Review of Books*, 15 December. Available at http://www.lrb.co.uk/v38/n24/tom-crewe/the-strange-death-of-municipal-england.

Cribb, J., Jesson, D., Sibieta, L., Skipp, A. and Vignoles, A. (2013) *Poor Grammar. Entry into Grammar Schools for Disadvantaged Pupils in England*. London: Sutton Trust.

Cullinane, C. (2016) *Gaps in Grammar*. Research Brief 15. London: Sutton Trust.

Cumbo, J. (2016a) Lifetime ISAs 'will benefit the wealthy most', *Financial Times Money*, 28 May: 3.

Cumbo, J. (2016b) IHT – and how the wealthy reduce it, *Financial Times Money*, 30 July: 4.

Cumbo, J. (2016c) OECD attacks Osborne's pension reforms, *Financial Times*, 8 December. Available at https://www.ft.com/content/97f1dd46-bc6c-11e6-8b45-b8b81dd5d080.

Curtis, P. (2008) Wider schools divide linked to higher rates of violent crime, *Guardian*, 28 February: 1.

Dabla-Norris, E., Kochhar, K., Suphaphiphat, N., Ricka, F. and Tsounta, E. (2015) *Causes and Consequences of Income Inequality: A Global Perspective*. IMF Staff Discussion Note SDN/15/13. Washington, DC: IMF.

D'Arcy, C., Corlett, A. and Gardiner, L. (2015) *Higher Ground. Who Gains from the National Living Wage?* London: Resolution Foundation.

Daudey, E. and Garcia-Penalosa, C. (2007) The personal and the factor distribution of incomes in a cross-section of countries, *The Journal of Development Studies*, 43 (5): 812–829.

Davies, G. (2016a) The global pivot towards fiscal policy, 25 September. Available at https://www.ft.com/content/612895b0-d22-3819-b7a6-e7ee33291450.

Davies, G. (2016b) The end of 'QE infinity'? 7 October. Available at https://www.ft.com/content/f36a1403-cfbc-3db9-a89c-14beef198e5f.

De Agostini, P., Hills, J. and Sutherland, H. (2015) *Were We Really All in it Together? The Distributional Effects of the Coalition Government's Tax-Benefit Changes*. Social Policy in a Cold Climate Working Paper No. 1, Centre for the Analysis of Social Exclusion, LSE and Institute for Social and Economic Research, University of Essex. Available at http://stiard.lse.ac.uk/case/_new/research/social_policy_in_a_Cold_Climate.asp.

Deaton, A. (2013) *The Great Escape: Health, Wealth and the Origins of Inequality.* Princeton, NJ and Oxford: Princeton University Press.

De Gregorio, J. and Lee, J.-W. (2002) Education and income inequality: new evidence from cross-country data, *Review of Income and Wealth*, 48 (3): 395–415.

Deloitte Shift Index (2013) Available at https://www2.deloitte.com/us/en/pages/center-for-the-edge/articles/shift-index-return-on-assets-business-performance.html.

Department for Business, Energy and Industrial Strategy (2016) *Corporate Governance Reform*. Green Paper. London: Department for Business, Energy and Industrial Strategy.

Department for Business, Energy and Industrial Strategy (2017a) *Sir David Metcalf named as the first Director of Labour Market Enforcement,* 5 January. Available at https://www.gov.uk/government/news/sir-david-metcalf-named-as-first-director-of-labour-market-enforcement.

Department for Business, Energy and Industrial Strategy (2017b) *Building Our Industrial Strategy.* Green Paper. London: Department for Business, Energy and Industrial Strategy.

Department for Education (2016a) *Educational Excellence Everywhere. Government consultation.* London: Department for Education.

Department for Education (2016b) *Schools that Work for Everyone. Government Consultation.* London: Department for Education.

Department for Work and Pensions (2014) *The Family Test: Guidance for Government Departments.* Available at http://www.gov.uk/government/uploads/system/uploads/attachment_data/file/368894/familt-test-guidance.pdf.

Dew-Becker, I. and Gordon, R.J. (2005) *Where Did the Productivity Growth Go? Inflation Dynamics and the Distribution of Income*. Brookings Papers on Economic Activities No. 2 2005: 67–127.

Dobbs, R., Lund, S., Woetzel, J. and Mutafchieva, M. (2015) *Debt and (Not Much) Deleveraging*. New York, NY: McKinsey Global Institute.

Dobbs, R., Madgavkar, A., Manyika, J., Woetzel, J., Bughin, J. Labaye, E. and Kashyap, P. (2016) *Poorer Than Their Parents? Flat or Falling Incomes in Advanced Economies*. New York, NY: McKinsey Global Institute.

Donovan, N. (2016) *A Unique Contribution: Reducing budget deficits and tackling inequality with a one-off wealth tax*. London: Fabian Society.

Dorling, D. (2011) *Injustice and the 1%*. London and New York, NY: Verso.

Dorling, D. (2012) *Fair Play. A Daniel Dorling Reader on Social Justice*, Bristol: Policy Press.

Dorling, D. (2014) *Inequality and the 1%*. London and New York, NY: Verso.

Dorling, D. (2015) Money changes everything, *Times Higher Education*, 12 February: 34–37.

Doward, J. (2016) Wave of top-level hirings fuels fear over Google's bid for political sway, *Observer*, 5 June: 8.

Doward, J. and Stevens, R. (2015) Britain's offshore tax havens at the heart of US investigation into World Cup corruption, *Observer*, 31 May: 5.

Drew, E. (2015) How money runs our politics, *New York Review of Books*, 4 June: 22–26.

Duncan, G.J. and Murnane, R.J. (2011) Introduction: The American dream, then and now, in G.J. Duncan and R.J. Murnane (eds) *Whither Opportunity? Rising Inequality, Schools, and Children's Life Chances*. New York, NY: Russell Sage Foundation, pp 3–23.

Drutman, L. (2015) *The Business of America is Lobbying: How Corporations Became Politicized and Politics Became More Corporate*. Oxford: University Press.

Eberstadt, R. (2016) *Men Without Work: America's Invisible Crisis*. West Conshohocken, PA: Templeton Press.

Economic Policy Institute (2016) *CEO Compensation, CEO-to-Worker Compensation Ratio, and stock prices, 1965–2015 (2015 dollars)*. Available at http://www.epi.org/publication/ceo-and-worker-pay-in-2015.

Economist (2015) America's elite. An hereditary meritocracy, 24 January 2015. Available at http://www.economist.com/news/briefing/21640316-children-rich-and-powerful-are-increasingly-well-suited-earning-wealth-and-power.

Eley, J. (2016) CGT rate proves we're not in it together, *Financial Times Money*, 9 April: 24.

Elliott, L. (2016) Cut taxes or invest? In the post-Brexit world, the answer to Hammond's dilemma is clear, *Guardian*, 29 August: 21.

Elming, W., Emmerson, C., Johnson, P. and Phillips, D. (2015) *An Assessment of the Potential Compensation Provided by the New 'National Living Wage'*. Briefing Note BN 175. London: IFS.

Elsby, M.W.L., Hobijn, B. and Sahin, A. (2013) *The Decline of the U.S. Labor Share*. Federal Reserve Bank of San Francisco Working Paper 2013-27. San Francisco, CA: Federal Reserve Bank.

Emmerson, C. (2017) *Two Parliaments of Pain: The UK Public Finances 2010 to 2017*. Briefing Note BN199. London: IFS.

End Child Poverty (2017) *4 Million Children Now Living in Poverty in the UK*. 16 March. Available at: http://www.endchildpoverty.org.uk/4-million-children-now-living-in-poverty-in-the-uk/.

Epstein, G. (ed) (2005) *Financialization and the World Economy*. Cheltenham: Edward Elgar.

Equality Trust (2014a) *About Inequality: Scale and Trends*. London: Equality Trust.

Equality Trust (2014b) *The Cost of Inequality*. London: Equality Trust.

Equality Trust (2017) *Inequality Set to Rise, Ignoring Experts Won't Make It Go Away*. 3 May. Available at: https://www.equalitytrust.org.uk/inequality-set-rise-ignoring-experts-wont-make-it-go-away.

Ermisch, J., Francesconi, M. and Siedler, T. (2005) *Intergenerational Economic Mobility and Assortative Mating*. Discussion Paper No. 1847. Munich: IZA.

Etherington, D. and Jones, M. (2016) The city-region chimera: the political economy of metagovernance failure in Britain, *Cambridge Journal of Regions, Economy and Society*, 9 (2): 259–268.

EY ITEM Club (2017) UK economy set for a 'hard rebalancing' says EY ITEM Club, 23 January. Available at http://www.ey.com/uk/en/newsroom/news-releases/17-01-23---uk-economy-set-for-a-hard-rebalancing-says-ey-item-club.

Fair Admissions Campaign (2013) Groundbreaking new research maps the segregating impact of faith school admissions, 3 December. Available at http://www.fairadmissions.org.uk/groundbreaking-new-research-maps-the-segregating-impact-of-faith-school-admissions.

Fair Education Alliance (2014) *Will We Ever Have a Fair Education For All?* London: Fair Education Alliance.

Farnsworth, K. (2013) Public policies for private corporations: the British corporate welfare state, *Renewal*, 21 (4): 51–65.

Farnsworth, K. (2015) *The British Corporate Welfare State: Public Provision for Private Businesses*. Sheffield Political Economy Research Institute Paper No. 24. Sheffield: University of Sheffield.

Financial Times (2016) The BoE has delivered: now for a fiscal response, 5 August: 10.

Finch, D. (2015) *Making the Most of Universal Credit. Final Report of the Resolution Foundation Review of Universal Credit*. London: Resolution Foundation.

Finch, D. (2016) *Hanging on. The Stresses and Strains of Britain's 'Just Managing' Families*. London: Resolution Foundation.

Fitoussi, J.P. and Saraceno, F. (2010) *Inequality and Macroeconomic Performance*. OFCE/POLHA Working Paper No. 2010-13. Available at https://ideas.repec.org/p/fec/doctra/1013.html.

Foerster, M.F. and Toth, I.G. (2015) Cross-country evidence of the multiple causes of inequality changes in the OECD Area. In A.B. Atkinson and F. Bourguignon (eds.) *Handbook of Income Distribution*, Vol. 2B, Amsterdam: Elsevier, pp 1729–1843.

Foerster, M., Llena-Nozal, A. and Nafilyan, V. (2014) *Trends in Top Incomes and Their Taxation in OECD Countries*. OECD Social, Employment and Migration Working Paper No. 159. Paris: OECD.

Ford, M. (2015) *The Rise of the Robots*. London: Oneworld Publications.

Foster, C.F. (2013) Wealth distribution and wealth creation in societies manufacturing cotton in Europe – Italy, Germany, Lancashire and Holland 1100 – 1780, in C.F. Foster and E.L. Jones *The Fabric of Society and How It Creates Wealth: Wealth Distribution and Wealth Creation in Europe 1000–1800*. Northwich, Cheshire: Arley Hall Press (pp. 37 – 115).

Fournier, J-M. and Koske, I. (2012) *Less Income Inequality and More Growth – Are They Compatible? Part 7. The Drivers of Labour Earnings Inequality – An Analysis Based on Conditional and Unconditional Quartile Regressions*. Economics Department Working Paper No. 930. Paris: OECD.

Francis, B. and Hutchings, M. (2013) *Parent Power? Using Money and Information to Boost Children's Chances of Educational Success*. London: Sutton Trust.

Frank, R.H. (1985) *Choosing the Right Pond: Human Behavior and the Quest for Status*. New York, NY: Oxford University Press.

Frank, R.H. (2007) In the real world of work and wages, trickle-down theories don't hold up, *New York Times*, 12 April: 16.

Frank, R.H. (2016) *Success and Luck: Good Fortune and the Myth of Meritocracy*. Princeton, NJ and Oxford: Princeton University Press.

Frank, R.H. and Cook, P.J. (2010) *The Winner-Take-All-Society: Why the Few at the Top Get So Much More Than the Rest of Us*. London: Virgin Books.

Frederiksen, K.B. (2012) *Less Income Inequality and More Growth – Are they Compatible? Part 6. The Distribution of Wealth*. Economics Department Working Paper No. 929. Paris: OECD.

Freeman, R. (1980) Unionism and the dispersion of wages, *Industrial and Labor Relations Review*, 34 (1): 3–23.

Freeman, R. (2006) *The Great Doubling: The Challenge of the New Global Labour Market*. Available at http://emlab.berkeley. edu/users/webfac/eichengreen/e183_sp07/great_doub.pdf.

Freeman, R. (2009) Globalization and Inequality. In W. Salverda, B. Nolan and T. Smeeding (eds) *Oxford Handbook of Economic Inequality*, Oxford: University Press, pp 575–589.

French, S. (2016) Four radical reforms to unleash a British productivity revolution, *The Times*, 27 December: 43.

Frey, C.B. and Osborne, M.A. (2013) *The Future of Employment: How Susceptible Are Jobs to Computerisation?* Available at http://www.oxfordmartin.ox.ac.uk/downloads/academic/The_Future_of_Employment.pdf.

Fritzell, J., Hertzman, J.B., Baekman, O., Borg, I., Ferrarini, T. and Nilson, K. (2014) Sweden: Increasing Income Inequalities and Changing Social Relations, in B. Nolan, W. Salverda, D. Checchi, I. Marx, A. McKnight, I.G. Toth and H. van de Werfhorst, H. (eds) *Changing Inequalities and Societal Impacts in Rich Countries: Thirty Countries' Experiences*, Oxford: University Press, pp 641–665.

Furceri, D. and Loungani, P. (2015) *Capital Account Liberalization and Inequality*. Working Paper 15/243. Washington, DC: IMF.

Furman, J. (2016) *The United States and Europe: Short-Run Divergences and Long-Run Challenges.* Remarks at Bruegel, Brussels, Belgium, 11 May. Available at http://bruegel.org/wp-content/uploads/2016/05/The-United-States-and-Europe-Short-Run-Divergence-and-Long-Run-Challenges-Jason-Furman.pdf.

Furman, J. and Orszag, P. (2015) *A Firm-Level Perspective on the Role of Rents in the Rise in Inequality*. Presentation at 'A Just Society' Centennial Event in Honor of Joseph Stiglitz, Columbia University, 16 October. Available at https://www.whitehouse.gov/sites/default/files/page/files/20151016_firm_level_perspective_on_role_of_rents_in_inequality.pdf.

Galbraith, J.K. (2007) Global inequality and global macroeconomics, *Journal of Policy Modelling*, 29: 587–607.

Galbraith, J.K. (2012) *Inequality and Instability: A Study of the World Economy Just Before the World Crisis.* Oxford and New York, NY: Oxford University Press.

Galbraith, J.K. (2016) *Inequality: What Everyone Needs to Know.* Oxford: University Press.

Galor, O. and Zeira, J. (1993) Income distribution and macroeconomics, *Review of Economic Studies*, 60: 35–52.

Gamble, A. (2014) *Crisis Without End? The Unravelling of Western Prosperity.* London and New York, NY: Palgrave Macmillan.

Gardiner, L. (2016) *Stagnation Generation: The Case for Renewing the Intergenerational Contract.* London: Resolution Foundation.

Garside, J. (2016a) Benefit fraud or tax evasion: row over Tories' targets, *Guardian*, 14 April: 1, 8.

Garside, J. (2016b) Duke's death prompts call for tax reform, *Guardian*, 12 August: 4.

Gates, B. (2014) Available at http://www.gatesnotes.com/Books/Why-Inequality-Matters-Capital-in-21st-Century-Review. 13 October 2014.

George, M. (2017a) The £53 million bill for 'related party transactions', *Times Educational Supplement*, 13 January: 14.

George, M. (2017b) Academies break pay rules by refusing to reveal salaries, *Times Educational Supplement*, 17 February: 12–13.

George, M. (2017c) Academy moves marred by 'conflicts of interest', *Times Educational Supplement*, 10 March: 8–9.

George, M. (2017d) 'There'd be outrage if this happened in the private sector', *Times Educational Supplement*, 9 June: 15–16.

Ghelani, D. (2016) *'Just About Managing' Families Hardest Hit by Welfare Reforms*. Press release, 21 November. Available at policyinpractice.co.uk/just-managing-families-hardest-hit-welfare-reforms-2020.

Gilens, M. and Page, B.I. (2014) Testing theories of American politics: elites, interest groups, and average citizens, *Perspectives on Politics*. Available at https://scholar.princeton.edu/sites/default/files/mgilens/files/gilens_and_page_2014-testing_theories_of_american_politics.

Gilens, M. and Page, B.I. (2016) Critics argued with our analysis of U.S. political inequality. Here are 5 ways they're wrong, *Washington Post*, 23 May. Available at https://www.washingtonpost.com/news/monkey-cage/wp/2016/05/23/critics-challenge-our-portrait-of-americas-political-inequality-here.

Glatter, R. (2010) Changing organisational structures: Will we never learn? *Education Review*, 23 (1): 15–24.

Glatter, R. (2014) Educational administration 1969–2014: reflections on pragmatism, agency and reform, *Journal of Educational Administration and History*, 46 (3): 351–366.

Goldin, C. and Katz, L.F. (2008) *The Race Between Education and Technology*. Cambridge, MA and London: Harvard University Press.

Goldrick-Rab, S. (2016) *Paying the Price: College Costs, Financial Aid, and the Betrayal of the American Dream*. Chicago: University Press.

Goodley, S. (2014) Britain slides down world equality table as gender gap widens in the workplace, *Guardian* 28 October: 3.

Goodley, S., Newman, M. and Mathiason, N. (2014) Revealed: How exclusive Tory ball plays matchmaker to donors and politicians, *Guardian*, 13 October: 3.

Goos, M. and Manning, A. (2003) *Lousy and Lovely Jobs: The Rising Polarization of Work in Britain*. Centre for Economic Performance Discussion Paper No. DP 0604, London: LSE.

Goos, M., Manning, A. and Salomons, A. (2011) *Explaining Job Polarisation: The Roles of Technology, Offshoring and Institutions*. Centre for Economic Studies Discussion Paper 11.34. Leuven: Katholieke Universiteit.

Gorard, S. (2013) *Growth of Academies and Free Schools Reinforces Student Segregation*. Available at http://theconversation.com/growth-of-academies-and-free-schools-reinforces-student-segregation-19411.

Gordon, R.J. (2012) *Is US Economic Growth over? Faltering Innovation Confronts the Six Headwinds*. Center for Economic Policy Research Policy Insight No. 63. Available at http://www.cepr.org/sites/default/files/policy_insights/PolciyInsight63.pdf.

Gordon, R.J. (2016) *The Rise and Fall of American Growth*. Princeton, NJ and Oxford: Princeton University Press.

Gosling, A. and Lemieux, T. (2001) *Labour Market Reforms and Changes in Wage Inequality in the United Kingdom and the United States*. NBER Working Paper No. 8413. Cambridge, MA: NBER.

Government Equalities Office (2010) *An Anatomy of Economic Inequality in the UK. Report of the National Equality Panel*. London: Government Equalities Office.

Green, F., Machin, S., Murphy, R. and Zhu, Y. (2008) Competition for private and state school teachers, *Journal of Education and Work*, 21 (5): 383–484.

Greenwood, R. and Scharfstein, D. (2013) The growth of finance, *Journal of Economic Perspectives*, 27 (2): 3–28.

Greenwood, J., Guner, N., Kocharkov, G. and Santos, C. (2014) Marry your like: Assortative mating and income inequality, *American Economic Review*, 104 (5): 348–353.

Gregory, T., Salomons, A. and Zierahn, U. (2016) *Racing with or against the machine? Evidence from Europe*. Discussion Paper No. 16-053. Mannheim: Centre for European Economic Research.

Gross, B. (2016) Central bankers are threatening the engine of the economy, *Financial Times*, 18 August: 14.

Guardian and Press Association (2014) Poorest UK households pay almost half their income in tax, campaigners say, 22 December 2014. Available at http://www.theguardian.com/money/2014/dec/22/poorest-uk-households-pay-half-income-tax-campaigners.

Hacker, J.S. and Pierson, P. (2010) *Winner-Take-All Politics: How Washington Made the Rich Richer and Turned Its Back on the Middle Class*. New York, NY and London: Simon and Shuster.

Haldane, A.G. (2015) *Labour's Share*. Speech at the Trades Union Congress, 12 November 2015. Available at http://www.bankofengland.co.uk/publications/Documents/speeches/2015/speech864.pdf.

Haldane, A.G. (2016a) *Whose Recovery?* Speech at Port Talbot, 30 June. Available at http://www.bankofengland.co.uk/publications/Pages/speeches/2016/916.aspx.

Haldane, A.G. (2016b) *One Car, Two Car, Red Car, Blue Car*. Speech at Redcar, 2 December. Available at http://www.bankofengland.co.uk/publications/Pages/speeches/2016/945.aspx.

Haldane, A., Brennan, S. and Madouros, V. (2010) What is the contribution of the financial sector: Miracle or mirage? In A. Turner et al. (eds) *The Future of Finance: The LSE Report*, London: LSE, pp 87–120.

Hall, B. and Murphy, K. (2003) The trouble with stock options, *Journal of Economic Perspectives*, 17 (3): 49–70.

Hanushek, E.A. and Woessmann, L. (2006) Does educational tracking affect performance and inequality? Differences-in-differences evidence across countries, *Economic Journal*, 116: C63-C76.

Hanushek, E.A. and Woessmann, L. (2012) Do better schools lead to more growth? Cognitive skills, economic outcomes, and causation, *Journal of Economic Growth*, 17: 267–321.

Harjes, T. (2007) *Globalization and Income Inequality: A European Perspective*. Working Paper WP/07/169, Washington, DC: IMF.

Harrington, B. (2016) *Capital Without Barriers: Wealth Managers and the One Percent*. Cambridge, MA and London: Harvard University Press.

Harrop, A. and Reed, H. (2016) *Inequality 2030. Britain's Choice for Living Standards and Poverty*. London: Fabian Society.

Hass, L.H., Liu, J., Young, S. and Zhang, Z. (2016) *Measuring and Rewarding Performance: Theory and Evidence in Relation to Executive Compensation*. Available at https://secure.cfauk.org/assets/1298/Remuneration_Report.pdf.

Hausman, J.A. and Sidak, J.G. (2004) Why do the poor and the less-educated pay more for long distance calls? *Contributions to Economic Analysis and Policy*, 3 (1): 1–27.

Hazell, W. (2017) The secret deals behind rocketing CEO salaries, *Times Educational Supplement,* 24 March, 18-21.

Heavy (2017) List of Goldman Sachs alumni in Donald Trump's administration. 5 January. Available at http://heavy.com/news/2017/01/donald-trump-goldman-sachs-drain-swamp-steve-bannon-steven-mnuchin-gary-cohn-jay-clayton.

Hein, E. and Mundt, M. (2013) Financialization, the financial and economic crisis, and the requirements and potentials for wage-led recovery, in M. Lavoie and E. Stockhammer (eds) *Wage-led Growth: An Equitable Strategy for Economic Recovery*. Basingstoke and New York, NY: Palgrave Macmillan, *pp* 153–186.

Helleiner, E. (1994) *States and the Re-emergence of Global Finance, from Bretton Woods to the 1990s*. Ithaca, NY: Cornell University Press.

Henry, S.G.B. (2014) The Coalition's economic strategy; has it made a bad thing worse? *Economic Outlook*, 38 (2): 14–20.

Herzer, D. and Vollmer, S. (2013) Rising top incomes do not raise the tide, *Journal of Policy Making*, 35 (4): 504–519.

High Pay Centre (2016) *HPC Submission to the BIS Select Committee Corporate Governance Enquiry October 2016, Executive Summary.* Available at http://highpaycentre.org/pubs/hpc-submission-to-the-bis-select-committee-corporate-governance-enquiry-october.

Hills, J. (2014) *Good Times, Bad Times: The Welfare Myth of Them and Us.* Bristol and Chicago, IL: Policy Press.

Hirsch, D. (2015) *Will the 2015 Summer Budget Improve Living Standards in 2020?* York: Joseph Rowntree Foundation.

Hirsch, F. (1976) *Social Limits to Growth.* Harvard, MA: Harvard University Press.

HMRC (2016a) *Tackling Tax Evasion: Legislation and Guidance for a Corporate Offence of Failure to Prevent the Criminal Facilitation of Tax Evasion.* Consultation document, 17 April. London: HMRC.

HMRC (2016b) *Strengthening Tax Avoidance Sanctions and Deterrents.* Discussion document, 17 August. London: HMRC.

HMRC (2016c) *Tackling Offshore Tax Evasion: A Requirement to Correct.* Consultation document, 24 August. London: HMRC.

HM Treasury (2013) *New Rules Use Government Buying Power against Tax Avoidance*, 14 February. Available at http://www.gov.uk/government/news/new-rules-use-government-buying-power-against-tax-avoidance, accessed 29 November 2016.

HM Treasury (2015a) *Reforms to the Taxation of Non-Domiciles*, 30 September. Available at https://www.gov.uk/government/consultations/reforms-to-the-taxation-of-non-domiciles.

HM Treasury (2015b) *Spending Review and Autumn Statement.* London: HM Treasury.

HM Treasury (2016a) *Autumn Statement 2016.* London: HM Treasury.

HM Treasury (2016b) *Reducing the Money Purchase Annual Allowance.* London: HM Treasury.

HM Treasury (2016c) *Reforms to the Taxation of Non-Domiciles: Response to Further Consultation.* London: HM Treasury.

HM Treasury (2017) *Spring Budget 2017.* HC 1025. London: HM Treasury.

Holmwood, J. (2014) Beyond capital? The challenge for sociology in Britain, *British Journal of Sociology*, 65 (4): 607–618.

Hood, A. and Johnson, P. (2016) *Are We 'All in this Together'?* London: IFS.

Hood, A. and Joyce, R. (2017) *Inheritances and Inequality across and within Generations.* Briefing Note BN 192. London: IFS.

Hood, A. and Waters, T. (2017) *Incomes and inequality: the last decade and the next parliament.* Briefing Note BN202. London: IFS.

Hopkins, N., Harding, L. and Mason, R. (2017) UK Banks Face Inquiry over Russian Scam, *The Guardian,* 22 March: 1, 15.

Houlder, V. (2014) Avoidance, evasion and other losses see tax gap rise to £34bn, *Financial Times*, 17 October, 6.

House of Commons Business, Energy and Industrial Strategy Committee (2016) *Employment Practices at Sports Direct.* Third Report of Session 2016–17. HC 219. London: The Stationery Office Limited.

House of Commons Committee of Public Accounts (2015a) *Tax Avoidance: The Role of Large Accountancy Firms – Follow-up.* Thirty-eighth Report of Session 2014–15. HC 1057. London: The Stationery Office Limited.

House of Commons Committee of Public Accounts (2015b) *HM Revenue and Customs Performance in 2014–15.* Sixth Report of Session 2015–16. HC 393. London: The Stationery Office Limited.

House of Commons Committee of Public Accounts (2016a) *Tackling Tax Fraud.* Thirty-fourth Report of Session 2015–16. HC 674. London: The Stationery Office Limited.

House of Commons Committee of Public Accounts (2016b) *The Apprenticeships Programme.* Twenty-eighth Report of Session 2016–17. HC 709. London: The Stationery Office Ltd.

House of Commons Committee of Public Accounts (2016c) *HM Revenue and Customs Performance in 2015–16.* Twenty-ninth Report of Session 2016–17. HC 712. London: The Stationery Office Limited.

House of Commons Committee of Public Accounts (2017) *Collecting Tax from High Net Worth Individuals.* Thirty-sixth Report of Session 2016–17. HC 774. London: The Stationery Office Limited.

House of Commons Committee on Standards in Public Life (2011) *Political Party Finance: Ending the Big Donor Culture*. Thirteenth Report. Cm 8208. London: The Stationery Office Limited.

Howson, J. (2010) How to cut millions of pounds without harming the chalk face, *Times Educational Supplement*, 17 September: 32–33.

Hutton, W. (2014) This pensions 'freedom' will be a long-term social disaster, *Observer*, 23 March: 38.

Hutton, W. (2015a) British capitalism is broken: Here's how to fix it, *Guardian*, 11 February: 27–29.

Hutton, W. (2015b) *How Good We Can Be: Ending the Mercenary Society and Building a Great Country*. London: Little, Brown.

Hutton, W. (2017) Overhaul our rotten tax system or we won't be able to sustain a healthy state, *The Observer*, 23 April: 38.

ILO (2014) *Global Wage Report 2014/15 Wages and Income Inequality*. Geneva: ILO.

ILO (2015) *The Labour Share in G20 Economies*. Geneva: ILO.

ILO (2016) *Non-Standard Employment Around the World*. Geneva: ILO.

IMF (2008) *Issues Brief. Globalization: A Brief Overview*. 02/08. Washington, DC: IMF.

IMF (2013) *Fiscal Monitor October 2013 Taxing Times*. Available at http://imf.org/external/pubs/ft/fm/2013/02/pdf/fm1302. pdf.

IMF (2015) *Financial Stability Report April 2015*. Washington, DC: IMF.

IMF (2016) *IMF Executive Board Concludes 2015 Article IV Consultation with the United Kingdom*, Press release, 24 February. Available at http://www.imf.org/externalnp/sec/pr/2016/pr1671.htm.

Impetus-PEF (2016) *Youth Jobs Index*. Available at http://www.impetus-pef.org.uk/policy-initiatives/youth-jobs-index.

Inman, P. (2016) We must borrow to build for young people's sake. Right now, *Observer*, 25 September, 42.

Institute for Government (2017) *General Election 2017: Five Key Manifesto Promises*. Available at: https://www.instituteforgovernment.org.uk/publications/general-election-2017-five-key-manifesto-promises.

Jack, S. (2017) May's social care pledge could be huge wealth tax, 19 May. Available at: http://www.bbc.co.uk/news/business-39977559.

Jacobs, M. and Mazzucato, M. (2016) *Rethinking Capitalism: Economics and Policy for Sustainable and Inclusive Growth.* Chichester: Wiley-Blackwell.

Jaumotte, F., Lall, S. and Papageorgiu, C. (2008) *Rising Income Inequality: Technology, or Trade and Financial Globalization?* Working Paper WP/08/185. Washington, DC: IMF.

Jaumotte, F. and Koske, I. (2014) Conclusion: Growth-enhancing policies and inequality, in P. Hoeller, I. Journard and I. Koske (eds) *Income Inequality in OECD Countries: What Are the Drivers and Policy Options?* New Jersey and London: World Scientific Publishing, pp 207–222.

Jaumotte, F. and Buitron, C.O. (2015) *Inequality and Labor Market Institutions.* Staff Discussion Note SDN/15/14. Washington, DC: IMF.

Jenkins, S.P. (2015) *The Income Distribution in the UK: A Picture of Advantage and Disadvantage.* Centre for the Analysis of Social Exclusion CASE Paper No. 186. London: LSE.

Jenkins, S.P., Micklewright, J. and Schnepf, S.V. (2006) *Social Segregation in Secondary Schools: How does England Compare with Other Countries?* Institute for Social and Economic Research. Colchester: University of Essex.

Jerrim, J. and Macmillan, L. (2014) *Income Inequality, Intergenerational Mobility and the Great Gatsby Curve: Is Education the Key?* Department of Quantitative Social Science, Working Paper No. 14-18. London: UCL Institute of Education.

Johnes, R. and Andrews, J. (2016) *Faith Schools, Pupil Performance and Social Selection.* Education Policy Institute, 2 December 2016. Available at http://epi.org.uk/report/faith-schools-pupil-performance-social-selection/#.

Johnson, B. (2013) *What Would Maggie do Today?* Boris Johnson's speech at the Margaret Thatcher lecture in full. Available at http://www.telegraph.co.uk/news/politics/london-mayor-election-mayor-of-london/10480321/Boris-Johnsons-speech-at-the -Margaret-Thatcher-lecture-in-full.html.

Johnson, P. (2015a) *Pension Policy – Where Have We Been, Where Are We Going,* 20 October. London: IFS.

Johnson, P. (2015b) *Autumn Statement 2015: IFS Briefing, Paul Johnson's Opening Remarks*, 26 November. Available at https://www.ifs.org/uploads/publications/budgets/Budgets%202015/Autumn/SR_Nov_2015_opening_remarks.pdf.

Johnson, P. (2016) *Autumn Statement 2016: IFS briefing, Paul Johnson's Opening remarks*, 24 November. Available at https://www.ifs.org.uk/uploads/budgets/as2016/as2016_pj.pdf.

Jones, O. (2014) *The Establishment*. London: Penguin.

Joseph Rowntree Foundation (2016) *A Minimum Income Standard for the UK*, 20 July. Available at https://www.jrf.org.uk/report/minimum-income-threshold-uk-2016.

Judt, T. (2010) *Ill Fares the Land,* London: Allen Lane.

Juhn, C., Murphy, K.M. and Pierce, B. (1993) Wage inequality and the returns to skill, *The Journal of Political Economy*, 101 (3): 410–442.

Kamm, O. (2016) Britain should seize this rare opportunity to borrow and spend, *The Times*, 27 September: 41.

Kaplan, J. (2015) *Humans Need Not Apply: A Guide to Wealth and Work in the Age of Artificial Intelligence*. New Haven, CT and London: Yale University Press.

Kaplan, S. and Rauh, J. (2010) *Wall Street and Main Street: What Contributes to the Rise in the Highest Incomes?* NBER Working Paper 13270. Available at http://www.nber.org/papers/w13270.

Karabarbounis, L. and Neiman, B. (2012) *Declining Labor Shares and the Global Rise of Corporate Saving*. NBER Working Paper w18154. Cambridge, MA: NBER.

Karabarbounis, L. and Neiman, B. (2013) The global decline of the labor share, *Quarterly Journal of Economics*, 129 (1): 61–103.

Katz, A. (2015) *The Influence Machine: The US Chamber of Commerce and the Corporate Capture of American Life*. New York, NY: Spiegel and Grau.

Kettle, M. (2017) Mayism has arrived, but where are the Mayites? *Guardian*, 19 May: 36.

King, I. (2016) Unpicking the triple lock is key to much-needed pension reform, *The Times*, 18 July: 39.

King, S.D. (2013) *When the Money Runs Out: The End of Western Affluence*. New Haven, CT and London: Yale University Press.

King, S.D. (2016) Why Theresa May is so critical of monetary policy, *Financial Times*, 12 October 2016. Available at https://www.ft.com/content/49164ebf-fc84-32e0-bf6d-71c130445b47.

Kington, T. (2017) Italy leaves Britain with £240m deal, *The Times*, 11 January: 15.

Klein, J. (2014) *Lessons of Hope: How to Fix Our Schools.* New York: HarperCollins.

Kliman, A. (2012) *The Failure of Capitalist Production. Underlying Causes of the Great Recession.* London: Pluto Press.

Kluve, J. (2010) The effectiveness of European active labor market programs, *Labor Economics*, 17: 904–918.

Kolev, A. and Saget, C. (2010) *Are Middle-Paid Jobs in OECD Countries Disappearing? An Overview.* Working Paper No. 96. Geneva: ILO.

Kotkin, J. (2015) Seven years ago, Wall Street was the villain. Now it gets to call the shots, *Observer*, 4 January: 29.

Krippner, G.R. (2011) *Capitalizating on Crisis: The Political Origins of the Rise of Finance*, Cambridge, MA: Harvard University Press.

Kristal, T. (2010) Good times, bad times: Postwar labor's share of national income in capitalist democracies, *American Sociological Review*, 75 (5): 729–763.

Krueger, A.B. (2012) *The Rise and Consequences of Inequality in the United States.* Speech delivered at the Center for American Progress, January 12. Available at http://www.whitehouse. gov/sites/default/files/krueger_cap_speech_final_remarks.pdf.

Krueger, A.B. (2013) *Land of Hope and Dreams: Rock and Roll, Economics and Rebuilding the Middle Class.* Remarks at the Rock and Roll Hall of Fame, Cleveland, Ohio, 12 June. Available at www.whitehouse.gov/blog/2013/06/12/rock-and-roll-economics-and-rebuilding-middle-class#fulltext.

Krueger, A.O. (1974) The political economy of the rent-seeking society, *American Economic Review*, 64 (3): 291–303.

Krugman, P. (2007) *The Conscience of a Liberal: Reclaiming America from the Right.* London: Allen Lane.

Krugman, P. (2014) Why We're in a New Gilded Age. Review of Thomas Piketty's *Capital in the Twenty-First Century. New York Review of Books*, 8 May: 15–18.

Krugman, P. (2015) Review of 'Saving Capitalism: For the Many, Not the Few'. Available at http://www.nybooks.com/articles/2015/12/12/12/17/robert-reich-challenging-oligarchy/?printpage=true.

Kumhof, M. and Ranciere, R. (2010) *Inequality, Leverage and Crises*. Working Paper WP/10/268. Washington, DC: IMF.

Kumhof, M., Lebarz, C., Ranciere, R., Richter, A.W. and Throckmorton, N.A. (2012) *Income Inequality and Current Account Balances*. Working Paper WP/12/08. Washington, DC: IMF.

Kuttner, R. (2014) Review of *The Fissured Workplace: Why Work Became So Bad For So Many and What Can Be Done To Improve It* by David Weil. *New York Review of Books*, October 23: 52–53.

Kuznets, S. (1955) Economic growth and income inequality, *American Economic Review*, 45 (1): 1–28.

Labour Party (2017) *For The Many, Not The Few. The Labour Party Manifesto 2017*. London: The Labour Party.

Lansley, S. (2011) *The Cost of Inequality: Three Decades of the Super-Rich and the Economy*. London: Gibson Square.

Lansley, S. (2016) *A Sharing Economy: How Social Wealth Funds Can Reduce Inequality and Help Balance the Books*. Bristol and Chicago, IL: Policy Press.

Lansley, S. and Reed, H. (2013) *How to Boost the Wage Share*. Touchstone Pamphlet#13. London: TUC.

Lavoie, M. and Stockhammer, E. (2013) Wage-led growth: Concept, theories and policies, in M. Lavoie and E. Stockhammer (eds) *Wage-Led Growth: An Equitable Strategy for Economic Recovery*. Basingstoke and New York, NY: Palgrave Macmillan, pp 13–39.

Lawrence, F. (2017) Who'll pay for the multinational tax grab? *The Guardian,* 26 May: 31.

Lazonick, W. (2013) The financialization of the U.S. corporation: What has been lost, and how it can be regained, *Seattle University Law Review*, 36: 857–910.

Lazonick, W. (2014) Profits without prosperity: Stock buybacks manipulate the market and leave most Americans worse off, *Harvard Business Review*, September: 47–55.

Legatum Institute and Centre for Social Justice (2016) *48:52 Healing a Divided Britain*. London: Legatum Institute and Centre for Social Justice.

Leigh, A. (2007) How closely do top income shares track other measures of inequality? *The Economic Journal*, 117: 619–633.

Lemieux, T. (2008) The changing nature of wage inequality, *Journal of Population Economics*, 21: 21–48.

Lemieux, T., MacLeod, W.B. and Parent, D. (2007) *Performance Pay and Wage Inequality*. NBER Working Paper No. 13128. Harvard, MA: NBER.

Leveson, L.J. (2012) *Leveson Inquiry: Culture, Practices and Ethics of the Press*. Available at http://www.official-documents.gov.uk/document/hc1213/hc07/0780/0780.asp.

Levin, S. (2016) Angry web post by US tech CEO reignites debate on inequality, *Guardian*, 4 June: 15.

Levy, F. and Temin, P. (2007) *Inequality and Institutions in 20th Century America*. MIT Department of Economics Working Paper 07-17. Available at http://ssrn.com/abstract=984330.

Longworth, R.C. (2009) *America's Heartland in the Age of Globalism*. London: Bloomsbury.

Lupton, R. and nine others (2015) *The Coalition's Social Policy Record: Policy, Spending and Outcomes 2010–2015*. Social Policy in a Cold Climate, Research Report 4. London: LSE.

Lynch, L.M. (2014) *Commentary: Polanyi's Paradox and the Shape of Employment Growth*. Available at https://www.kansascityfed.org/publicat/sympos/2014/2014lynch.pdf.

Machin, S. (2009) Education and inequality, in W. Salverda, B. Nolan and T. Smeeding (eds) *The Oxford Handbook of Inequality*. Oxford: University Press, pp 261–307.

Maguire, J. (2014) How increasing income inequality is dampening U.S. economic growth and possible ways to change the tide. *Economic Research*, 5 August. Available at https://www.globalcreditportal.com/ratingsdirect.

Manyika, J., Chui, M., Bughin, J., Dobbs, R., Bisson, P. and Marrs, A. (2013) *Disruptive Technologies: Advances that Will Transform Life, Business and the Global Economy*. New York, NY: McKinsey Global Institute.

Marmot, M. (2015) *The Health Gap: The Challenge of an Unequal World*. London: Bloomsbury.

Marshall, A. (1890) *Principles of Economics.* London: Macmillan.

Marshall, P. (2015) Blame the rise of the plutocrats on politics not capitalism, *Financial Times*, 9 January: 13.

Martin, D. (2015) We're ruled by a cosy elite who all go to the same dinner parties, says former No 10 policy guru chief Steve Hilton, *Mail Online*, 17 May. Available at http://www.dailymail.co.uk/news/article-3085342/Stop-listening-insular-ruling-elite-help-poor-Cameron-s-ex-guru-Steve-Hilton-warns-Tory-PM.html.

Martin, J. and Grubb, D. (2001) *What Works and for Whom: A Review of OECD Countries' Experiences with Active Labour Market Policies.* IFAU – Office of Labour Market Policy Evaluation Working Paper 2001:14. Paris: OECD.

Martin, J. and Immervoll, H. (2007) The minimum wage: Making it pay. *OECD Observer* No. 261.

Marx, I. and Van Rie, T. (2014) The policy response to inequality: Redistributing income, in W. Salverda, B. Nolan, D. Checchi, I. Marx, A. McKnight, I.G. Toth, and H. van de Werfhorst (eds) *Changing Inequalities in Rich Countries: Analytical and Comparative Perspectives.* Oxford: University Press, pp 239–264.

Marx, I. and Verbist, G. (2014) The policy response: Boosting employment and social investment, in W. Salverda, B. Nolan, D. Checchi, I. Marx, A. McKnight, I.G. Toth, and H. van de Werfhorst (eds) *Changing Inequalities in Rich Countries: Analytical and Comparative Perspectives.* Oxford: University Press, pp 265–293.

Marx, I., Nolan, B. and Olivera, J. (2014) *The Welfare State and Anti-Poverty Policy in Rich Countries.* IZA Discussion Paper No. 8154. Antwerp: Forschungsinstitut zur Zukunft der Arbeit.

Mason, R. (2015) Election surge in political donations sees record total for past year of over £100m, *Guardian*, 29 May: 14.

May, T. (2016a) Economy must work for everyone in a truly Great Britain, *The Times*, 11 July: 7.

May, T. (2016b) *Statement from the new Prime Minister Theresa May*, 13 July. Available at https://www.gov.uk/government/speeches/statement-from-the-new-prime-minister-theresa-may.

May, T. (2016c) *Britain the Great Meritocracy: Prime Minister's speech*, 9 September. Available at https://www.gov.uk/government/speeches/britain-the-great-meritocracy-prime-ministers-speech.

May, T. (2016d) *Speech to the Conservative Party Conference*, 5 October. Available at https://www.politicshome.com/news/uk/political-parties/conservative-party/conferences/nes/79596/read-thersa-mays-full-speech.

May, T. (2016e) *Speech to the CBI Conference*, 21 November. Available at https://www.gov.uk/government/speeches/cbi-annual-conference-2016-prime-ministers-speech.

May, T. (2017a) *The Shared Society: Prime Minister's speech at the Charity Commission annual meeting*, 9 January. Available at https://www.gov.uk/government/speeches/the-shared-society-prime-ministers-speech-at-the-charity-commission-annual-meeting.

May, T. (2017b) *Theresa May's Brexit speech in full*, 17 January. Available at http://www.telegraph.co.uk/news/2017/01/17/theresa-mays-brexit-speech-full/.

Mayer, C. (2013) *Firm Commitment: Why the Corporation is Failing Us.* Oxford: University Press.

Mazzucato, M. (2013) *The Entrepreneurial State: Debunking Public vs. Private Sector Myths.* London, New York, NY and Delhi: Anthem Books.

McCall, A. and Watts, R. (2017) Five of UK's richest men bankrolled Brexit, *The Sunday Times*, 23 April: 4.

McCarty, N., Poole, K. and Rosenthal, H. (2006) *Polarized America: The Dance of Ideology and Unequal Riches.* Harvard: MIT Press.

McKnight, A. and Cowell, F. (2014) Social Impacts: Health, Housing, Intergenerational Mobility, in W. Salverda, B. Nolan, D. Checchi, I. Marx, A. McKnight, I.G. Toth and H. van de Werfhorst (eds) *Changing Inequalities in Rich Countries: Analytical and Comparative Perspectives*, Oxford: University Press, pp 169–194.

McLanahan, S. (2004) Diverging destinies: How children are faring under the second demographic transition, *Demography*, 41 (4): 607–627.

McNally, A. (2015) *Debtonator: How Debt Favours the Few and Equity Can Work For All of Us.* London: Elliott and Thompson Limited.

Media Reform Coalition (2015) *Who Owns the UK Media?* Available at http://www.mediareform.org.uk/wp-content/uploads/2015/10/Who-_owns_the_UK_media-report_plus_appendix1.pdf.

Meek, J. (2012) *Human Revenue Stream*, 20 March 2012. Available at http://www.lrb.co.uk/blog/2012/03/20/james-meek/human-revenue-stream.

Meek, J. (2014) Where will we live? *London Review of Books.* 9 January. Available at http://www.lrb.co.uk/v36/n01/james-meek/where-will-we-live.

Mell, A., Radford, S. and Thevoz, S.A. (2015) *Is There a Market for Peerages?* Discussion Paper No. 744. Oxford: Department of Economics.

Merrick, R. (2016) Electoral Commission warns of 'lost' voters, 18 July. Available at http://www.ukauthority.com/news/6347/electoral-commission-warns-of-lost-voters#.

Mettler, S. (2014) *Degrees of Inequality: How the Politics of Higher Education Sabotaged the American Dream.* New York: Basic Books.

Mian, A. and Sufi, A. (2014) *House of Debt: How They (and You) Caused the Great Recession, and How We Can Prevent It from Happening Again.* Chicago, IL and London: University of Chicago Press.

Milanovic, B. (2011) *The Haves and the Have-Nots: A Brief and Idiosyncratic History of Global Inequality.* New York: Basic Books.

Milanovic, B. (2016) *Global Inequality: A New Approach for the Age of Globalization.* Cambridge, MA: Harvard University Press.

Ministry of Justice (2017) *Review of the Introduction of Fees in the Employment Tribunals: Consultation on Proposals for Reform.* Cm 9373. London: Ministry of Justice.

Minton, A. (2015) Locals left hungry: Why Britain's 'broken' planning system allows speculators to benefit from rising land values instead of communities, *Financial Times, House and Home,* 24/25 January: 10.

Mirrlees, J., Adam, S., Besley, T., Blundell, R., Bond, S., Chote, R., Gammie, M., Johnson, P., Myles, G. and Poterba, J. (2011) *Tax by Design*. Oxford: University Press.

Mishel, L., Bivens, J., Gould, E. and Shierholz, H. (2012) *The State of Working America*. Ithaca, NY and London: ILR Press.

Mishel, L., Shierholz, H. and Schmitt, J. (2013) *Don't Blame the Robots: Assessing the Job Polarization Explanation of Growing Wage Inequality*. Washington, DC: Economic Policy Institute.

Mishkin, S. and Chon, G. (2014) Google overtakes Goldman Sachs in US political lobbying stakes, *Financial Times*, 17 October: 1, 8.

Mitchell, A. and Sikka, P. (2014) The nonsense of shareholder ownership: What we should know, 3 September. Available at http://leftfootforward.org/2014/09/the-nonsense-of-shareholder-ownership-what-we-should-know/#more-87768 (accessed 7 September 2014).

Monaghan, A. (2017) Aviva: savings reveal growing gap between rich and poor, *The Guardian*, 20 February, 4.

Moody's (2016) Announcement: Moody's: US corporate cash pile, led by tech sector, to grow to $1.77 trillion by end of 2016, 3 November. Available at https://www.moodys.com/research/Moodys-US-corporate-cash-pile-led-by-tech-sector-to--PR_357576.

Monbiot, G. (2017) Dark money is pushing democracy in the UK over the edge, *The Guardian*, 17 May. Available at https://www.theguardian.com/commentisfree/2017/may/17/dark-money-democracy-billionaires-funding.

Morgenson, G. (2016) Portland adopts surcharge on C.E.O. pay in move vs. income inequality, *New York Times*, 7 December. Available at https://www.nytimes.com/2016/12/07/business/economy/portland-oregon-tax-executive-pay.html.

Mosseri-Marlio, W. (2016) Available at https://socialshorthand.com/wmossermarlio/j2Mb6mtF1P/cost-of-the-triple-lock-is-set-to-surpass-pound20-billion.

Murphy, R. (2014) The tax gap. Available at http://www.taxresearch.org.uk/Documents/PCSTaxGap2014.pdf.

Murphy, R. (2015) Flush out the cash caches. Review of *The Hidden Wealth of Nations* by Gabriel Zucman, *Times Higher Education*, 5 November: 44–45.

Murphy, R. (2017) Why becoming a tax haven would be bad news for Britain, *The Guardian2,* 24 March: 10-11.

NAO (2014a) *Tax Reliefs.* London: NAO.

NAO (2014b) *The Effective Management of Tax Reliefs.* London: NAO.

NAO (2016a) *HMRC's Approach to Collecting Tax from High Net Worth Individuals.* London: NAO.

NAO (2016b) *Financial Sustainability of Schools.* London: NAO.

NAO (2017) *Capital Funding for Schools.* London: NAO.

Nat Cen Social Research (2016) Britain divided? Public attitudes after seven years of austerity, 30 June. Available at http://www.natcen.ac.uk/news-media/press-releases/2016/june/britain-divided-public-attitudes-after-seven-years-of-austerity.

Nolan, B., Salverda, W., Checchi, D., Marx, I., McKnight, A., Toth, I.G. and van de Werfhorst, H. (eds) (2014) *Changing Inequalities and Societal Impacts in Rich Countries: Thirty Countries' Experiences.* Oxford: University Press.

Nordhaus, W.D. (2015) *Are We Approaching an Economic Singularity? IT and the Future of Economic Growth.* NBER Working Paper No. 21547. Harvard, MA: NBER.

Nordhaus, W.D. (2016) Review of *The Rise and Fall of American Growth: The US Standard of Living Since the Civil War* by Robert J. Gordon, *New York Review of Books,* August 18. Available at http://www.nybooks.com/articles/2016/08/18/why-economic-growth-will-fall/?printpage=true.

OECD (2008) *Growing Unequal? Income Distribution and Poverty in OECD Countries,* Paris: OECD.

OECD (2010a) *PISA 2009 Results: Overcoming Social Background: Equity in Learning Opportunities and Outcomes. Volume II,* Paris: OECD.

OECD (2010b) *Viewing the United Kingdom School System Through the Prism of PISA,* Paris: OECD.

OECD (2011a) *An Overview of Growing Income Inequalities in OECD Countries: Main Findings.* Paris: OECD.

OECD (2011b) *Going for Growth. Part II Chapter 4 Housing and the Economy: Policies for Renovation.* Paris: OECD.

OECD (2012) *Going for Growth. Part II Chapter 5 Reducing Income Inequality while Boosting Economic Growth: Can it Be Done?* Paris: OECD.

OECD (2014) *All On Board: Making Inclusive Growth Happen*. Paris: OECD.

OECD (2015a) *Going for Growth 2015*. Paris: OECD.

OECD (2015b) *In It Together: Why Less Inequality Benefits All*. Paris: OECD.

OECD (2015c) *Universal Basic Skills: What Countries Stand to Gain*. Paris: OECD.

OECD (2016a) *Tax Policy Reforms in the OECD 2016*. Paris: OECD.

OECD (2016b) *Economic Outlook*, 2, 2, Chapter 2. Paris: OECD.

OECD (2016c) *The Productivity-Inclusiveness Nexus* Meeting of the OECD Council at Ministerial Level Paris, 1–2 June. Available at http://www.oecd.org/mcm/documents/The-productivity-inclusiveness-nexus.pdf.

OECD (2016d) *Social Expenditure Update 2016*. Paris: OECD.

OECD (2016e) *Income Inequality Update 2016*. Paris: OECD.

Ofcom (2015) *Measurement Framework for Media Plurality*. Available at https://www.ofcom.org.uk/_data/assets/for_media_plurality_statement.pdf.

OECD (2017) *OECD Economic Outlook, Volume 2017 Issue 1 United Kingdom*. Paris: OECD.

Office for Fair Access (2014) *Report and Accounts, 2013–14*. Bristol: Office for Fair Access.

Office of the Schools Adjudicator (2014) *Annual Report September 2013 to August 2014*. Available at http://www.gov.uk/government/uploads/system/uploads/attachment_data/file/393886/OSA_Annual_Report_2014.pdf.

O'Hara, M. (2014) US adds poverty to dangerous reading list, *Guardian*, 22 October, 42.

Okun, A. (1975) *Equality and Efficiency: The Big Trade-Off*. Washington, DC: Brookings Institution Press.

Oldenski, L. (2014) Offshoring and the polarization of the U.S. labor market. *ILR Review 67 (Supplement)*. Ithaca, NY: Cornell University.

Onaran, O. and Galanis, G. (2013) Is Aggregate demand wage-led or profit-led? In M. Lavoie and E. Stockhammer (eds) *Wage-Led Growth: An Equitable Strategy for Economic Recovery*. Basingstoke and New York, NY: Palgrave Macmillan, pp 71–99.

Onaran, O., Stockhammer, E. and Grafl, L. (2011) Financialisation, income distribution and aggregate demand in the USA, *Cambridge Journal of Economics*, 35 (4): 637–661.

ONS (2016a) *The Effect of Taxes and Benefits on Household Income: Financial Year Ending 2015*. London: ONS

ONS (2016b) *Statistical Bulletin: Health Expectancies at Birth and at Age 65 in the UK, Based on 2011 Census Health and Disability Prevalence Data: 2010 to 2012*. London: ONS.

ONS (2016c) *Statistical Bulletin: Profitability of UK Companies, April to June 2016*. London: ONS.

ONS (2017) *Household Disposable Income and Inequality in the UK: Financial Year Ending 2016*. London: ONS.

Osborne, H. (2016a) Big businesses see 25% drop in tax rates, *Guardian*, 29 February: 15.

Osborne, H. (2016b) Ueber loses right to classify UK drivers as self-employed, *Guardian*, 28 October. Available at https://www.theguardian.com/technology/2016/oct/28/uber-tribunal-self-employed-status.

Osborne, H. and Gayle, D. (2015) More UK workers now paid below living wage, *Guardian*, 13 October: 16.

Osbourne, H. (2015) Landlords taking advantage of £26.7bn a year in subsidies, say rental campaigners, *Guardian*, 9 February: 18.

Ostry, J. (2014) We do not have to live with the scourge of inequality, *Financial Times*, 3 March: 14.

Ostry, J.D., Berg, A. and Tsangarides, C.G. (2014) *Redistribution, Inequality and Growth*. Staff Discussion Note SDN/14/02. Washington, DC: IMF.

Ostry, J.D., Loungani, P. and Furceri, D. (2016) Neoliberalism: Oversold? *Finance and Development* June. Washington, DC: IMF.

Ottaviano, G.I.P. and Peri, G. (2011) Rethinking the effect of immigration on wages, *Journal of the European Economic Association*, 10 (1): 152–197.

Oxfam (2016) How to close Great Britain's great divide. Media Briefing, 13 September. Available at http://policy-practice.oxfam.org.uk/publications/how-to-close-great-britains-great-divide-the-business-of-tackling-inequality-620059.

Page, B.I., Bartels, L.M., and Seawright, J. (2013) Democracy and the policy preferences of wealthy Americans, *Perspectives on Politics*, 11 (1): 51–73.

Palley, T.I. (2012) *From Financial Crisis to Stagnation: The Destruction of Shared Prosperity and the Role of Economics.* Cambridge: Cambridge University Press.

Palley, T.I. (2015) The US economy: Explaining stagnation and why it will persist. Available at http//:www.thomaspalley. com/docs/research/Interpretation%20of%20the%20Crisis%20 WEBSITE.pdf.

Parker, A. (2015) Governance, fragmentation and chaos. In *What's Next for Education?* London: New Visions Group, pp 11–17.

Peet, R. (2011) Inequality, crisis and austerity in finance capitalism, *Cambridge Journal of Regions, Economy and Society*, 4 (3): 383–399.

Percy, S. (2016) *Companies Have Saved £42.2bn since 2008 by Cutting Investment and Retaining Earnings.* Available at https:// www.treasurers.org/node/9413.

Performance and Innovation Unit (2001) *Social Mobility: A Discussion Paper.* London: Cabinet Office.

Persson, T. and Tabellini, G. (1991) *Is Inequality Harmful for Growth? Theory and Evidence.* NBER Working Paper No. 3599. Cambridge, MA: NBER.

Pessoa, J.P. (2016) *International Competition and Labor Market Adjustment.* Centre for Economic Performance. Discussion Paper No. 1411. London: LSE

Peters, J. (2010) The rise of finance and the decline of organised labour in the advanced capitalist countries, *New Political Economy*, 16 (1): 73–99.

Pettifor, A. (2006) *The Coming First World Debt Crisis.* Basingstoke: Palgrave Macmillan.

Pew Research Center (2015) *The American Middle Class is Losing Ground.* Available at http://www.pewsocialtrends. org/2015/12/09/the-american-middle-class-is-losing-ground/.

Philippon, T. (2014) *Has the U.S. Finance Industry Become Less Efficient? On the Theory and Measurement of Financial Intermediation.* Available at pages.stern.nyu.edu/~tphilipp/research.htm.

Philippon, T. and Reshef, A. (2009) *Wages and Human Capital in the U.S. Financial Industry: 1909–2006.* NBER Working Paper No. 14644. Available at http://www.nber.org/papers/w14644.

Philippon, T. and Reshef, A. (2013) An international look at the growth of modern finance, *Journal of Economic Perspectives*, 27 (2): 73 – 96.

Pickard, J. (2015) Party donors recognised in royal honours, *Financial Times*, 11–12 June: 4.

Piketty, T. (2014a) *Capital in the Twenty-First Century.* Cambridge, MA and London: The Belknap Press of Harvard University Press.

Piketty, T. (2014b) *Capital in the Twenty-First Century*: a multidimensional approach to the history of capital and social classes, *British Journal of Sociology*, 65 (4): 736–747.

Piketty, T. (2015) Review of *Inequality: What Can Be Done? New York Review of Books*, 25 June. Available at http://www.nybooks.com/articles/2015/06/25/practical-vision-more-equal-society.

Piketty, T. and Saez, E. (2003) Income inequality in the United States, 1913–1998, *The Quarterly Journal of Economics*, 118: 1–39.

Piketty, T. and Saez, E. (2006) *The Evolution of Top Incomes: A Historical and International Perspective.* NBER Working Paper No. 11955. Cambridge, MA: NBER.

Piketty, T. and Zucman, G. (2014) Capital is back: wealth–income ratios in rich countries 1700–2010, *The Quarterly Journal of Economics.* Available at http://qje.oxfordjournals.org.

Piketty, T., Saez, E. and Stantcheva, S. (2011) *Optimal Taxation of Top Labor Incomes: A Tale of Three Elasticities.* NBER Working Paper No. 17616, Cambridge, MA NBER.

Piketty, T., Saez, E. and Zucman, G. (2016) *Distributional National Accounts: Methods and Estimates for the United States.* Washington, DC: Washington Center for Equitable Growth.

Pincus, S.C.A. and Robinson, J.A. (2010) *What Really Happened During the Glorious Revolution?* Unpublished. Available at http://scholar.harvard.edu/jrobinson.

Pollin, R. (2010) The case against deficit hawks: austerity is not a solution, why the deficit hawks are wrong, *Challenge*, November–December: 6–36.

Posen, A. (2014) The economic inequality debate avoids asking who is harmed, *Financial Times*, 5 August: 23.

Prasad, M. (2006) *The Politics of Free Markets*. Chicago, IL: University of Chicago Press.

Prasad, M. (2012) *The Land of Too Much: American Abundance and the Paradox of Poverty*. Cambridge, MA and London: Harvard University Press.

Pratley, N. (2015) Long road ahead for banks, *Guardian*, 19 March: 13.

Press Association (2015) *Two-Fifths of British Political Donations Made by just 76 People*. 14 June. Available at https://www. theguardian.com/politics/2015/jun/14/two-fifths-of-british-political-donations-made -by-just-76-people.

Rajan, R.G. (2010) *Fault Lines. How Hidden Fractures Still Threaten the World Economy*. Princeton, NJ and Oxford: Princeton University Press.

Rajan, R.G. (2013) *A Step in the Dark: Unconventional Monetary Policy after the Crisis*. Andrew Crockett Memorial Lecture. The University of Chicago Booth School of Business. 23 June. Available at http://www.bis.org/events/agm2013/sp130623. pdf.

Rankin, J. (2016) UK contests EU tax haven blacklist of 'treasure islands' despite Brexit, *Guardian*, 8 November: 20.

Rawls, J. (1971) *A Theory of Justice*. Cambridge, MA: The Belknap Press of Harvard University Press.

Reardon, S.F. (2011) The widening academic achievement gap between the rich and the poor: New evidence and possible explanations, in G.J. Duncan and R.J. Murnane (eds) *Whither Opportunity? Rising Inequality, Schools, and Children's Life Chances*. New York, NY: Russell Sage Foundation, pp 91–116.

Reardon, S. and Waldvogel, J. (2016) *Research Brief: International Inequalities*. London: Sutton Trust.

Reay, D. (2012) *What Would a Socially Just Education System Look Like?* London: Centre for Labour and Social Studies.

Redfern (2016) *The Redfern Review into the Decline of Home Ownership.* 16 November. Available at http:www.redfernreview. org.

Reed, H. and Himmelweit, J.M. (2012) *Where Have All the Wages Gone? Lost Pay and Profits outside Financial Services.* Touchstone Extras. London: TUC.

Reed, H. and Lansley, S. (2016) *Universal Basic Income: An Idea Whose Time Has Come?* London: Compass.

Reeves, R. (2017) Cutting inheritance tax now exposes a warped sense of priorities, *Guardian,* 28 February. Available at: https://www.theguardian.com/commentisfree/2017/feb/28/ inheritance-tax-north-south-divide.

Reich, R. (2016) *Saving Capitalism: For the Many, Not the Few.* London: Icon Books.

Relman, A. (2014) A challenge to American doctors, *New York Review of Books*, 14 August: 32–33.

Reno, R.R. (2014) *Inequality and Agency.* 1 March. Available at https://www.firstthings.com/article/2014/03/the-public-squ are?gclid=CNTwv67zqs8CFfMV0wodplkA3g.

Resolution Foundation (2016) *Budget 2016 Response.* London: Resolution Foundation.

Rosen, S. (1981) The economics of superstars, *The American Economic Review*, 71 (5): 845–858.

Rothstein, J. (2010) Is the EITC as good as an NIT? Conditional cash transfers and tax incidence, *American Economic Journal: Economic Policy*, 2 (1): 177–208.

Saez, E. (2008) *Striking it Richer: The Evolution of Top Incomes in the United States (Update using 2006 preliminary estimates).* University of California, Berkeley: Department of Economics.

Saez, E. (2013) *Striking it Richer: The Evolution of Top Incomes in the United States (Updated with preliminary estimates).* Available at http://128.32.105.3/~saez/saez-UStopincomes-2012.pdf.

Saez, E. and Piketty, T. (2013) Why the 1% should pay tax at 80%, *Guardian*, 24 October 2013. Available at http://www. theguardian.com/commentisfree/2013/oct/24/1percent-pay-tax-rate-80percent.

Saez, E. and Zucman, G. (2014) *Wealth Inequality in the United States since 1913: Evidence from Capitalized Income Tax Data.* NBER Working Paper No. 20625. Cambridge, MA: NBER.

Salverda, W., Nolan, B. and Smeeding, T. (2009) Introduction, in W. Salverda, B. Nolan and T. Smeeding (eds) *The Oxford Handbook of Economic Inequality*. Oxford: University Press, pp 3–23.

Salverda, W., Nolan, B., Checchi, D., Marx, I., McKNight, A., Toth, I.G. and van de Werfhorst, H. (2014) Introduction, in W. Salverda, B. Nolan, D. Checchi, I. Marx, A. McKnight, I.G. Toth, and H. van de Werfhorst (eds) *Changing Inequalities in Rich Countries: Analytical and Comparative Perspectives*. Oxford: University Press, pp 1–14.

Sammons, P., Toth, K. and Sylva, K. (2015) *Subject to Background: What Promotes Better Achievement for Bright but Disadvantaged Students?* London: Sutton Trust.

Sant'Anna, A.A. (2015) *A Spectre Has Haunted the West: Did Socialism Discipline Income Inequality?* Munich Personal RePEc Archive Paper No. 64756. Available at http://mpra.ub.uni-muenchen.de/64756 (accessed 23 November 2016).

Saunders, M. (2017) *The Labour Market*. Speech given at the Resolution Foundation, 13 January. Available at http://www.bankofengland.co.uk/publications/Pages/speeches/2017/953.aspx.

Savage, M. (2015) Labour wants more tax from non-doms, *The Times*, 4 March, 20.

Sayer, A. (2016) *Why We Can't Afford the Rich*. Bristol: Policy Press.

Scheidel, W. (2017) *The Great Leveler: Violence and the History of Inequality from the Stone Age to the Twenty-First Century*. Princeton, NJ and Oxford: Princeton University Press.

Schwartz, C.R. (2010) Earnings inequality and the changing association between spouses' earnings, *American Journal of Sociology*, 115 (5): 1524–1557.

Securities Exchange Commission (2015) *SEC Adopts Rule for Pay Ratio Disclosure*, Press release, 5 August. Available at https://www.sec.gov/news/pressrelease/2015–160.html.

Sen, A. (2015) The economic consequences of austerity, *New Statesman*, 4 June. Available at http://www.newstatesman.com/print/node/227892.

Sharma, Y. (2010) Swedish smiles turn sour as rift, *Times Educational Supplement*, 12 March: 32–33.

Shaw, M. (2013) Case study: Finland, *Times Educational Supplement*, 6 December: 10.

Shepherd, J. (2010) Private school teachers receive pension subsidy, data shows, *Guardian*, 6 November: 9.

Shestakovsky, B. (2015) *High-Tech hand Work: When Humans Replace Computers, What Does It Mean for Jobs and for Technological Change?* Available at http://blog.castac.org/2015/07/high-tech-handwork/.

Shiller, R.J. (2003) *The New Financial Order*. Princeton, NJ and London: Princeton University Press.

Shutt, H. (2014) *Responding to the Great Disintegration: Denial or Renewal?* Available at http://harryshutt.com/2014/11/27/responding-to-the-great-disintegration-denial-or-renewal.

Sikka, P. (2013) Without curbing corporate power the G8 have no chance of combating tax avoidance, 12 June. Available at https://theconversation.com/columns/prem-sikka-4302.

Sikka, P. (2014a) We can't afford corporate welfare, 18 March. Available at http://www.huffingtonpost.co.uk/prem-sikka/budget-2014-corporate-welfare-_b_4986497.html?just_reloaded=1.

Sikka, P. (2014b) Break the stranglehold of shareholders, *Guardian*, 11 December: 26.

Sikka, P. (2015a) As HSBC shows, we've been timid and pathetic in dealing with tax dodgers, *Guardian* 12 February. Available at http://theguardian.com/commentisfree/2015/feb/12/hsbc-pathetic-dealing-tax-dodgers-evaders-barely-punished.

Sikka, P. (2015b) Tax cheats cost far more than benefits cheats – yet far fewer are prosecuted, 17 February. Available at http://leftfootforward.org/2015/02/tax-cheats-cost-far-more-than-benefits-cheats-yet-far-fewer-are-prosecuted.

Sikka, P. (2016a) How serious is David Cameron about tackling corruption? 12 May. Available at http://leftfootforward.org/2016/05/how-serious-is-david-cameron-about-tackling-corruption.

Sikka, P. (2016b) BHS was a cash-generating machine for Philip Green and his family, 15 June. Available at http://leftfootforward.org/2016/06/bhs-was-a-cash-generating-machine-for-philip-green-and-his-family.

Sikka, P. (2016c) Britain is on the road to being a corporate tax haven, 31 October. Available at https;//leftfootforward. org/2016/10/Britain-is-a-tax-haven-where-corporate-greed-is-rewarded.

Sikka, P. (2017a) An energy price cap won't fix corporate abuses, 9 May. Available at: http://www.huffingtonpost.co.uk/prem-sikka/energy-price-cap_b_16504836.html.

Sikka, P. (2017b) The Tories promise to be tough on tax evasion. Where's the evidence? 22 May. Available at https://www.theguardian.com/commentisfree/2017/may/22/tories-promise-tough-tax-evasion-manifesto-tax-avoidance.

Sikka, P. and 13 others (2016) *Reforming HMRC: Making It Fit for the Twenty-First Century, First Stage Report.* London: Labour Party.

Smith, N.A., Phillips, D. and Simpson, P. (2016) *Council-Level Figures on Spending Cuts and Business Rates Income.* London: IFS.

Smithers, A. (2013) *The Road to Recovery: How and Why Economic Policy Must Change.* London and New York: Wiley.

Social Integration Commission (2015) *Kingdom United? Thirteen Steps to Tackle Social Segregation.* Available at http://socialintegrationcommission.org/images/sic_Kingdomunited.pdf.

Social Market Foundation (2016a) *Educational Inequalities in England and Wales.* London: Social Market Foundation.

Social Market Foundation (2016b) *Social Inequalities in Access to Teachers.* London: Social Market Foundation.

Social Mobility and Child Poverty Commission (2014b) *Elitist Britain.* London: Social Mobility and Child Poverty Commission.

Social Mobility Commission (2016) *State of the Nation: Social Mobility in Britain.* London: Social Mobility Commission.

Song, J., Price, D.J., Guvenen, F. and Bloom, N. (2015) *Firming Up Inequality.* Centre for Economic Performance CEP Discussion Paper No 1354. London: LSE.

Stewart, W. (2016) Education rankings: hitting a home run or swing and a miss? *Times Educational Supplement*, 25 November, 29–35.

Stiglitz, J. (2007) *Making Globalization Work.* New York, NY, and London: W.W. Norton and Co.

Stiglitz, J. (2013a) *The Price of Inequality*. London: Penguin.

Stiglitz, J. (2013b) Inequality is a choice, *New York Times*, 13 October. Available at http://opinionator.blogs.nytimes.com/2013/10/13/inequality-is-a-choice/?r=0.

Stiglitz, J. (2014) The myth of America's golden age. Available at http://www.politico.com/magazine/story/2014/06/the-myth-of-americas-golden-age-108013_full.html.

Stiglitz, J. (2015) *The Great Divide*. London: Allen Lane.

Stockhammer, E. (2012) Financialization, income distribution and the crisis, *Investigacion Economica*, 71 (279): 39–70.

Stockhammer, E. (2013) Why have wage shares fallen? An analysis of the determinants of functional income distribution, in M. Lavoie and E. Stockhammer (eds) *Wage-led Growth: An Equitable Strategy for Economic Recovery*. Basingstoke and New York, NY: Palgrave Macmillan, pp 40–70.

Storm, S. and Naastepad, C.W.M. (2013) Wage-led or profit-led supply: Wages, productivity and investment, in M. Lavoie and E. Stockhammer (eds) *Wage-led Growth: An Equitable Strategy for Economic Recovery*. Basingstoke and New York, NY: Palgrave Macmillan, pp 100–124.

Sturn, S. and van Treeck, T. (2013) The role of income inequality as a cause of the great recession and global imbalances, in M. Lavoie and E. Stockhammer (eds) *Wage-led Growth: An Equitable Strategy for Economic Recovery*. Basingstoke and New York, NY: Palgrave Macmillan, pp 125–152.

Summers, L. (2013) *Transcript of Larry Summers speech at the IMF Economic Forum*, November 8. Available at http://www.facebook.com/notes/randy-fellmy/transcript-of-larry-summers-speech-at-the-imf-economic-forum-nov-8-2013/585630634864563.

Summers, L. (2015) It can be morning again for the world's middle class, *Financial Times*, 18 January. Available at http://www.ft.com/cms/s/2/826202e2-9d85-11e4-8946-00144feabdc0.html#axzz3SBynHbbd.

Summers, L. (2016) The age of secular stagnation: what it is and what to do about it, *Foreign Affairs*, 15 February. Available at https://www.foreignaffairs.com/print/1116485.

Susskind, R. and Susskind, D. (2015) *The Future of the Professions*. Oxford: Oxford University Press.

Sutton Trust (2009) *Attainment Gaps between the Most Deprived and Advantaged Schools. A Summary and Discussion of Research by the Education Research Group at the London School of Economics.* London: Sutton Trust.

Sweney, M. (2016) Sorrell's £70m is no 'superstar' salary, WPP pay chief tells MPs, *Guardian*, 7 December: 1.

Sweney, M. (2017) Sorrell's pay curbed in WPP, *Guardian*, 29 April: 23.

Syal, R. (2014) Secretive club boosts Tory fundraiser in aid of marginal seats, *Guardian*, 17 October: 11.

Syal, R. (2016) Minister admits Google tax deal 'not glorious, *Guardian*, 1 February: 11.

Tawney, R.H. (1964) *Equality.* London: Unwin Books.

Taylor-Gooby, P. and Straker, G. (2011) The coalition programme: a new vision for Britain or politics as usual? *The Political Quarterly*, 82 (1): 8–18.

Tetlow, G. (2017) Affluent families pass on wealth to next generation, *Financial Times*, 6 January. Available at https://www.ft.com/content/b73da2ca-d33c-11e6-9341-7393bb2e1b51.

Tetlow, G. and O'Connor, S. (2016) British workers face worst decade for pay in 70 years, *Financial Times*, 24 November. Available at https://www.ft.com/content/d56b46f6-b237–11e6–9c37–5787335499a0.

Tett, G. (2015) An export economy that fails to import jobs, *Financial Times*, 9 January: 13.

Thompson, M.J. (2007) *The Politics of Inequality: A Political History of the Idea of Economic Inequality in America.* New York, NY: Columbia University Press.

Thrupp, M. (1999) *Schools Making a Difference: Let's Be Realistic! School Mix, School Effectiveness and the Social Limits of Reform.* Buckingham and Philadelphia, PA: Open University Press.

Timmer, M.P., Erumban, A.A., Los, B., Stehrer, R. and de Vries, G.J. (2014) Slicing up global value chains, *Journal of Economic Perspectives*, 28 (2): 99–118.

Tinbergen, J. (1975) *Income Distribution: Analysis and Policies.* Amsterdam: North Holland.

Toynbee, P. and Walker, D. (2015) Cameron's coup: Has he finished what she started? *Guardian*, 28 January: 28–30.

Trading Economics (2016) *United Kingdom Household Saving Ratio*. Available at http://www.tradingeconomics.com/united-kingdom-personal-savings.

Trading Economics (2017) *United Kingdom Corporate Profits 1955–2017*. Available at http://www.tradingeconomics.com/united-kingdom/corporate-profits.

TUC (2016) *The UK's Highest Paid CEO Earns the Average Salary in under 45 Minutes, TUC Analysis Finds*. Press release, 11 September. Available at https://www.tuc.org.uk/print/125592.

Turner, J. (2015) Barely under control, Jenny Turner on the privatisation of schools, *London Review of Books*, 7 May: 6–14.

Urzua, C.M. (2013) Distributive and regional effects of monopoly power, *Economica Mexicana Nueva Epoca*, 2: 279–295.

Van Clief, M., O'Byrne, S. and Leeflang, K. (2014) *The Alignment Gap between Creating Value, Performance Measurement and Long-Term Incentive Design*. Research Report. New York, NY: Investor Responsibility Research Center Institute.

Van der Weide, R. and Milanovic, B. (2014) *Inequality Is Bad for Growth of the Poor (But Not for That of the Rich)*. Policy Research Working Paper No. 6963. Washington, DC: World Bank.

Vasagar, J. (2010) No league table, no inspections, no private schools, *Guardian*, 6 December: 15.

Vaughan, A. (2017) Energy firms lobby Tories to weaken promise of price cap, *Guardian*, 23 May: 23.

Veblen, T. (1934) *The Theory of the Leisure Class*. New York: Modern Library.

Voitchovsky, S. (2005) Does the profile of income inequality matter for economic growth? *Journal of Economic Growth*, 10: 273–296.

Walker, P. (2016) Concern as Sure Start centre closures surge, *Guardian*, 8 December: 18.

Waslander, S., Pater, C. and van der Weide, M. (2010) *Markets in Education: An Analytical Review of Empirical Research on Market Mechanisms in Education*. Available at http://www.oecd.org/officialdocuments/publicdisplaydocumentpdf/?cote=EDU/WKP%282010%2915&docLanguage=En.

Waters, T. (2016) *Autumn Statement November 2016, Distributional Analysis*. Available at https://www.ifs.org.uk/publications/8767.

Watt, H. (2017) Electoral Commission to scrutinise Leave.EU's referendum spending, *Guardian,* 22 April: 2.

Watt, H. and Pegg, D. (2016) Tax inquiries for 22 people after Panama Papers, says Hammond, *Guardian*, 9 November: 8.

Watt, N. and Wintour, P. (2015) Conservative Party 'bankrolled by hedge fund managers', *Guardian*, 5 February. Available at https://www.theguardian.com/politics/2015/feb/05/conservatives-bankrolled-hedge-fund-managers.

Weale, S. (2015) Swedish free schools: famed for success and a beacon for Britain ... so what's gone wrong? *Guardian*, 11 June: 13.

Weale, S. (2017) What society gives their youngest less chance than their parents had? *Guardian*, 31 January: 34.

Webb, M.S. (2015a) A generation game with the wrong winners, *Financial Times Money*, 6 March: 8.

Webb, M.S. (2015b) Light holiday reading with a heavy message, *Financial Times Money* 18 July: 6.

Webb, M.S. (2015c) Vast cost of charity sector is squirrelled away, *Financial Times Money* 8 August: 6.

Webb, M.S. (2015d) Our pension regime is so stupidly complicated, *Financial Times Money*, 10 October: 24.

Webb, M.S. (2016) Wake up and listen to the politicians, *Financial Times Money*, 8 October: 20.

Weeden, K.A. and Grusky, D.B. (2014) Inequality and market failure, *American Behavioral Scientist*, 58 (3): 473–491.

Weil, D. (2014) *The Fissured Workplace: Why Work Became so Bad for so Many and What Can Be Done to Improve It*. Cambridge, MA and London: Harvard University Press.

Welch, F. (1999) In defense of inequality, *The American Economic Review*, 89, 2, 1–17.

White, W.R. (2012) *Ultra Easy Monetary Policy and the Law of Unintended Consequences*. Federal Reserve Bank of Dallas Globalization and Monetary Policy Institute Working Paper No. 126. Available at http://www.dallasfed.org/assets/documents/institute/wpapers/2012/0126.pdf.

Whittaker, M. (2015) *Time to Catch Up? Living Standards in the Downturn and Recovery*. Available at http://www.resolutionfoundation.org/wp-content/uploads/2015/03/Living-standards-slide-pack.pdf.

Wilby, P. (2015) Review of *How Good Can We Be? Guardian Review*, 21 February: 9.

Wilkinson, R. and Pickett, K. (2009) *The Spirit Level: Why Equal Societies almost Always Do Better*. London and New York, NY: Allen Lane.

Wilkinson, R. and Pickett, K. (2014) *A Convenient Truth. A Better Society for Us and the Planet*. London: Fabian Society.

Winston, G.C. (2000) *Economic Stratification and Hierarchy Among US Elite Colleges and Universities*. Discussion Paper No. 58, Williams Project on the Economics of Higher Education. Williamstown, MA: Williams College.

Wintour, P. and Syal, R. (2014) Conservatives raise funds to fight a possible second election next year, *Guardian*, 19 December: 2.

Wolf, M. (2014a) *The Shifts and the Shocks: What We've Learned – and Have Still to Learn – from the Financial Crisis*. London: Allen Lane.

Wolf, M. (2014b) Why inequality is such a drag on economies, *Financial Times*, 30 September: 23.

Wolf, M. (2015) Corporate surpluses are contributing to the savings glut, *Financial Times*, 18 November: 16.

Wolf, M. (2016) Monetary policy in a low rate world, *Financial Times*, 13 September: 13.

Wolf, M. (2017) The long and painful journey to world disorder, *Financial Times*, 5 January. Available at https://www.ft.com/content/ef13e61a-ccec-11e6-b8ce-b9c03770f8b1.

Woolf, N. (2014) The United States, *Guardian 2*, 30 October: 10.

World Economic Forum (2017) *The Inclusive Growth and Development Report 2017*. Davos: World Economic Forum.

Wren-Lewis, S. (2015a) The austerity con, *London Review of Books*, 19 February: 9–11.

Wren-Lewis, S. (2015b) The macroeconomic record of the coalition government, *National Institute Economic Review*, 231: R5–R16.

Xing, Y. and Detert, N. (2010) *How iPhone Widens the US Trade Deficits with PRC*. Discussion Paper 10-21. Tokyo: National Graduate Institute for Policy Studies.

Young, D. and Scott, P. (2004) *Having Their Cake: How the City and Top Managers are Consuming British Industry*. London: Kogan Page.

Younge, G. (2014) Republicans have called him a dictator. So why can't Obama get his own way? *Guardian*, 17 November: 29.

Zucman, G. (2013) The missing wealth of nations: Are Europe and the U.S. net debtors or net creditors? *The Quarterly Journal of Economics*, 128 (3): 1321–1364.

Zingales, L. (2015) *Does Finance Benefit Society?* Presidential Address to the American Finance Association, January. Available at faculty.chicagobooth.edu/luigi.zingales/papers/research/finance.pdf.

INDEX

References to the endnotes are shown as the page number followed by the note number (eg 213n3)

A

academies 195–6, 197, 224n11
Acemoglu, D. 45–6
Achur, J. 87
active labour market programmes (ALMPs) 141–3
Adam, S. 127, 128
Aghion, P. 32–3
Alcock, P. 132
Aldrick, P. 212n6
Allen, R. 154
Alvaredo, F. 11–12
Andrews, J. 157
Apple 212n3
apprenticeships 183–4, 219n1
Aronoff, D. 97
assortative mating 65
Atkinson, A.B. 10, 11, 39, 111, 115, 122, 126, 130, 135, 143, 145, 146, 210n10, 213n3
Attanasio, O. 15
austerity 82, 102–4, 160
   see also public deficit

B

banks 90, 103, 161, 177, 218n14, 220n6
   see also financialisation

Barker, K. 125
Bartels, L.M. 20, 44–5, 100
Barth, E. 133
Bassanini, A. 141–2
Bazot, G. 92
Bebchuk, L. 88
Bell, B. 92–3
benefit fraud 116
benefits
   capping 184, 225n17
   Conservative policy 184–90, 218n15
   fraud 116
   necessity of 134
   and pensions 136
   and rent seeking 99
   see also social expenditure
Bertrand, M. 38
Blanchflower, D. 213n4
Blau, F.D. 55
Bogliacino, F. 105–6
Bowles, S. 25, 38
Bowman, A. 150
Brewer, M. 203
Brexit 177, 199–201
Brooks, R. 113–14, 116, 117, 118, 119, 131, 176
Broughton, N. 129
Browne, J. 128

Buchanan, J. 63
Burgess, S. 157
Butler, P. 225n17

C

Cameron, D. 40, 170, 171
capital gains tax 125, 126, 179,
 216n8
capital returns 64–5
capitalism 73–7
Card, D. 67, 86
Carney, M. 17, 163
carried interest 216n7
Case, A. 59
CEO pay 93
 ratio to average worker pay 62,
 73, 86–7, 147–9
Chang, H-J. 27
Chen, W-H. 65
Chennells, L. 68
Chetty, R. 30
childcare 202–3
Chusseau, N. 55
Cingano, F. 14, 23–4, 36, 66
*Citizens United v. Federal Election
 Commission* 40
Clarke, S. 189
collective bargaining 143–4
Collinson, P. 180, 181
Commission on Inequality in
 Education 34
common-interest states 83–4
competition 145–7
Conservative Party, current policy
 169–206
 2015 election manifesto 172,
 178, 180, 182, 184, 190, 192, 195,
 197–8, 199
 2017 election manifesto 174,
 177–8, 178–9, 182, 184, 186–7,
 189–90, 191–2, 194–5, 196, 198,
 201, 223–4n10, 224n13, 225n18
 and loss of majority 205–6
 negative effects of 203–5
consumption inequality 15–16, 38
consumption tax 129, 138
Cook, P. 70, 71, 72
Corak, M. 31
Corlett, A. 188–9
Cornia, G.A. 215n13

corporate governance 147–50, 166,
 192–4, 204
corporate profits 64–5, 76–7, 80,
 89, 90, 131, 217n13
corporate structures 95
corporate welfare 98–9
 see also rent seeking
corporation tax 120, 130–1, 138,
 181–2, 217n14
 see also tax avoidance
council tax 126, 165, 217n9
Coutts, K. 81
Cowell, F. 32
Creedy, J. 146
Cribb, J. 156

D

Dabla-Norris, E. 22–3
Daudey, E. 16
Deaton, A. 28, 59, 211n9
debt 210n3
demand regimes 88–9
Dew-Becker, I. 67, 73
DiNardo, J.E. 67
direct and indirect taxes 127–8
diverted profits tax 215n2
Dixon, R. 146
Donovan, N. 124
Dorling, D. 26, 38–9, 83, 92, 95,
 213n2, 219n1
Drew, E. 41
Duncan, G.J. 31
DUP 205–6
Duval, R. 141–2

E

Earned Income Tax Credits 133–4,
 218n17
economic growth
 and Brexit 200
 and inequality 22–3, 36–8
 see also macroeconomic policies
economic impact of inequality
 34–8
education
 access to 65–6
 Conservative policy 194–7, 204
 impact of inequality on 23–4,
 32–4

policy to tackle inequality
152–9, 166
school funding 195, 197, 223n10
school admissions 156–8, 196–7,
223n9
and social mobility 28–9, 31
supply of 65–6
winner-take-all-markets 71–3
and women 65–6
Education and Adoption Act 2016
195
Eley, J. 179
Elsby, M.W.L. 55
employment portfolios 63–4
energy prices 177–8
environmental sustainability 39–40
Equality Trust 27, 217n9
European Union
Brexit 177, 199–201
and tax avoidance 176, 177
executive pay 62, 70, 88, 93, 147–9,
192–4, 212n6, 220n3
see also top incomes

F

Fabian Society 124, 188
Fair Admissions Campaign 157
faith schools 157–8, 196
Farnsworth, K. 98–9
financial globalisation 54
financial intermediation 90, 92
financialisation 90–7, 162
Conservative policy 192–4
and globalisation 54
international financial relations
104–6
rent seeking 97–9
Finland 153, 215n12
fiscal policy 162–3, 198–9
see also macroeconomic policies
fissuring 61–3
Fitoussi, J.P. 36
Foerster, M. 69, 120, 123, 125,
215n11
Foreign Direct Investment (FDI)
54
Foster, C.F. 211n8
France 108
Francis, B. 31
Frank, R.H. 70, 71, 72, 129, 212n6

Frederiksen, K.B. 74
free schools 196
Freeman, R. 52–3, 85–6
French, S. 214n5
Fried, J. 88
functional income inequality 16–17
Furman, J. 64–5, 98, 143, 146

G

Galbraith, J.K. 85, 94–5, 100, 104–5
Garcia-Penalosa, C. 16
Gates, B. 75
geographical segregation 30, 38–9
George, M. 224n11
Germany 108
Gilens, M. 42
Gini coefficient 6–7, 10, 13–14, 22,
29–30, 127–8
Glatter, R. 154
globalisation 52–6
and skill-biased technological
change (SBTC) 69–70
Goldin, C. 66
Google 41, 215n2
Gorard, S. 154
Gordon, R.J. 67, 73
grammar schools 156–7
Great Gatsby Curve 29–30
Great Recession 15, 34, 63, 76–7,
82
austerity 82, 102–4, 160
see also public deficit
Grubb, D. 142
Grusky, D.B. 97
guard labour 25–6
Gudgin, G. 81

H

Hacker, J.S. 41, 84–5
Harjes, T. 86
Harrington, B. 176
Harrop, A. 188
Hausman, J.A. 146
Hazell, W. 224n11
health, impact of inequality on 26
Hein, E. 162
higher education 71–3, 196
Hills, J. 13
HMRC

budget cuts in 115, 174
and living wage 183
and tax avoidance 115–16, 174–5
and tax reliefs 120
Hobijn, B. 55
Holmwood, J. 76, 108
Hood, A. 124, 186, 189
Hood, Sir John 220n3
Houlder, V. 113–14
House of Commons Committee of
Public Accounts 117, 120, 175
House of Commons Committee on
Standards in Public Life 150–1
household structure 65–7
housing 38–9, 224n15
housing benefit 99
housing services tax 127
human capital accumulation theory
36
Hume, D. 24
Hutchings, M. 31
Hutton, W. 131, 149, 224n15

I

IFS (Institute for Fiscal Studies) 14,
124, 127, 128, 185, 186, 189, 203
ILO (International Labour
Organisation) 16–17, 60–1
IMF (International Monetary Fund)
22, 24, 52, 86, 102, 122–3
Immervoll, H. 144
immigration 55
income tax
personal allowance 178–9, 202
rates of 216n8
top incomes 11, 82–3, 122–3,
138, 178–9, 203
incorporation 222n3
indirect taxes 127–8
industrial action 190–1, 204
industrial and competition policy
145–7
industrial strategy 191–2
inequality
case against 24–47
case for 19–24
as Conservative policy priority
170–1
of consumption 15–16
cost of 27

definition of 5
economic impact of 34–8
educational impact of 32–4
environmental sustainability
39–40
extent of 5–6
future for 202–6
impact on health 26
impact on housing 38–9
of income 9–17
increasing 3–4
institutional causes 79–109
internationally 5–9, 7
measuring 6–9
policy reforms 164–7
political impacts of 40–7
and recession 15
social impacts of 25–32
and squeezed middle 14–15
structural causes of 49–77
of wealth 11, 12–14, 74–7
information and transparency
112–13, 164, 170–1
inheritance tax 118, 124, 126, 172,
180, 204
Intergenerational Income Elasticity
(IGE) 29, 29–30
intergenerational social mobility
29–32
International Clearing Union 162
international financial relations
104–6

J

Jaumotte, F. 54
Jayadev, A. 25
jobs, Conservative policy 182–4
Johnes, R. 157
Johnson, B. 20
Johnson, P. 185, 186
Jones, O. 44
Joseph Rowntree Foundation
218n18
Joyce, R. 124
Judt, T. 26, 45
just managing families 186–90

K

Kahn, L.M. 55
Kaplan, S. 91, 93
Katz, L.F. 66
Kettle, M. 205
King, S.D. 103, 160–2
Kliman, A. 76–7
knowledge, and globalisation 53
Kotkin, J. 90, 96–7
Krippner, G.R. 214n9
Kristal, T. 87
Krueger, A.B. 29–30
Krugman, P. 11, 41, 44, 64, 74, 86–7, 88
Kumhof, M. 105
Kuznets, S. 105, 215n11

L

labour force participation 58–9
labour market
    active labour market programmes (ALMPs) 141–3
    deregulation of 80, 85
    and globalisation 52–5
labour market institutions 85–90, 143–5, 165
    Conservative policy 190–1
labour share 16–17, 55, 58
land value tax 126
Lansley, S. 20, 80, 81, 82, 96
Lavoie, M. 88–9
Leigh, A. 209n8
Lemieux, T. 88
Leveson Inquiry 221n7
limited liability 149
Living Wage 182–3, 202, 214n6
    see also Minimum Wage; National Living Wage
lobbying 84
luck 212n6
Lupto, R. 218n15
Lynch, L.M. 61

M

macroeconomic policies 99–102, 159–64, 167
    see also austerity
    Conservative policy 197–9, 205
Maestri, V. 105–6

Malik, S. 225n17
Marmot, M. 26
Marshall, P. 214n10
Martin, J. 142, 144
Marx, I. 132–3, 133–4, 135, 144, 145
Marxism 76–7
Mason, R. 43
May, T.
    and Brexit 199, 200
    and corporate governance 192–3
    and education 196
    and inequality 169, 171, 202
    and 'just managing families' 186–7
    loss of majority 205–6
    and tax avoidance 173
Mayer, C. 220n6
Mazzucato, M. 145–6
McKnight, A. 32
McNally, A. 131
media
    ownership of 44, 151
    portray of inequality 27
Meek, J. 83
Mell, A. 43
Milanovic, B. 5–6, 21–2, 25, 37, 69, 215n11
Minimum Wage (now National Living Wage) 88, 144–5, 181, 182–3, 202
Mirrlees Review 128
Mishel, L. 67–8
Mitchell, A. 220n4
Moene, K.O. 133
monetary policy 15, 100, 103, 163
    see also macroeconomic policies
money laundering 177
Morse, A. 38
Mundt, M. 162
Murnane, R.J. 31

N

national insurance 122, 179
National Living Wage (formerly Minimum Wage) 183, 185, 214n6
neoliberal policies 80–5, 101–2, 107–8
non-domiciled status 118–19, 172
non-standard work 59–63

O

OECD
and changes in household
structure 65
and economic growth 23–4, 35,
121
and education 141–2, 153–4
extent of inequality 6–9
fiscal policy 162–3
and non-standard work 59–60
and real wages 17
and recession 15
and social expenditure 133
and wealth inequality 74
off-shoring 55
ONS 127–8
Orszag, P. 64–5
Osborne, H. 182
Ostry, J. 36, 102

P

Page, B.I. 42
Palley, T. 47, 100–1, 101–2
Panama Papers 173
Park, Y. 38
participation income 135–6
path dependencies 107–9, 201
Peet, R. 82–3, 90
pensions
Conservative policy 189–90
cost of 136
deregulation 217n12
and private schools 158–9
tax reliefs 121–2, 204
triple lock 132, 136, 165,
189–90, 202, 219n19
personal income tax allowance
178–9, 202
personal savings 129–30, 138, 165,
181, 202
Pettifor, A. 52, 104, 214n9
Philippon, T. 90, 91, 92, 93
Pickett, K. 25, 28–9, 33, 39
Pierson, P. 41, 84–5
Piketty, T. 11, 14, 19, 49, 73–6,
99–100, 122, 126
political impacts of inequality 40–7
donations to political parties
41–3, 96–7, 150–1, 166, 201
political system 108–9, 201–2

Posen, A. 209n2
poverty porn 27
Prasad, M. 108–9, 201
PriceWaterhouseCoopers 117
private schools 158–9, 196
privatisation 83
property market 224n15
property taxes 125–7, 138
Public Accounts Committee
(PAC), see House of Commons
Committee of Public Accounts
public deficit
austerity 82, 102–4, 160
Conservative policy 197–8
macroeconomic policies 197–8
and personal taxes 129
and social expenditure 132–6,
138–9, 184–6, 186–90
public sector employment 145
public utilities, privatisation 83

Q

quantitative easing 103
Queen's Speech 169

R

Rajan, R.G. 81–2
Rauh, J. 91, 93
Rawls, J. 20
real wages 17
Reay, D. 152
Reed, H. 96, 188
Reeves, R. 180
Reich, R. 64
Relman, A. 164
Reno, R.R. 46
rent seeking 97–9, 119–20, 137,
164–5
Conservative policy 177–8
definition of 211n4
Reshef, A. 90, 91, 93
Resolution Foundation 182–3, 186,
187, 188–9
Robinson, J.A. 45–6
Rothstein, J. 218n17

S

Saez, E. 9–10, 12–13
Sahin, A. 55

Salverda, W. 106
Sant'Anna, A.A. 83–4
Saraceno, F. 36
savings, personal 129–30, 138, 165, 181, 202
Sayer, D. 27, 39
schools *see* education
second machine age 56–7
secular stagnation 35, 160
segmentation 37
selective schools 196
self-employment 179
shareholders 96, 147–8, 192–3, 220n3, 220n4, 220n6
Sidak, J.G. 146
Sikka, P. 98, 115–16, 117, 177, 181, 193, 216n4, 220n4
skill-biased technological change (SBTC)
  critique of 67–70
  and economic inequality 56–9
  and globalisation 69–70
  and non-standard work 60
Smithers, A. 93, 97
social expenditure 132–6, 138–9
  Conservative policy 184–90, 204
  just managing families 186–90
social impacts of inequality 25–32
social mobility 28–32, 100
social separation 37
squeezed middle 14–15
Stiglitz, J. 34, 35, 40, 53–4, 79
Stockhammer, E. 16, 88–9, 95–6
strikes 190–1
subsidies 98–9
Summers, L. 35, 210n9
sustainable employment portfolios 63–4
Sweden 153, 215n12

T
Tawney, R.H. 152
tax avoidance 113–19, 137, 164–5
  Conservative policy 172–7
  critique of government action 174–5
  steps to reduce 115–19
tax credits 133–4, 185, 187
tax evasion *see* tax avoidance
tax havens 176–7

tax rates 216n8
  capital gains 126, 179, 216n8
  Conservative policy 178–9
  corporation tax 131, 182
  declining 120–1
  and economic growth 35–6, 37–8
  tax burden on working class 82–3
  on top incomes 11, 82–3, 120–1, 122–3, 138, 178–9, 203
tax reliefs 120, 121–2, 131, 158, 180, 204, 216n6
taxation
  of capital gains 125, 126, 179, 216n8
  Conservative policy 172–82, 185–9
  on consumption 129, 138
  corporate 120, 130–1, 138, 181–2, 217n14
  direct and indirect 127–8, 137
  on inheritances 118, 124, 126, 172, 180, 204
  and private schools 158
  of property 99, 125–7, 138
  of wealth 123–5, 138, 179–80
technological change 56–9, 67–70
Thompson, M.J. 24
top incomes
  executive pay 62, 70, 88, 93, 147–9, 192–4, 212n6, 220n3
  financialisation 91–5
  increasing 9–14, 62, 84
  ratio to average pay 62, 73, 86–7, 147–9
  tax rates 11, 82–3, 120–1, 122–3, 138, 178–9, 203
  and wealth 12–14
  winner-take-all-markets 70–3, 212n6, 213n10
Toth, I.G. 69, 215n11
Toynbee, P. 99
Trade Union Act 2016 190–1
trade unions 85–8, 143–4, 204
  Conservative policy 190–1, 224n13

U

United States
  economic growth 37
  education 33, 66
  extent of inequality 8–9
  financialisation 90–5
  globalisation 52–3, 55, 56
  income distribution 14–15
  labour force participation 58–9
  macroeconomic policies 100–1
  neoliberal policies 84–5, 107–9
  non-standard work 61–2
  political impacts of inequality
    40–2, 44–5, 96–7
  skill-biased technological change
    (SBTC) 67–8
  social mobility 29, 30–1, 32
  top incomes 9–13, 62, 84
  unions 86–7
  wealth distribution 77
  winner-take-all-markets 73
Universal Credit 184, 185, 187,
  188, 223n5

V

Van der Weide, R. 37
Van Reenen, J. 68, 92–3
Van Rie, T. 132, 133–4, 144
VAT 127–8
Veblen, T. 38
Verbist, G. 135, 145
Voitchovsky, S. 10

W

wage share 16–17
wages
  executive pay 62, 70, 88, 93,
    147–9, 192–4, 212n6, 220n3
  and financialisation 91–3, 96
  and globalisation 55, 69
  and immigration 55
  labour market institutions 85–90,
    190–1
  Living Wage 182–3, 202, 214n6
  Minimum Wage 88, 144–5, 181,
    182–3, 202
  National Living Wage 183, 185,
    214n6
  and non-standard work 61–3

  real wages 17
  and SBTC 67–8, 69
  and trade unions 85–8, 97
  wage share 16–17
  see also top incomes
Walker, D. 99
Walmart 86, 214n8
Waters, T. 189
wealth distribution 11, 12–14, 74–7
wealth taxation 123–5, 138, 179–80
Webb, M.S. 120, 136, 212n3
Weeden, K.A. 97
Weil, D. 61–2, 63
Welch, F. 21
welfare state 132–6, 138–9, 184–90,
  204
  see also benefits; social
  expenditure
Wilby, P. 194
Wilkinson, R. 25, 28–9, 33, 39
winner-take-all-markets 70–3,
  212n6, 213n10
Wolf, M. 34, 106, 225n16

Z

Zucman, G. 12–13, 75, 176